Social and Community Development Practice

Social and Community Development Practice

Manohar Pawar

SAGE www.sagepublications.com
Los Angeles • London • New Delhi • Singapore • Washington DC

First published in 2014 by

 SAGE Publications India Pvt Ltd
B1/I-1 Mohan Cooperative Industrial Area
Mathura Road, New Delhi 110 044, India
www.sagepub.in

SAGE Publications Inc
2455 Teller Road
Thousand Oaks, California 91320, USA

SAGE Publications Ltd
1 Oliver's Yard, 55 City Road
London EC1Y 1SP, United Kingdom

SAGE Publications Asia-Pacific Pte Ltd
3 Church Street
#10-04 Samsung Hub
Singapore 049483

Published by Vivek Mehra for SAGE Publications India Pvt. Ltd, Phototypeset in 10.5/12.5pt Times New Roman by Diligent Typesetter, Delhi and printed at Saurabh Printers Pvt. Ltd., New Delhi.

Library of Congress Cataloging-in-Publication Data

Pawar, Manohar S.
  Social and community development practice / Manohar Pawar.
      pages cm
  Includes bibliographical references and index.
    1. Social service. 2. Social planning. 3. Community development. I. Title.
  HV40.P324   361.6'1—dc23   2014   2014009891

ISBN: 978-81-321-1845-9 (HB)

The SAGE Team: Shambhu Sahu, Alekha Chandra Jena, Anju Saxena and Dally Verghese

To
My Grandmother
Mrs Gangubai Babu Shinde

*During my travel in America, I ran short of 36 hours
to see her alive, a promise I failed to keep, which has
made me live with that guilt throughout!*

Thank you for choosing a SAGE product! If you have any comment,
observation or feedback, I would like to personally hear from you.
Please write to me at <u>contactceo@sagepub.in</u>

—Vivek Mehra, Managing Director and CEO,
SAGE Publications India Pvt. Ltd, New Delhi

Bulk Sales

SAGE India offers special discounts for purchase of books in bulk.
We also make available special imprints and excerpts from our
books on demand.

For orders and enquiries, write to us at

Marketing Department
SAGE Publications India Pvt. Ltd
B1/I-1, Mohan Cooperative Industrial Area
Mathura Road, Post Bag 7
New Delhi 110044, India
E-mail us at <u>marketing@sagepub.in</u>

Get to know more about SAGE, be invited to SAGE events, get on
our mailing list. Write today to <u>marketing@sagepub.in</u>

This book is also available as an e-book.

Contents

Section IV
The Future of SCD

List of Tables, Figures and Boxes

Tables

Figures

Boxes

List of Abbreviations

ADB	Asian Development Bank
APASWE	Asia Pacific Association of Social Work Education
ASEAN	Association of South East Asian Countries
ASSWI	Association of Schools of Social Work in India
BATSW	Bombay Association of Trained Social Workers
BE	Budget Estimates
BRAC	Bangladesh Rural Advancement Committee
BSW	Bachelors in social work
CBO	Community-based organization
CESCR	Committee of Economic, Social and Cultural Rights
COS	Charity Organization Society
DFID	Department for International Development
DNTs	De-notified tribes
DSPD	Division for Social Policy and Development
EXIM Bank	Export-Import Bank
GDP	Gross domestic product
GO	Government organization
GOI	Government of India
HRCA	Human Rights Council of Australia
IASSW	International Association of Schools of Social Work
ICSD	International Consortium for Social Development
ICSW	International Council on Social Welfare

IFSW	International Federation of Social Workers
IGNOU	Indira Gandhi National Open University
ILO	International Labour Organization
IMF	International Monetary Fund
INGO	International non-government organization
ISPSW	Indian Society of Professional Social Work
ISW	International social work
ITEC	Indian Technical and Economic Cooperation
IWGIA	International Working Group on Indigenous Affairs
KAPSW	Karnataka Association of Professional Social Workers
LOC	Letters of Credit
MATSWE	Maharashtra Association of Social Work Educators
MSW	Masters in social work
NAPSWI	National Association of Professional Social Workers in India
NNSSWQESWEI	National Network of Schools of Social Work for Quality Enhancement of Social Work Education in India
NGOs	Non-government organizations
NREGA	National Rural Employment Guarantee Act
OBCs	Other backward classes
ODA	Official development assistance
OPHI	Oxford Poverty and Human Development Initiative
PEP	Profession, education and practice
PO	People's organization
PSWFC	Professional Social Workers Forum, Chennai
PWDs	Persons with disabilities
SAARC	South Asian Association of Regional Cooperation
SCAAP	Special Commonwealth Assistance for Africa Programme
SCs	Scheduled castes
SDA	Social Development Advisers
SF	Solution-focused
SPF	Social Protection Floor

STs	Scheduled tribes
SWOT	Strengths, weaknesses, opportunities and threats
TISS	Tata Institute of Social Sciences
UGC	University Grants Commission
UN	United Nations
UN-DESA	United Nations Department of Economic and Social Affairs
UNDP	United Nations Development Programme (UNDP)
UNDSPD	United Nations Division for Special Policy and Development
UNESCAP	United Nations Economic and Social Commission for Asia and the Pacific
UNGA	United Nations General Assembly
UNHCR	UN High Commissioner for Refugees
UNRISD	United Nations Research Institute for Social Development
UNSDN	United Nations Social Development Network
UNUDHR	United Nations Universal Declaration of Human Rights
USWSSA	Unorganised Sector Workers' Social Security Act

Foreword

In the early 1990s I had the good fortune to visit and study, on behalf of ESCAP (the UN Economic and Social Commission for Asia and the Pacific), some 12 local social development initiatives across a range of countries, selected because they had been deemed to be highly successful. I was tremendously impressed by how they operated and what they were achieving, and frequently by the calibre of the workers involved. I of course appreciated that these initiatives were covering but a tiny fraction of the local communities in need of such work, but they were vital in showing the road ahead. My only disappointment was that no qualified social workers were involved in the work that I visited, leaving me a little ashamed of my own profession.

Then in the mid-1990s, the United Nations convened a top government-level consultation on social development, and its report made exciting reading. This was followed a few years later by the leaders of the world endorsing a set of Millennium Development Goals. It seemed clear to many of us that the international community as a whole knew what social development called for, could readily identify an appropriate and agreed-upon set of goals, and possessed the knowledge and expertise to implement social development at various levels of society and in a range of contexts. All this was both exciting and extremely promising for the future well-being of the still disadvantaged peoples of the world.

However, I was very aware that local-level social development required a pool of workers who, preferably, did not have to be trained on the job. One possibility was the formation of a social development profession. More expeditious though would be to expand social work's community development stream to embrace social development; and, at the same time, modify social work's entry and education arrangements to ensure that potential social workers, and especially those who might elect to go into social development work, came from a much wider range of social strata and from rural and remote areas. I therefore anticipated a huge expansion of social work across the Asia-Pacific region along these lines. Certainly it was clear that the workers for this local-level social development had to emanate, as far as was possible, from those countries possessing the greatest need for such development. If cross-border collaboration was called for, which was likely to be the case, it should be in the form of collaboration between countries within a sub-region, such as South Asia. Much less frequently, collaboration between developed and developing countries would be called for, to mutual benefit.

Looking back on that period of the 1990s from 2013 I find myself feeling disappointed. Despite considerable alleviation of poverty at national levels, high economic growth rates in some countries, and significant progress on many of the Millennium Development Goals, it is apparent that little has changed at many local levels. Local poverty levels have often fallen to some degree because younger people have left many rural communities and send money back to their families, sometimes at significant cost to themselves, but the field of comprehensive local-level social development is still very much in its infancy. Moreover, while the numbers of schools of social work have increased quite dramatically across our region, very few schools are based in the most poverty-stricken areas, very few draw students from marginalized populations, and almost none focus significantly on social development. Why this remains the situation, especially given social work's stated values, is something of a mystery.

For these reasons, Professor Manohar Pawar's book, in terms of its content and place of publication, is very timely and welcome. It does not purport to offer all the answers for a meaningful entry of social work into social development across South Asia, but it does provide the kind of material to motivate those social workers who are concerned about their region's level of social development, and let us hope there are many of these, to sit down and think about the potential of local-level social development in South Asia and how that potential might best be realized.

We should all appreciate the work that Manohar Pawar has put into furthering the cause of local-level social development in the Asia-Pacific region over the last few decades, and we must seek to ensure that his efforts have not been in vain. I feel confident that this book will contribute significantly to that goal.

Dr David Cox
Retired Professor of Social Work
Australia

Preface

The main motivation for writing this book was to disseminate ideas for further discussion, debate and testing. I would not have thought of preparing such a book if my colleagues, students and friends had not expressed so much interest in my writing and publications. Over a period of 30 years, my writing has been published mostly in the form of refereed journal articles and books. Unfortunately, however, the unfair market acts as a distribution barrier, and hence those publications are not readily accessible to readers in India and the South Asian region, though promotional and periodic free download is a recent helpful development and I hope that in the future all such publications may be made available free to readers as has already occurred with some journals. Reflecting on and drawing from my previous work, this book is especially designed for readers in India and South Asia generally, as well as for similar countries beyond the South Asian region. This book is about my reflections on social and community development practice. It discusses the concept of a social development approach and why such an approach is relevant to the needs in many local-level communities or grassroots-level villages. Within its focus on social and community development practice, the book considers certain strategies for the social work profession, for social work and social and community development students, for educators and practitioners, and, for that matter, anyone interested in the whole area of social development and its implementation at a local level.

When I reflect on my life from a social and community development practice perspective, it looks like my life has revolved around self-interest—self-seeking, self-fulfilment, self-centredness. If everyone is like me, I wonder how such beautiful communities and societies as we often encounter have been built; communities in which we are born, consume, grow, learn, educate, work, earn, and build self- and social-centred networks. In practice, effective communities are the foundation of our successful day-to-day living. Having now turned the fifty-first page of my life, I believe it is a right time for me to examine what my contribution to these wonderful societies and communities has been. On reflection, it seems to be miniscule. Therefore, if I may be permitted, I would like this book to be treated as my small contribution to the creation of effective societies and communities, and I dedicate it to that goal. Yet in doing so, I must immediately qualify this by saying that many of the ideas contained in this book are not entirely my own. Many good ideas regarding social and community development have been with us for a long time. However, in a world where life so often revolves around the proverbial rat race, with many negative and destructive forces, it is crucial to resurrect good ideas from the past that may contribute to countering destructive forces today. For this reason, I can justify the exercise of repeating good ideas from the past, with the sincere hope that if they have not been adequately heeded prior to now, their potential may yet be realized. Many of these ideas around social and community development are highly relevant to our day and age, and they need to be central in our thoughts and action as concerned citizens and social workers. I hope that this book will assist its readers to explore these good ideas again with reference to our current situation. If I have contributed to the thinking and action of tomorrow's social and community development workers, I shall hopefully have contributed to the development of better communities in the future.

As any book-writing project is a difficult, challenging, time-consuming and demanding task, it cannot be completed without the help and cooperation of others. I would like to sincerely thank Professor David Cox for reading the draft of the book, offering valuable suggestions and kindly agreeing to introduce the book by writing the foreword. This book would not have been possible without the compact grant provided by the Faculty of Arts, Charles Sturt University (CSU), which partly released me from teaching tasks and helped me focus on completing this book. I would like to thank Professor Jennifer McKinnon, Executive Dean of the Faculty of Arts, CSU (former head of the School of Humanities and Social Sciences), and Associate Professor Margaret Woodward, Associate

Dean, Research, Faculty of Arts, CSU. The basic concept for this book in a way emerged from my friendship with Mr Chandrakant Kore, a well-accomplished engineer, who has no idea of this, but I thank him for his appreciation of my work and our friendship. I would like to thank all my social work colleagues at the school of Humanities and Social Sciences, particularly, Dr Bill Anscombe for his thoughts on the role of virtues in social work practice and Associate Professor Wendy Bowles for allowing me to reproduce her table on comparative analysis of social work codes of ethics. I also would like to appreciate and acknowledge reprint permissions granted by the publishers of my previous work, the detailed list of which is provided at the end of the book. The commissioning, editorial and production teams at SAGE Publications, New Delhi, were wonderful to work with and their contribution to publishing this book is very much appreciated. Finally, most of my writing results from denying well-deserved time to my family—my wife, Jaya and our children, Neel and Tulasi, who bore the brunt of it. Without their love, understanding, cooperation and support, this book and other writing projects would not have been possible and I am very grateful to them.

Manohar Pawar

Section I

Social and Community Development (SCD) Practice

The first section of the book considers social and community development practice and is organized into four chapters. The first chapter discusses social development approach. Any content on social development in social work curriculum is not as common as content on community organization and development. However, given that many developing countries need a developmental perspective in social work education and practice, some understanding of social development knowledge and skills is relevant and useful for all social workers. The main message this first chapter aims to convey is that social development is not an ideal or utopian concept, as sometimes suggested, but one that can be practised in the field with very positive outcomes. To demonstrate this point, the first part of the chapter discusses the meaning and definitions of social development. In the second part, by exploring the historical origins of social development, it is argued that social development is not new and that the ideas inherent in it have been present in the Indian heritage and culture, as well as in other cultures, for thousands of years. The evolution of social development ideas during the colonial period and the purposeful use of these ideas later on by the United Nations (UN) and similar agencies are noteworthy. Several ideologies, such as individualist, collectivist and partnership, have influenced the development of social development thought. Drawing on the available literature and its analysis, in the third part I have discussed the social development approach and argued that it can be practised effectively. Practising social development calls for understanding existing conditions and changing them where necessary by setting clear goals; following values, principles, processes and strategies at various levels of the society; and covering all dimensions of social development.

The second chapter focuses on how social development approach, as set out in the first chapter, can be applied to the development of local-level communities. For conceptual clarity, it discusses the meaning of local level, the changing nature of communities and community development. By pointing out how grassroots-level communities have been neglected for a long time, it justifies the need to work with those communities and shows how social development approach can help to facilitate their comprehensive development. Furthermore, it suggests some basic strategies to be used within community development practice. The essence of the application of social development approach is that all dimensions of the community need to be developed, not just one or two, so that people experience a better quality of life and well-being.

By merging the values and principles together, the third chapter discusses four core values and principles for community development practice. In view of their extensive depth and breadth, challenges and difficulties in using them and their usefulness and effectiveness, the four values and principles discussed are human rights, self-reliance, self-determination and participation. Each of the values and principles is discussed in terms of its meaning, critiques of, and obstacles to, its use and what strategies can be employed to practise them.

The final chapter of the section focuses on the dynamics of community development practice. Although social workers and social and community development workers experience several complex dynamics in their practice, the chapter has categorized such dynamics into four broad areas, which, while neither exhaustive nor exclusive, are common and crucial. First, it is suggested that the application of values and principles to community development practice is challenging as it is likely to produce different reactions from different groups in communities. Second, entry into the community and beginning community development work has its own dynamics. Third, awareness raising and capacity building, as basic activities in the community, will pose several challenges to the worker. Following a range of community development work, the fourth dynamic is around the sustainability of community as well as community development programmes and projects in terms of their continuity.

I hope these first four chapters provide some basic knowledge, skills and insights into practising the social development approach and, thus, enhancing the social development of communities.

1

A Social Development Approach

Introduction

Although social development is not new in social work literature, its study and application by social work and welfare students and educators appear to have been somewhat limited in India and the Asian region generally. When I was studying social work at the Tata Institute of Social Sciences (TISS), I often saw a book entitled *Some Aspects of Social Development* (authored by Professor M.S. Gore, 1973) displayed at the publications department and issues of the journal *Social Development Issues* at the TISS library, but I hardly remember studying social development in my social work course. Why such a fascinating and comprehensive subject has not been taught in social work schools is an important question that keeps bothering me. When I began working as a lecturer in international social work at the Regional Social Development Centre, La Trobe University, Professor David Cox introduced me to the subject of social development. I attended his lectures in his Master of International Social Work course and taught with him some lecture sessions.

As a new student of social development, I read *Social Change and Development* by So (1990), United Nations Economic and Social Commission for Asia and the Pacific's (UNESCAP, 1992) Social Development Strategy for the ESCAP region towards the year 2000 and beyond, and Professor James Midgley's (1995) book, *Social Development: The Developmental Perspective in Social Welfare*. I reviewed Midgley's book, and the review article appeared in the *Indian*

Journal of Social Work (Pawar, 1997). I also assisted Professor Cox in organizing a regional workshop on social development-oriented courses in social work and co-authored two reports entitled *Introducing a Social Development Perspective into Social Work Curricula at All levels* (Cox et al., 1997b) and *Social Development in Social Work Education* (Cox et al., 1997c). My initial exposure to this basic literature and the experiences and opportunities offered by Professor Cox drew me into the field of social development.

For nearly two decades I have been reading social development literature and teaching the subject to social work and welfare students. My contemplation of the subject and my life experiences and observations of communities suggest that social development is not merely a philosophy or an ideal state. The ideas inherent in social development are practical, and social development can be practised within local-level communities. Professor Cox and I have developed and discussed this argument earlier (Pawar and Cox, 2010a, b and c), and this chapter substantially draws on that work. Midgley's (2014) new book, *Social Development: Theory and Practice*, reflects this practice focus in its title and content. My own reflections on the subject over a period suggest that, despite conceptual ambiguity and varied understanding of it, social development as a goal, strategy, idea and ideal is achievable. Towards this end, the first section of the chapter analyzes several meanings of social development. The second traces its historical evolution and shows how social development draws strength from various theoretical and ideological traditions, and the final section discusses an emerging approach to social development. Achieving social development at all levels on a global scale is a challenging task, but it is a practical and necessary task, and social work and social development workers can play important roles in understanding it and influencing their institutions and communities to practise social development in a committed way.

Meaning(s) of Social Development

It is important to understand the meaning of social development in such a way that it can be practised. As the concept of social development is broad, flexible and all-encompassing, its understanding varies depending on our own disciplinary traditions, orientations and limited thinking. For example, it reminds us of a story of the description of an elephant by visually disabled persons whose description was dependent on the part of the elephant they touched and the way they sensed it. In response to one survey on social development content in social work education, a respondent from a developed country stated (see Cox et al., 1997c):

> Anyway, at first it was difficult for me to understand the definition of so called 'social development'. In Japan we always use this term when we think of developing countries.

Earlier, when I invited a colleague to write on social development, his response was:

> Unless the war in Iraq stops, writing about social development does not make any sense to me.

I also have seen some social work educators' disinclination to consider social development. Some unfortunately think that it is not a clear and practical subject, and they reject it outright. Even when just the concept is utilized, it is often contested. Although in the current socio-economic and political environment it is a real challenge to develop an acceptable and practical view of social development, it is important to do so. To develop the conceptual clarity, first the terms 'social' and 'development' have been briefly discussed; second, several scholars' definitions of social development have been considered; and finally, their thinking has been further progressed with the ultimate aims of promoting its understanding and practice.

The word 'social', as a prefix to development, is generic, broad and all-encompassing, and wherever the word 'social' is attached to other words in a way similar to its use in social development, the meaning gets diffused and generally creates confusion among users of this word to the extent that it is often taken lightly or casually (e.g. 'social' work). The root of the word social is found in Latin, where 'socius' (noun) means 'ally, confederate', and also, by extension, 'sharer, partner and companion'. Its adjective 'socialis' means 'of or belonging to companionship, sociable, social'. Another Latin word associated with 'socius' is 'socio', which means 'to join or unite together, to associate: to do or hold in common, to share with'.

The Shorter Oxford English Dictionary lists four meanings for the word 'social' that emphasize, respectively, belonging, mutuality, group living and activities to improve conditions of a society by addressing problems and issues.

Similarly, the noun 'development' as a suffix has different meanings and is used in a range of different fields such as biology, music, drama, sports, mining, building/housing, photography, politics and economics. Its dictionary meaning is derived from the verb 'develop', which means 'grow gradually; become or make more mature, advanced or organised' (Hornby, 1993). Develop also means 'to bring out the capabilities or possibilities of; bring to a more advanced or effective state; to cause to grow; to elaborate or expand in detail; and to bring into being or activity; generate; evolve'. Thus, development connotes an act and/or a process: an act of improving by expanding or enlarging or refining, and a process in which something passes by degrees to a different stage, especially a more advanced or mature stage (Dictionary.com, 2007).

To understand 'social development' in a simplistic way, by combining the lexical meanings of the two words, one thing is very clear, namely, that social development does not mean development of just one individual, one family, one neighbourhood, one community, one corporation, one nation, one nation-state, or one region. It also does not mean development of just one aspect of any entity, such as economic or political, to the neglect of other aspects. Social development means the collective development of the whole entity, whatever that entity might be; thus, it means growing, advancing, maturing step by step or stage by stage in a unified way and comprehensively covering all aspects and dimensions of such entities as a society. For example, despite prosperity, the growing inequality in many societies in fact indicates the absence of social development. Growth, advancement and maturity may be readily understood in a biological sense, but does this understanding apply to communities, societies and institutions? What is advancement? Is it progressing from one stage to a relatively better stage? Do well-developed regions within a country or countries present a matured better stage, while many countries in Africa, Asia and Latin America present a poorer stage that needs to be changed to a 'matured, advanced stage' as portrayed by developed countries? Do extreme increases in material production

and wealth, to the extent of adversely affecting the climate, triggering violence within and between countries, increasing child poverty
and leading to growth in the number of the isolated elderly, as we see
in many developed countries, such as the USA and Japan, constitute
an advanced matured stage, and therefore, the ultimate attainments
of social development? Look also at vast disparities between rural
and urban India and in many Asian countries. Certainly, impressive
economic growth and development, though necessary, is not social
development. The world's collective growth, change, advancement,
maturity and development raise fundamental questions in terms of
development for what, for whom, how and for how long. Keeping
these debatable questions in mind, it would be interesting to see
whether these questions are addressed in the following definitions of
social development.

As stated earlier, definitions of social development are varied
and many, and they may be flexibly grouped under three categories
depending on the approach they follow. One category of definitions
emphasize, among other things, systematic planning and the link
between social and economic development. A second group of definitions shows that bringing about structural change is the core element of social development; and a third focus is on realizing human
potential, meeting needs of the community population and achieving
a satisfactory quality of life. One of the critical issues in defining
social development is its relationship with economic development. Is
economic development embedded in social development, or is social
development complementary to economic development? The 1995
World Summit on Social Development distinguishes the two and sees
social development, without defining it, as a necessary complement
to economic development, and so do the United Nations Development Programme (UNDP) Human Development reports in many
ways. Some definitions seem to capture this issue by suggesting that
social development and economic development are different but at
the same time juxtaposed.

A critical examination of these definitions clearly shows that the
conception of social development differs from author to author (see
Boxes 1.1 to 1.3). Some focus on the process, some on the outcome
and some both. Some definitions include the meaning and purpose of
social development and what needs to be done to achieve it, whereas

Box 1.1:
Definitions that focus on systematic planning and linking social and economic development

The concept of social development is inclusive of economic development but differs from it in the sense that it emphasises the development of the totality of society in its economic, political, social, and cultural aspects. (Gore, 1973)

Social development is a process of planned social change designed to promote the well-being of the population as a whole in conjunction with the dynamic process of economic development. (Midgley, 1995)

In 2014, Midgley (2014, p. 13) revised the definition as follows: a process of planned social change designed to promote the well-being of the whole population as whole within the context of a dynamic multifaceted development process.

[Social development is] planned comprehensive social change designed to improve people's general welfare. The interrelatedness of major social problems requires the economic and cultural efforts of national and international government structures and society's institutions and all its citizens. (Barker, 2003)

Box 1.2:
Definitions that focus on structural change

Social development is a comprehensive concept which implies major structural changes—political, economic and cultural, which are introduced as part of deliberate action to transform society. (Pathak, 1987)

Development should be perceived as a multidimensional process involving the re-organisation and reorientation of entire economic and social systems. . . . [it] involves radical changes in institutional, social and administrative structures as well as in popular attitudes and even customs and beliefs. (Todaro, 1997, p. 69)

(Box 1.2 Contd.)

(Box 1.2 Contd.)

New social development (NSD) is conceptualised as a post-material process of human-societal transformation that seeks to build identities of people, communities and nations. Universalisation of equality and justice, on the one hand, and annihilation of violence, war and disease, on the other hand, will go a long way to ensure NSD's substance, contours and contents. (Mohan, 2010, pp. 205, 221)

Box 1.3:
Definitions that focus on realizing the human potential, needs and quality of life

Social development includes improvement in the quality of life of people . . . (a more) equitable distribution of resources . . . broad-based participation . . . in the process of decision making; and special measures that will enable marginal groups and communities to move into the mainstream. (Pandey, 1981)

Social development has two interrelated dimensions: the first is the capacity of people to work continuously for their welfare and that of society; the second is the alteration or development of a society's institutions so that human needs are met at all levels, especially at the lowest level, through a process of improving the relationships between people and social economic institutions. (Paiva, 1982)

Social development is the process of planned change designed to bring about a better fit between human needs and social policies and programs. (Hollister, 1982)

Social development implies evolution and transformation through which people and societies maximise their opportunities, and become empowered to handle their affairs. (Mohan and Sharma, 1985)

Social development is directed towards the release of human potential in order to eliminate social inequities and problems. (Meinert and Kohn, 1987)

(Box 1.3 Contd.)

(Box 1.3 Contd.)

The three basic components of core values of development are life-sustenance, self-esteem and freedom. (Goulet in Thirlwall, 1989, p. 8)

Social development is focused not only on the well-being of individuals, but more frequently than not on the achievement of the well-being and fullest possible human realisation of the potentials of individuals, groups, communities, and masses of people. (Billups, 1994, from Lowe, 1995)

[Social development is] a participatory process of planned social change designed to promote the well-being of the people, and which, as such, offers an effective response to the innate needs and aspirations of the whole population for the enhancement of their quality of life. (Cox et al., 1997b)

The term social development can refer to: improvement in the welfare and quality of life of individuals; or changes in societies—in their norms and institutions—that make development more equitable and inclusive for all members of a society. (Davis, 2004)

others cover only one aspect of it. The conceptual analysis suggests that social development is about systematically introducing a planned (sometimes radical) change process, releasing human potential, transforming people's determination, reorganizing and reorientating structures and strengthening the capacity of people and their institutions to meet human needs. Additional goals include: to reduce inequalities and problems, create opportunities and empower people, achieve human welfare and well-being, improve relationships between people and their institutions and, finally, ensure economic development. Along with these concepts it is also useful to look at the eight characteristics of social development presented by Midgley (1995), although some of them may overlap with the above concepts, as in reality they emanate from them. Four of these characteristics address the issue of process, clarifying what the process is about.

These are positive change, progressive development, intervention through organized efforts and economic development. The other four characteristics refer to interdisciplinary theoretical bases, ideologically oriented strategies, an inclusive or universal scope and the welfare goals of social development.

Although the precise nature of the concept of social development may be contested, controversial and debatable, few would disagree with its goals. Yet the social development literature offers little clarity about how these goals, values, strategies and the process of social development can be implemented and achieved in the field. In other words, these concepts do not cover the 'how' and 'how long' of development and social development. Due to the lack of discussion on, or uncertainty regarding, the practical aspects of social development, some people may perceive it as utopian or idealistic, and so, not realistic. Thus, the greatest challenge for social development thinkers is to demonstrate that social development can be practised and achieved in the real world. It is not a vague concept or relevant only to developing countries. Focusing on this issue of the practicality of social development, we may gain some insights from the historical origins and theoretical basis of social development.

Historical Origins of Social Development

Early Civilizations

Readers of the history of social development may wonder whether it is possible to trace authentic and convincing historical origins of the term 'social development' and how it was practised. The idea of change and social development—not the exact nomenclature itself—was there with the ancient Chinese, Greek and Indian civilizations. Pathak (1987) notes that social development ideas have been part of Western social thought for more than 2,500 years. They were also present during the Buddhist period and in the writings of Manu and Kautilya (Pathak, 1987). The goal of the welfare and well-being of the whole universe was part of the Indian culture thousands of years earlier. For example, *Lokah Samastha Sukhino Bhavantu*, which means, 'May all the beings in all the worlds become happy,' is part of many Hindu people's every-day prayer. However, what causes change and development and what kinds of change and development lead to welfare and well-being are not conclusively revealed in human history.

Biological Change Ideas

From a biological point of view, change, development and decay are the essence of life and occur in a cyclical form. There is nothing static in the universe. The application of these biological phenomena to non-biological aspects of life, society and cultures suggests that they too undergo similar cycles, and thus, the concept of a golden age arises. History shows that many civilizations have achieved a period of great advancement, reached a peak and then gradually experienced a decline. Is social development part of this cycle? Midgley (1995) contends that social development is not retrogressive, but progressive. It is an important assumption that may hinge on the precise cause of social development. In biological science, growth, change, development and decay are attributed to natural causes or forces, though some of this kind of change and development process may be facilitated or manoeuvred by human intervention. Change due to natural causes is not part of social development, but conscious human efforts to deal with the consequences of natural change certainly can be. Midgley (1995) traces the theory of social change to ancient Greek thinkers, particularly Heraclitus' view that when opposite elements fuse (dialectic) and produce a new phenomenon, change occurs. He traces it also to St Augustine's view on stages of progressive change caused by both material and spiritual forces. Finally, he refers to Ibn Khaldun's thoughts on human conflict (between nomadic tribes and settled dwellers) and change.

Social and Economic Change Ideas

During the era of the Renaissance or Enlightenment in the 18th and 19th centuries, many thinkers rejected the traditional, dogmatic and religious explanations of social change, often formulated in terms of advancement followed by decline, and instead emphasized that social change occurs stage by stage in an ongoing, progressive manner. Perhaps drawing on the work of early Greek philosophers, the cause of change and progress was attributed, on one hand, to ideas in terms of thesis, antithesis and synthesis (see George Hegel's and his followers' thoughts) and, on the other, to economic and social forces in terms of materialism (see thoughts of Adam Smith, Karl Marx and Friedrich Engels). Although these two causes at that time appeared different, on reflection one may see the link between ideas and material forces capable of influencing the other but keeping their own entities intact.

Planned Social Change

It appears that these and similar thoughts laid an initial rudimentary foundation for planned human intervention that sought to bring about social change and development. Further developments, such as ideas of creating a perfect society, birth of the sociology discipline and Auguste Comte's views on the use of the scientific method to solve social problems, gradually overcame non-intervention thoughts (see Herbert Spencer's views) and influenced many Fabian socialists and sociologists who supported planned intervention for people's welfare. One such sociologist was Leonard Hobhouse who coined the term 'social development' to connote a process of planned social change (Dean, 2010; Midgley, 1995, pp. 29, 45). Although in the 19th and 20th centuries the extent to which governments should and should not intervene was a controversial issue, the industrial revolution, growing mechanization, industrialization, migration of people from rural to urban areas and consequent urbanization together resulted in governments' planned intervention through various welfare programmes and services (e.g. Bismarck's social insurance and poor laws) primarily relating to health, education and housing. However, the extent of coverage, operation and delivery differed significantly from one country to another. Reaction to the impact of the great depression and World War II led to some additional and important welfare measures, such as a New Deal and the Social Security Act in the USA and the Beveridge Report and its implementation in the UK and its influence beyond, eventually evolved into the concept of the welfare state.

Colonial Period and Social and Community Development

Although Hobhouse first used the term 'social development' in the UK, it appears that European colonies provided fertile ground for practising social development. Whether social development in many colonies in Africa, Asia and Latin America was either a well-planned approach of colonial administrators or a necessity of the time is not clear. However, the process, impact and outcome of colonization and decolonization were a mixed blessing for colonies and the whole experience was generally negative for the colonized, although colonizers may hold an entirely different view. The initial exciting entry into the new world, in the name of exploration and adventure, gradually resulted in creating a place for trade and commerce. It also eventually established colonizers' rule by suppressing and subjugating people by several means, including violence, resisting independent movements to the maximum, sowing the seeds of divisions and conflicts, and finally surrendering to the local people. Such developments are often narrated as colonial history that no one would recall with pleasure and pride.

However, European colonizers have also been widely acknowledged for contributing to infrastructure development and laying the foundations of educational systems, health services, postal systems and welfare services—particularly through missionaries, prison building, tax systems and the rule of law—however self-benefitting these may have been for the colonizers. The main motivation in doing all this was really to exploit the resources of the colonies and export them to Europe and not to promote the welfare and well-being of the people. Although such colonization practices were prevalent for a few hundred years, during the 16th to the 18th centuries, new developments in the West, particularly during the era of the Enlightenment, industrial revolution and industrialization and an increase in manufacturing and production increasingly influenced colonial administrators. To colonial administrators, 19th- and 20th-century colonies were not just places for exploitation but also markets for the consumption of goods produced in Europe through growing industrialization. To promote a market in the colonies for such products, systematic economic development measures and limited welfare services were needed and were, therefore, initiated. Exporting raw materials from, and importing finished products to, colonies was almost the rule of that time and remains so for some countries even today. Thus, strategic economic development in colonies was the need at the time to strengthen the industrial base in the industrialized countries.

It is this socio-economic situation that appears to have provided a fertile ground for practising social development in some colonies. Midgley (1994, 1995), drawing on the colonizer-promoted mass literacy and related activities to improve conditions in Western Africa in the 1940s, suggests that the emergence of a social development perspective, one that transcended mere literacy and education to endorse community development, was a product of these times. However, we are uncertain about attributing the origin of social development to Western Africa in the 1940s. Much before that period the British had established a relatively good educational system in India and had promoted agriculture and exported cotton from India and from many other colonies to the UK, and within this whole process, economic development, community development and welfare were inextricably closely connected. However, we are unsure whether colonial administrators consciously planned and combined economic and welfare activities in colonies. During those colonial times, many countries in Africa and Asia achieved neither satisfactory economic development nor adequate welfare services. Moreover, the development of welfare services often remained subsidiary to economic development in many colonies. Nonetheless, the idea and the potential of combining economic and welfare development, with all its potential benefits, may be sensed from the trial-and-error economic and community development experiments that occurred in the colonies, whatever the mixture of motives.

Colonial administrators exported not only raw materials but also people. Some people were exported to other colonies to enhance agriculture and economic development activities, and some others, particularly elites, went to the UK for further learning and education (e.g. Mahatma Gandhi and Jawaharlal Nehru and his dynasty from India). Exposure to the West enlightened them with ideas of freedom, democracy and the rule of law. On their return as 'finished products', some of them joined and led the growing independence movements in several colonies. Seeking to attain their dreams of freedom from colonizers, of independence and of nation building, their long struggle and sacrifices eventually yielded results. Many colonies became independent nations and established political and administrative systems with varied strengths.

However, the legacy of colonization and the links with coloniz-ers continued. In the decolonized countries, social, economic and political power structures were concentrated in the hands of elites, who, drawing on their own economic and community development experiences and their exposure to Western welfare systems, initi-ated grand nation-building projects. These elites lured the masses by promising that they would build a strong nation, achieve economic prosperity and eradicate poverty, adopt a Russian central planning model, develop welfare provisions and employ community develop-ment as an important approach to achieve all this. Perhaps watching these promising developments in decolonized nations, as Midgley (1994) notes, in 1954 the British government formally adopted the term 'social development' to connote the combination of traditional social welfare and community development. Midgley quotes an offi-cial British document that states that social development involves "nothing less than the whole process of change and advancement of a territory considered in terms of the progressive well-being of society and the individual" (United Kingdom, Colonial Office, 1954, p. 14, cited from Midgley, 1994, p. 6).

United Nations and Social Development

Although some countries achieved impressive economic prosper-ity, they often remained far behind the developed Western coun-tries, and such prosperity as did eventuate hardly percolated down to many local levels. Issues such as poverty, lack of health services, access to education and low standard of living did not reduce but continued unabated, and in addition, some of the poor countries were also not able to repay their debts. This kind of lopsided eco-nomic development, exacerbated in some countries by the debt crisis, was a great challenge not only for many new nation-states but also for the UN, which significantly changed its strategy from limited remedial welfare services to a social development strategy that emphasized social services and not just economic develop-ment. Since the 1960s, the UN has played a key role in popularizing the social development approach. It renamed one of its sections as the Commission for Social development in 1966, established the Research Institute for Social Development, organized meetings of experts and published their work on social planning, supported the ILO's (International Labour Organization) adoption of a basic needs approach in 1976, convened the World Summit on Social Development in 1995, and in 2000, developed the Millennium Development Goals that clearly emphasize social development (UNDP, 2003). The ILO's social protection floor initiative is also noteworthy (ILO, 2013; Social Protection Floor, 2013). In 2013, the Division for Social Policy and Development (DSPD) of the United Nations Department of Economic and Social Affairs (UN-DESA) has launched a web portal (http://www.unsdn.org) called United Nations Social Development Network (UNSDN, 2013) to share knowledge and good practices among social development professionals. These significant social development milestones and initiatives within the UN have resulted in several notable activities, which would require another chapter to elaborate. However, such activities appear to have encouraged many organizations and countries to adopt a social development perspective in their work.

These early and contemporary developments in the UN and actions by the UN have clearly influenced the World Bank. Davis (2004), in his paper, *A History of the Social Development Network in the World Bank, 1973–2002*, clearly shows how the World Bank was initially obsessed with the effectiveness of projects and how that obsession gradually changed in the mid-1980s to include a social development perspective in the World Bank's work. It further states that the establishment of the World Bank's social development network in 1997 and its work typically reflect and embody

- a focus on people and societies—rather than specific sectors or the economy;
- in-depth country and local knowledge—permitting adaptation to diverse conditions;
- a bottom-up perspective—including support for participatory approaches that encourage people to solve problems and that empower the poor;
- a concern with social systems and with the economic, social and political factors that support inclusion, social integration and sustainable social development; and
- support for a strong government role in reducing social barriers and making development more equitable and inclusive.

Publications on Social Development

Along with the popularization of the social development concept by the UN, several scholars (e.g. Cuyvers, 2001; Gore, 1988; Jones and Pandey, 1981; Midgley, 1995, 2014; Midgley and Conley, 2010; Patel, 2005; Pawar and Cox, 2010c) and UN organizations (e.g. the Research Institute for Social Development and the Economic and Social Commission for Asia and the Pacific) have published on the social development theme. As mentioned earlier, the UN has launched a web portal called UNSDN to share knowledge and good practices among social development professionals (see http://www.unsdn. org; United Nations Division for Special Policy and Development [UNDSPD], 2013). The International Consortium for Social Development (formerly known as the Inter University Consortium for International Social Development) has regularly published the journal *Social Development Issues* since the 1970s. Oxfam has published a journal entitled *Development in Practice* since the 1990s. The Asian and Pacific Association of Social Work Education has recently changed its journal name to *Asia-Pacific Journal of Social Work and Development*. Recently, in India, the Rajagiri College of Social Sciences initiated a new journal known as *Rajagiri Journal of Social Development*. In Africa, the *Journal of Social Development in Africa* has been published out of the School of Social Work in Zimbabwe since 1985. Both Indian and American encyclopaedias on social work have a chapter on social development. International professional bodies such as International Federation of Social Workers (IFSW), International Association of Schools of Social Work (IASSW) and the International Council on Social Welfare (ICSW) unitedly embraced the social development approach (for details, see Chapter 10).

Ideologies and Social Development

Historically, many aspects of social development and its implementation may be traced to four ideologies. These are individualist or liberal, populist, collectivist and partnership/institutional (Midgley, 1995, 2003). The organizations of the nation-states and societies are also influenced by these ideologies. The individualist or liberal ideology gives prime importance to individuals at the cost of neglecting or ignoring other entities in the society. In its extreme form, it does not accept any form of control of the individual. As it poses practical difficulties in organizing societies and helping other individuals in a dignified way, this ideology is used with moderation; thus, the emergence of neoliberals and related versions of the ideology. This neoliberal ideology emphasizes the individual's liberty, freedom, rational choice and natural rights. It is the mother of capitalism that pervades the globe today. It is a very powerful ideology and perhaps both the cause and the cure for a number of contemporary social problems. Those societies that follow an individualist or liberal ideology hold the individual responsible (to blame) for her or his situation and expect the individual to struggle, become self-reliant and create her or his own destiny. The social development goals of welfare and well-being are then achieved by enabling the individual to develop, that is, by developing capacities and by developing institutions along certain lines (e.g. reflecting the free market and privatization and ending regulatory regimes) and introducing policies and programmes that uphold the individual's liberty and freedom to develop knowledge and skills, to start enterprises, to compete in the market, to exploit opportunities, to contribute to capital formation and, thereby, generally, to achieve one's own welfare and well-being. When all individuals do so, social development goals can be achieved. For those who are incapable of participating within these liberal societies, through, for example, some incapacity, help is provided on a charitable and remedial basis with the option of buying welfare services in the market.

By contrast, populist ideology emphasizes the well-being of people and their communities at local levels. Midgley (1995, p. 90, 2003) states, "Populism champions the cause of ordinary people against the establishment, seeks to serve their interests and represents the popular will." Followers of this ideology follow and lead people's interests and mobilize people to organize communities and initiate change or action, sometimes by radical means. In many postcolonial newly formed states (e.g. India), some leaders have emerged from among the ordinary people, gained power by popularizing people's interests, relating developments to their needs, issues and aspirations and by developing and using slogans that reflect these interests. This ideology is helpful in bringing together and organizing neglected groups such as women, children and the elderly, and hence, focusing on the issues of these neglected groups. Many policies and programmes have been developed to meet peoples' interests. The populist ideology lends itself to community organization, community development and social action approaches to achieve social development goals or to improve conditions (see Chapter 2). It also operates as a bottom-up approach and one that is effective at local levels. One of the core aspects of social development, namely participation, stems from this ideology. Many non-government organizations (NGOs), community organizations and community and social development workers implicitly or explicitly use this ideology to improve the conditions of the people and communities with which they work.

Differing from the above two ideologies, the collectivist or socialist ideology emphasizes collectives of people, collective ownership of property and collective decision-making. Labour movements, trade unions and cooperatives are partly influenced by such ideology. According to this ideology, the state is a form of collective that can effectively manage economic and social development and meet peoples' needs. It is based on the assumption that "the state embodies the interests of society as a whole, and that it has a responsibility to promote the well-being of all citizens; government is collectively owned by citizens and represents their interests; the state is therefore the ultimate collective" (Midgley, 1995, p. 125). This ideology sounds somewhat idealistic, as there are many governments that are not accountable to citizens and in turn suppress them. However, by and large, the state as a collective, whether it be liberal, democratic and communist, has played a remarkable role in the economic development of countries as well as introduced various welfare measures, though the balance between the two—economic development and welfare—significantly differs from one country to another. In fact, the general trend suggests that some states and international agencies have overemphasized economic development by neglecting social dimensions of societies and by damaging the ecology, though they appear to be moving towards correcting the imbalance. However, it may be noted that collectivist or socialist ideology is an umbrella kind of ideology that encompasses many other significant aspects. For example, there are both democratic and communist states; some follow highly centralized planning and some follow decentralized planning, some are highly authoritarian and top-down and some encourage participation of citizens and others do not. Yet all of them aim to improve living conditions and achieve social development.

The fourth ideology is the partnership ideology, which Midgley (1995) calls the institutional perspective. Since the term 'institution' in this context may confuse readers, we have replaced it with the term 'partnership ideology'. All the above-presented ideologies have their strengths and weaknesses and can be found in practice in different forms and to varying degrees in all societies and communities. For heuristic purposes, they may be delineated separately, but in practice and for achieving social development goals, the best elements of all the three ideologies may be combined or at least accepted in such a way that partnership among these ideologies may be developed to better achieve social development goals. The essence of the partnership ideology is that partnership among the ideologies, theories, nation-states and national and international agencies needs to be nurtured to achieve social development goals. Although the state needs to steer the partnership, the market, state and community have to be the main drivers. There are many examples to show how all three are needed, for an emphasis on only one type of ideologically oriented development is seen to lead to distorted development. For example, in self-help groups and microfinance schemes, individuals' awareness, capacity and skills need to be developed; individuals have to come together in groups around some norms, with the group ensuring that it meets the needs and interests of the members; and the state should work to create an enabling environment so that individuals and groups can perform effectively, and thus, meet their needs and achieve well-being. However, because some communities and nation-states are capable of generating their own resources and others are not, partnerships between internal and external members and agencies need to be developed. When needed, this process may include external aid and personnel who work with communities at various levels to facilitate social development. Partnership is also needed among all the sectors of development, as they are all inextricably linked, and achieving one at the neglect of the others is detrimental and will result in distorted development.

The question is, can individualist, populist and collectivist ideologies coexist in societies so as to change current conditions and achieve social development goals? The partnership ideology suggests that it is possible to plan a combination of the three ideologies and apply them in such ways as to introduce social change and achieve social development goals.

On the whole, the historical evolution of the concept of social development suggests that, although the concept is not new, it has gradually emerged from a natural phenomenon to a planned phenomenon, with various scholars, institutions and socio-economic and political contexts and ideologies influencing its current form and shape. Contemporarily, social development is an important agenda of many governments. For example, in the UK, the Overseas Development Administration, now known as the Department for International Development (DFID), first appointed its Social Development Advisers (SDA) in 1975. However, it did not employ them in great numbers, as their number grew from two in 1987 to only seven in 1991. However, by 1997, DFID was employing more than 40 SDAs who have been significantly contributing to DFID's policy development from a social development perspective (Eyben, 2003). Many governments also have established a ministry or department of social development (e.g. New Zealand, Thailand, China and Trinidad and Tobago) to achieve the goals of social development. Although conservative governments in the 1980s, through their free market, liberalization and privatization policies, limited the application of the social development approach to some extent, such governments were also attracted to the idea of community participation and self-reliance. However, conservative governments' policies in some areas in fact led to negative social consequences in terms of growing poverty and inequality, both in developed and developing countries. This situation has been further compounded by climate change issues, yet it has again created excellent opportunities for social development thinking and practice.

Emergence of a Widely Held and Implemented Understanding of a Social Development Approach

Is there an appropriate theoretical basis to social development that can guide our understanding of the essential nature of and reasons for this approach? Are there any theories of social development? To these basic questions responses would differ depending on how one understands social development. Some may argue that social development as a field of practice draws from various disciplines and that it does not have its own knowledge base or its own theory. Adopting a contrary view, however, some suggest that social development does have its own theoretical base. This is one of the most difficult and controversial issues in social development.

We argue here that, in a strict sense and from a positivistic framework, there is no social development theory, though some scholars have used the term, 'social development paradigm' (Karger, 1994), which suggests that there is a grand theory of social development, but we think that is not the case. The current status of the underdevelopment or lack of social development theories does, however, provide great opportunities for building social development theories, and we believe that this can be done. Towards that end, we must consider some pre-stages of theory development that include identifying, and conceptualizing with clarity, concepts and variables, probable relationships and non-relationships among them, and values, ideologies and goals that influence those concepts and variables and their inter-relationships. As presented in this chapter, a brief exposition of the varied concepts, historical evolution and ideological orientations of social development may suggest that none of them is clear, convincing and conclusive. However, drawing from such an analysis, it may be possible to identify some core elements of, and an approach to, social development. Within a broad approach to social development, we locate seven composite concepts and variables as presented in Figure 1.1 and Box 1.4. These are existing conditions, goals, values, processes, strategies, levels and dimensions, and the figure shows the linkages among them.

The main purpose of the suggested approach to social development in Box 1.4 is to demonstrate that it is practical to progress social

Figure 1.1:
An approach to social development

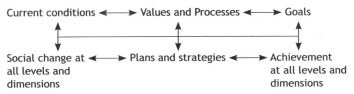

Box 1.4:
An approach to social development

Existing conditions
- Social change, progress and development

Goals
- Promotion of people's well-being or quality of life
- Enabling people to experience freedom to satisfy their aspirations and realize their potential

Values
- Respect for people and belief in their capacity to grow and develop
- An holistic understanding of human existence—physical to spiritual
- Acceptance of social and cultural pluralism and incorporation of the centrality of people's cultures and values
- Acknowledging the importance of ecological issues and people's link with nature and their environment
- Acknowledging that social relations are based on the right and obligation to participate, equality of opportunity and the right of all to social justice

Processes
- A participatory process
- An empowering process

Strategies
- Capacity building of individuals, groups and communities
- Local institution building and support for people's organizations
- Fostering self-reliance
- Creating an enabling environment within which all people can develop
- Participation in the development and functioning of social institutions
- Promoting the provision of adequate resources and services accessible to all
- Promoting a proactive role for the state in supporting participatory planning

(Box 1.4 Contd.)

(Box 1.4 Contd.)

- Engaging in the development and implementation of policies to enhance social development
- Coordinating development initiatives at all levels
- Strengthening civil society in all its various aspects

Levels
- International
- National
- Within the nation, regions
- States and provinces
- Districts
- The lowest administrative unit of governments
- Local-level or grassroots-level communities and villages

Dimensions
- Cultural
- Political
- Economic
- Ecological
- Education
- Health
- Housing
- Equity groups
- Citizens and their institutions

Source: Adapted from Cox et al. (1997b).

development. The approach first begins with an understanding of existing conditions and causes of such conditions, with a view to initiating social change, progress and development. First, it is clear that social development is about individuals, families however viewed, groups, communities and societies within their environment (including the ecological environment). All these entities have a current status or condition. That condition may be delineated in terms of geographic location, history, culture, political type and level, economy, infrastructure, resources, health, education, opportunities for development and major problems. The cause of any condition needs to be critically examined. Existing conditions may also be analyzed on the basis of a wide range of variables, including peoples' standard of living, societies' and communities' experience of minimal progress or further deterioration, decline due to distorted development resulting in concentration of wealth and resources, inequality, a class-based society, stress and isolation and lack of or inadequate access to the necessities of life such as food generally, nutritious healthy food, shelter, clothing and health and education services. Factors contributing to such conditions may then include gender discriminatory practices, dictatorial regimes, natural or human-made calamities such as war and conflict, tsunamis, floods, earthquakes, droughts and famines, or industrial and technological accidents.

To understand current conditions, two questions may be posed: what are the current conditions, and why do such conditions exist? Addressing the first question is relatively simpler than the second. Several epistemological and theoretical orientations may be utilized to understand current conditions. These mainly emerge from research approaches that include quantitative research, survey analysis, census data, development indicators, qualitative research, observation, ethnographic studies, case studies, participatory research, appreciative enquiry, media reports and so on. Descriptions of the current conditions at the macro level are often readily available and can be used to develop a better understanding of current conditions. For example, the UNDP's Human Development Index, which is based on several variables, classifies countries into those with low, medium and high levels of human development. However, this is at the societal level: at the grassroots or local community levels such an understanding needs also to be developed because of significant diversity. There is in practice considerable debate about the way these levels are reported, measured and understood and achievements claimed.

The perceived macro causes of current conditions that require social development have been attributed to several theories such as modernization, dependency and world systems (see So, 1990). These are controversial and evolving, with supporters constantly correcting their positions as a response to critiques and new evidence. All the relevant theories may be categorized as endogenous or exogenous. Theories that attribute the current conditions to internal factors, such as culture, tradition, subsistence farming, ignorance, lack of resources, leadership, governance, the level of use of technology, lack of innovation and so on may be treated as endogenous theories.

Modernization theories clearly fit here. Theories that attribute the current conditions to external factors, such as exploitation by industrialized countries in the West, international trade and aid regulations set by the international agencies (e.g. International Monetary Fund [IMF] and World Bank, World Trade Organization [WTO]) and globalization may be regarded as exogenous theories. Dependency and world systems theories clearly argue that these external factors are the cause of current and deteriorating conditions in the world. In reality, however, the causes of conditions that cry out for social development are a combination of both types of theories—clearly evident, for example, in the causes of climate change, and such conditions exist in many countries, both developed and developing, albeit to different degrees.

Second, it is important to set goals. To change conditions, systematic planned efforts need to be made to enable people to experience freedom and realize their potential, so as to ensure their well-being and quality of life, which are important general goals of social development. Specific goals may include the welfare, well-being, standard of living, human rights and equality and equity pertaining to any or all entities—individuals, families, groups, communities and societies, along with sustaining the ecological context. Goals are the foundations of social development practice, but no goals can be discussed without their value dimensions and ideological orientations. Goals are also based on the assumption that current conditions are unsatisfactory and need to be improved, so that achieving better conditions is expressed through goals. The theory-building process calls for a clear conceptual development of goals that are tangible, practical, measurable and verifiable, yet goals of social development are often criticized as unclear and unattainable. The complexity of clearly conceptualizing these goals stems from how material goals (e.g. meeting basic needs, increasing literacy rates and education, life expectancy etc.) and ideational goals (e.g. social justice, peace, welfare, well-being, equality, equity and empowerment) are inextricably combined in an interdependent way (see Midgley, 1995). Ideational goals, such as social justice, equality and distribution, have value and ideological connotations. The literature indicates considerable debate and controversy around social development goals (see supporting and opposing arguments by Midgley, 1995, pp. 92–101), but is it now time for us to get over that debate and focus on specific goals? For example, the Millennium Development Goals, relating to poverty, health, education, discrimination, ecology, cooperation and coordination may be viewed as social development goals. Yet who sets social development goals or agendas, and how, are vexing questions. Are they international community agencies or, at the national and local levels, a few individuals or a few elites, or all people and communities? How can people participate in setting social development goals? What are the value and ideological orientations of the goal setters? If social development goals are already set externally, how do we convince people and communities to own them? These questions have significant implications for planning and processes.

Third, the discussion of goals clearly includes values and ideologies. The set goals need to be achieved by adhering to the values of human dignity and worth, diversity, sustaining ecology, rights and obligations, and holism. Fourth, such values are closely connected to the processes of people's participation and empowerment, which are among the foundations of social development. Fifth, several strategies in the approach, which are self-explanatory, need to be implemented by following such processes as exemplified in the four above. Although the overall goals may be the same, that is, the welfare and well-being of all people, specific plans, strategies and processes to achieve the goals and thereby improve conditions differ significantly, depending on existing ideological orientations and beliefs as to the causes of existing conditions.

Sixth, such strategies need to be employed at multiple levels and in multiple sectors or dimensions (Cox and Pawar, 2006, 2013). Our conceptualization of multi-level includes international, national and, within the nation, regions, states or provinces, districts (the lowest administrative unit of governance) and grassroots-level communities and villages. The most important aspect of the multi-level approach currently, because of its comparative neglect to date, is the local level, which may be the grassroots-level communities or villages under the lowest administrative unit of governments. Although the other levels, including district, state or region, and nation, are important, a short history of development has unequivocally demonstrated that development endeavours at those levels alone, undertaken in a centralized manner, have not helped social development at the local level. The majority of grassroots-level communities, villages, rural areas and parts of urban areas have failed to receive the benefits of economic development to the extent they should have received, and thus, have remained far from achieving social development goals. In view of this apparent outcome, we are strongly convinced that, although social development at the national and regional levels within the nation has to be planned and promoted, the priority and focus should be the local community levels. Equally, priority also should be given to certain regions that have by and large remained underdeveloped in comparison with some other regions within a country.

Finally, social development work at multi-levels should also focus on multi-dimensions or sectors that mainly include cultural, political, economic, ecological, education, health, housing, equity groups and citizens and their institutions. Although these sectors are well planned and developed at national levels in many countries, most of the countries have overemphasized economic development, assuming that such development will percolate down, and hence, solve all problems and contribute to the development of the other dimensions at all levels, but such is not the case.

The cultural dimension of social development is a comprehensive, complex and controversial one, as conceptually it could include all other dimensions. However, for the purpose of delineation and discussion, we may separate out the other dimensions, though they are connected to the cultural dimension in that every aspect of society is connected to its culture. Early modernization theorists argued that, in order to become modern, to develop and to Westernize, traditional people and communities should get rid of their traditions, customs and beliefs as constituting the major hurdles in their progress. Contrary to this theory, the development of the Asian tigers and of some regions within countries showed that development and traditions can coexist. This development experience suggests that culture, customs, traditions and beliefs and development per se can exist together. Achieving one by losing the other is no development at all. Moreover, external agents' advice to give up one's culture to develop does not appear humane and is likely to undermine well-intended development efforts. Thus, to initiate social development, it is necessary and important for both external and internal development agents to understand people's and communities' culture, traditions, customs and religious and spiritual practices and beliefs. How do people and communities gain strengths from their culture and use them in all the other dimensions? Culture appears to be a foundation for all other dimensions. Understanding with sensitivity and developing people's and communities' culture in terms of religion, spirituality, arts and customs and beliefs contribute to people's welfare and well-being, and thereby, helps to achieve social development goals.

Developing the political dimension includes awareness raising, sensitizing around issues and needs and ways of addressing them, and developing the desire and abilities of people to participate in affairs and decision-making that affect their lives. The most important aspect of political development is leadership development at various levels and dimensions. Leadership needs to be developed in such a way that leaders are able to appreciate the importance of all dimensions and drive them. In fact, the whole development rests on the strength of the political dimension as in effect the centre of 'democratic' decision-making, though such decision-making needs to be truly participatory and people based.

Developing the economic dimension at all levels is vital. It is important to understand and work on people's economic aspirations. What are the resources of people and communities at all levels? What are the sources of livelihood? Are communities in any ways self-sufficient in meeting their needs? How are the existing resources distributed? What are the major blocks for economic development? These blocks could be inadequate infrastructure, underdeveloped or lack of markets and unemployment or a lack of employment opportunities. Depending on many factors, in most cases development of the economic dimension requires the mobilization of both internal and external resources by a range of agents, including governments, businesses, NGOs and, if necessary, international agencies. Development of primary industries, micro-enterprises (see Chapters 8 and 9 in Midgley, 2014) and fair market mechanisms are often the essence of economic development. Although it appears challenging, once economic development is generated, its rapid and unbridled growth can make or mar the social change process if it is not appropriately planned and implemented so as to enable the development of other dimensions.

The development of long-term and sustainable economic development primarily depends on sustainable ecological systems and human resources. Economic development that has exploited natural resources and neglected and damaged ecological systems has come under considerable criticism and rightly so. Thus, it is important to ensure that while pursuing economic development ecological development is equally emphasized. It may include watershed development and management; tree planting and the growth and protection of forests, seeds and species; developing green zones; controlling and preventing pollution (CO_2 emissions) and preventing both wastage and stagnation of natural resources, such as water and soil. It is well demonstrated that good ecological development results in good economic development (e.g. see the results of watershed development projects). Recent climate change issues and actions and green economy are pertinent to this dimension.

The development of human resources calls for the development of health and educational dimensions. Good health is vital for all living beings. The development of all the other dimensions depends on the development of healthy people and communities. To develop the health dimension, more preventive and promotive approaches need to be employed. Access to healthy, nutritious food and safe drinking water; development of healthy habits; prevention of at least the excessive consumption of alcohol, tobacco and similar other substances; and measures to reduce maternal mortality and child mortality and increase life expectancy are needed at all levels. Although these are repeatedly stated in national plans and programmes, they are often not translated to the local level.

Broadly and realistically, awareness is education. The education of people can readily trigger the social change process. Thus, it is important to provide both formal and informal education. Primary education has been made universal and compulsory in many countries, but such quality education needs to be realized particularly at the local level. Educating people about their culture, economy, political systems, ecology, health and how they can contribute to their development should be the goal. Developing educational infrastructure and facilitating pathways for further education need also to be given priority. The education dimension will then in turn contribute to the other dimensions.

Adequate, functional and quality housing is an important aspect of development. This dimension is closely related to health, economic and cultural dimensions. For good health and comfort, a good house and related infrastructure such as water and sanitation are essential. Millions of individuals live in mud-walled and thatched-roof houses, which are far from satisfactory. Also unsatisfactory is the situation in large urban centres where a large number of people live in slums. Poor housing certainly has implications for health. The housing development should be culturally suitable. Peoples' economic situation needs to be strengthened to the extent that they can afford their own house. Also, housing needs to be planned in such a way that it has functional sanitation arrangements. In many communities where water services are provided without sanitation, the water runs onto streets or gets blocked in gutters, making an excellent breeding ground for mosquitos, which has serious health implications.

Life experiences and some current distorted development patterns clearly show that some members and groups of the community, such as children, women, the elderly, the physically challenged, victims of disasters and people with illness, are particularly vulnerable and often miss out on the gains of development. They may be considered as equity groups for whom necessary services need to be provided in terms of the dimensions presented here to ensure their inclusion into the society's mainstream.

The development of cultural, political, economic, ecological, health, educational, housing and equity group dimensions should be geared towards developing good citizenship and institutions at all levels. Citizenship entails rights and responsibilities and ownership of the community. Thus, the development of all these dimensions may aim to develop individual capacities, thus contributing to turning people into good citizens who constructively engage in building their communities. Similarly, the development of these dimensions needs to create good governance institutions. Each dimension should have a role in governance institutions that are effective, efficient and free from corrupt practices. The development of good citizenship and good institutions go hand in hand and, in turn, should help in addressing all other dimensions. I hope that practising social development on a global scale by following this approach at all levels, particularly in local-level communities, will help to achieve universal social development.

Conclusion

As stated in the introduction, this chapter has looked at the concept and historical evolution of social development and an emerging approach to social development practice. Although there are various definitions of social development, common themes may be identified in terms of goals, values, processes that may advance structural change, the juxtaposing of social with economic development and the participation and empowerment of people and communities. The historical analysis has shown that the idea of social development has evolved over a long time. Many scholars and evolving socioeconomic and political contexts and institutions have contributed to social development, and several ideologies have embraced social development from their own perspectives. The partnership ideology appears to be the most promising as it appears to capture the best elements of all other major ideologies. Drawing from such an analysis, we have presented a social development approach that focuses on improving the existing conditions, such as distorted development, with the clear goal of enhancing human welfare and well-being. It also incorporates a value orientation and empowering and participatory processes and suggests effective strategies for implementation at all levels and all dimensions with an emphasis on local levels. We believe that such an approach enhances the conceptual clarity of social development and affirms that social development can be practised anywhere and its goals achieved.

2

Local-level Community Development

Introduction

My own life experiences in villages and observation of the overall development process suggest that local-level community development (these concepts are defined in what follows) through the social development approach (presented in Chapter 1) is very much needed today. I was brought up in a large-size (with a population of about 10,000) village in India and lived in villages for nearly two decades. I keep reflecting on village life, with its persisting needs and problems. It was a very old and traditional village where farming was the main source of livelihood for the majority of people. The majority of children turned to farming, and only a small number of them went on to higher education after year 10 of their schooling. Most of the mud- or mud-and-stone-built houses were clustered according to caste groups. Houses belonging to scheduled castes and tribes were located outside the village, though a very small number of families have recently brought houses inside the village. Occupations were linked to castes, though this situation has now been significantly diluted, at least in some places. People used to access doctors only when they were seriously ill, and they also followed spiritual healing methods. The majority of people lived in poverty. Poverty and subsistence farming; seasonal employment; underemployment and unemployment; lack of or inadequate infrastructure, including basic roads and sanitation; health issues; and lack of quality education were then very common in villages.

In recent times, life in some villages has changed through general development processes and more particularly through gram panchayats. Poverty level has come down and wages have relatively improved; more children go to school; transportation has become better; people's access to health services has relatively increased, whether private or public; and some gram panchayats have developed some public, albeit often minimal, infrastructure such as roads and sanitation. Stratification based on caste has also become diluted. The government's public distribution system has also improved. The expected change in the occupational structure is occurring as more people are moving from agriculture to service or manufacturing sectors. There is both surplus labour and a shortage of labour, and some people have begun commenting that labourers' attitude towards commitment to work is changing as they seem to be happy with government provisions. Increasing rural-urban interaction, urbanization, information and communication technology and purchasing power in a relative sense are all contributing to more consumerism. Some of these changes that are occurring in some villages are bringing other problems. For example, the provision of tap water without sanitation has led to waste water flowing on streets and providing an excellent breeding ground for mosquitoes, whereas easy access to plastic products has led to inappropriate disposal of plastic bags and cups in villages, and, third, the labour force departing from the agriculture sector has no planned employment outlet. Educated youth have migrated to urban areas. Communities' informal care, welfare practices (Pawar and Cox, 2004) and art and cultural activities, all appear to be diminishing.

Although significant development has occurred at several levels, including at the village level with varied degree and speed, the general conditions in large number of villages in India and South Asia generally have not changed to the extent that they should have, although there are few individual exceptions. When I visit villages in India, I often cannot see any discernible change in them, and, from what I see, I am not convinced that the quality of life is improving in these villages, notwithstanding India's high economic growth rate and higher wages. I keep asking myself, why is this so and what can be done? There may be many ways of addressing this issue, but I would like to suggest the use of the social development approach for local-level community development. In developing this idea, first this chapter discusses the concept of local level and community development and the changing nature of community development. Then it discusses the significance, rationale and goals of local-level community development. Finally, the last section shows how social development approach can be employed for furthering local-level community development and related strategies and programmes.

Basic Concepts

Local Level

It is important to understand the concepts of local level and community development. In Chapter 1, under Box 1.4, seven levels of social development, from international to local, have been identified (see Figure 2.1). Although all levels are important and social development should occur at all levels, here our focus is on understanding what local level is. The word 'local' in local-level community development does not carry any one specific connotation. Uphoff (1986, p. 11) saw it as signifying any or all of the following: locality level (a set of interrelated communities having cooperative or commercial relations), community level (a relatively self-contained socio-economic residential unit), or group level (a self-identified set of persons with a common interest, may be a small residential group like a hamlet or neighbourhood, an occupational group, or some ethnic, caste, age, sex, or other grouping), household level and individual level. As briefly stated in Chapter 1, local level refers to the majority of grassroots-level communities and villages in both rural areas and parts of urban areas. Specifically, it refers to the bottom of the pyramid as shown in Figure 2.1. Similarly, those who keep commuting between rural and urban areas for work or trade maintain in fact two community bases. Under each taluka there are many gram panchayats and gram panchayats that consist of thousands of villages and communities. The local level refers to such villages and

Figure 2.1:
Multi-levels for social development practice and the local level

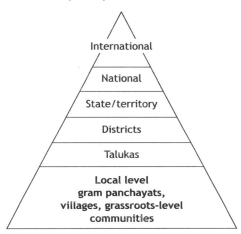

communities under gram panchayats and similar communities falling under urban development authorities or municipal corporations (this nomenclature may differ from state to state).

The local level may also be conceptualized in terms of individuals, families, groups and communities, given the importance of all these types of units in their engagement in the majority of situations covered under local-level community development. In addition to their significance as local units or entities, in our 2013 text (Cox and Pawar, 2013, pp. 182–184) we regard individuals, families and communities as one sector of society alongside three others, namely, the marketplace or economic sector, the governance of the state or institutional sector and the civil society sector (these sectors go well with several dimensions of the social development approach), and we go on to argue that this individuals–families–communities sector and its development constitute the foundation of any society. The following is a summary of our argument:

> If we wish to be more specific, we can discuss several ways in which important aspects of society depend on the foundations established at the local level. One argument is that ultimately it is people who constitute a society's most important resource, but like all other resources, people

require development, and this development begins at the local level. A crucial aspect of this is capacity building at the individual, family, and community levels. A second argument is that important societal qualities, such as social capital and social integration, cannot ultimately be imposed from above but rely on local-level developments (World Bank, 2000/2001, 2001). A third argument is that macroeconomic development is, to a significant degree, dependent on economic developments at the local level, such as the household economy, the community economy, and the informal economy, while other levels of economic development require that the local level functions effectively as producers and consumers within the economic system. (Cox and Pawar, 2013, p. 184)

In social development terms, it is important to see the development of local level as not only the development of the very foundations of a society but also as building at the local level a receptivity to national development initiatives. There is thus a two-way process. On one hand, national-level development creates opportunities that then exist for individuals and groups to take advantage of. These may be capacity-building opportunities, as through accessing education and training systems, income earning opportunities, as through engaging in the emerging employment market, or the pursuance of personal and group interests through the opportunities made available by national-level development, such as those offered by urbanization and international links. On the other hand, effective national-level development also reaches out to localities through the provision of services and opportunities; however, the ability of the local level to be receptive to these will depend in large part on the extent of existing local capacity building and local organizational development. That is to say, a locality needs to be prepared for participation in mainstream national development. Hence, the role of local-level community development through a social development approach is to achieve both of these goals, namely, the preparation of localities for full and effective participation in whatever national- and state-level development offers, and preparation of the entities that constitute a locality to enable them to reach out and take advantage of emerging opportunities beyond the local level. Where, however, national- and state-level social development is either virtually non-existent or exists but excludes certain population groupings, the focus of local-level community development will be significantly on self-reliant development.

Community Development

To understand the concept of community development, it is neces-sary to look at the concept of community. The term 'community' is a general, complex, contested (Pierson and Thomas, 2010) and com-prehensive one as different people and professionals use it in differ-ent ways for different purposes. Effrat (1974, p. 2) rightly commented that "much of the problem in identifying the various definitions lies in separating the content of the conception from value-laden imagery of warmth and camaraderie attached to it in many cases." Hillery's (1955) analysis of 94 definitions of community showed three most common elements of the concept of community. These were area, common ties and social interaction. Similarly, recent authors of two community development textbooks (Ife, 2013; Stepney and Popple, 2008) have discussed the concept of community in terms of five core character-istics. These are size of the population, commonality among people, identity and belonging, primary relationships and attachment and local culture. A shift from defining community to describing community characteristics suggests difficulties in capturing the dynamic objective and subjective phenomena of the community.

In contemporary modern and postmodern life do we have commu-nities with these characteristics or do we live in such communities? The progressive 21st century with the baggage of successful coloni-zation and subjugation of local populations, significant achievement of industrialization, modernization, production and prosperity, urbaniza-tion, controlled geographical location of communities based on some criteria, such as caste or occupation (particularly in rural areas and villages), and such communities' integration and politicization have rendered the constitution of community complex, challenging and diffused. As people's lifestyles have changed over recent times, so have their communities and their conception of the community. For example, people who live in highly urbanized and so-called devel-oped centres and heavily engaged in their work and their own lives without knowing who their neighbours are and what is happening in their neighbourhood cannot fit within the traditional meaning of community that focuses on locality, belonging and local culture. Such peoples' sense of belonging often lies elsewhere, not necessarily in the locality. The new concept and reconstruction of the community must, therefore, reflect the constantly changing nature of people and their communities. How are communities changing and what kinds of communities exist at the local level? Rather than following the definitions of community as defined in the West, it is important to observe and understand how communities exist and how they are changing at the local level, within a specific context.

Contemporary communities may be understood in terms of three overlapping types that may or may not be connected to each other. The first and most fundamental aspects of community are people and place in terms of geography or locality, close or distant, and mutual or otherwise interaction among people that creates a relative sense of belongingness and attachment both with people and the place. Sociological definitions have mostly covered geographic locality, belongingness among people and their interactions. The concept of community should also include belongingness and attachment to the place, as people also have belongingness to their place in terms of their land, water and vegetation. Such an understanding of community is important from the ecological point of view, which is gaining increasing significance in contemporary times. Such types of communities are most common at the local level in rural areas. It may be noted that geographic or locality-based community appears to be under threat and likely to gradually disappear as urbanization and its influences penetrate traditional community-living styles at the local level. Both rural and urban communities have strengths and weaknesses. Rural communities are often conservative, have strong belief systems and their groupings and relationships are often based on religion, caste and similar identity, and some of these may work as barriers when working with them initially. By contrast, urban communities are more anonymous, more contractual in their dealings and more likely to look at what people are rather than prejudiced by factors such as caste, origin and so on (Pierson and Thomas, 2010).

In the second type, there are communities of people with or without any specified geographic locality, but their sense of community is developed on the basis of common background, interests or issues, such as religion, ethnicity, place of origin, language, sports or hobbies, disability, child care, youth, ageing and so on. The second type may be labelled as 'target and/or interest-based community'.

The third type is a virtual community that has spread the community net by drastically reducing time and space where interactions occur and relationships develop, with or without physical proximity and often beyond geographic locality. For example, such communities develop through the use of the internet, social media such as Facebook and smartphones, through which people interact, develop relationships, devise action plans and fight for specific causes.

Keeping in mind these very different types of communities, from a normative perspective, community development is defined as "a participatory people-centred process that involves bringing together, mobilizing or organizing people, keeping them together and enabling them to work together to address their needs and issues and thus to facilitate their own, their communities' and society's comprehensive development as per the social development approach" (Pawar, 2010). However, it does not imply that community development is always or often practised according to this definition, though it ought to be. It may also be challenging to practise this type of community development within the last two types of communities.

The great hopes of earlier community development efforts in independent India, and its spread in many countries largely failed due to several complex factors. Power structures from village to upper levels resisted community development initiatives, and these structures siphoned off most of the benefits. It was also difficult to access the thousands of villages. Furthermore, the lack of coordination among inter-ministerial bureaucracies, an overemphasis on social services, centrally led bureaucratic and reporting procedures and a lack of involvement of communities with their linkages to higher-level regional units diminished the prospects of community development in India (see analysis of Korten, 1980) and the same may also have happened in other Asian countries. Most important, influenced by Western economic development theories (e.g. see Rostow's stages of growth and the Lewis theory of development in Todaro, 1997) and modernization theories, the nation-building priority was dominated by centrally led economic growth and development that offered little room for community development practice at the local level. In the mid-1960s, most community development programmes were terminated or drastically reduced. In his analysis Korten (1980) states, "Community development had promised much, yet delivered little." Let us, therefore, now turn our attention to the significance of and rationale behind focusing on local-level community development.

Significance, Rationale and Goals of Local-level Community Development

The Large Size and Unaddressed Needs and Issues of Vulnerable and Improvised Populations

The significance of and rationale for local-level community development stem from the scale of the potential and unaddressed needs and issues of vulnerable and impoverished populations that have existed for a long time. Thousands of villages in India and in the Asian region are yet to fully share the fruits of development occurring at other levels (see Figure 2.1). Although it has been estimated that in the near future about 50 per cent of people will be living in urban areas, still 50 to 65 per cent of people will live in villages in rural and remote areas, and meeting their needs and addressing their issues are important. In the 21st century, or as some people are calling it 'the Asian century', in the midst of prosperity and consistent high growth rates, the current impoverished state of many local communities cannot be justified. About one billion poverty-stricken and vulnerable people are unable to secure an acceptable standard of living or realize their full potential. Moreover, given all the resources that have gone into development to date, we can only conclude that this unacceptable situation will be rectified only when serious direct attempts are made to alleviate poverty, reduce insecurity, raise standard of living and expand the range of available opportunities at all those local levels where there is a dire need for development.

The Place of the Local Level in Social Development

The basic understanding of social development as it has emerged in the recent decades is that the three levels of international, national and local are by themselves and in their own right key levels of development. There is no intrinsic logic as to why any benefits of previous international- or national-level development should invariably trickle down to each and every local level, partly because of the inherent nature of international and national levels and the emphasis given to their development. Local levels will often require direct targeting if they are to be receptive to developments at other levels. Despite a certain level of outreach, global- and especially national-level, developments create opportunities that the constituent elements of a society need to take advantage of, usually taking the initiative by themselves, if they are to get a share in the benefits. Hence, even when outreach does occur, the process must be reciprocal, with the local level being also able and ready to reach out through the process of bottom-up development.

The Significance of Pluralism in Society

The modern society is almost invariably pluralistic in a range of ways, and it is very common for political and economic developments, plus the ability to benefit from them, to follow the particular social patterns in a society resulting from its pluralistic nature. Almost invariably some categories or groups of people are effectively excluded from some developments or significantly discriminated against, and although this state of affairs can be tackled through anti-discrimination measures at the national level, these will not always work, unless, at the same time, disadvantaged groups are appropriately strengthened to take their rightful place within the society. Local-level community development will, therefore, often be very important in addressing inequalities and imbalances within pluralistic societies.

The Existence of Remote Communities

Many nations possess areas that are remote or cut-off in ways that render participation in national level development, as contributors or beneficiaries, a difficult process. These may be island communities separated from mainland or national centres, mountain communities cut off by rugged terrain and often heavy winters, remote areas in far-flung corners of the nation, or poverty-entrenched areas whose very poverty isolates them from developments elsewhere. Although modern nations may develop appropriate responses to all kinds of barriers, some areas can still be forgotten or overlooked when their remoteness coincides with other characteristics such as the possession of a particular tribal-ethnic-racial-religious characteristic that sets them apart and even renders them unpopular. In most such situations, local-level community development will need to focus on achieving a high degree of self-reliant development as the basis initially of survival but ultimately of significant progress.

The Importance of Building Community Networks and Strengths and Civil Society at the Local Level

Community strengths and networks (some scholars refer to it as social capital; see Hoff, 1998; Korten, 1995, p. 279; Putnam, 1993, p. 235) are crucial ingredients in social development. The World Bank (1999/2000, p. 18) sees social capital reflected at the local level, for example, in citizen and parental involvement in education, health and local credit schemes, and so on, and manifested in a high level of "participation in village level social organizations" (World Bank, 1997, p. 115). According to Cox (2006, pp. 14–15),

> At the civil society level, social capital is again not the level of capacity building and so on that has occurred within the many social organizations but that which binds these organizations together in terms of how they network with each other, trust each other, relate to each other and ultimately how they work together within social processes. Moreover, social capital will result in certain types of social organizations that might not otherwise emerge: that is to say, organizations that reflect a community-based or community-wide approach, whether political, economic, social, cultural or welfare in nature, will emerge in societies with strong social capital. Midgley (1995, ɔ. 160) refers to such developments as social capital stock.

The importance of community bonds and the foundations of civil society are crucial to both the local level and ultimately the society as a whole, and it is through local-level community development essentially that these two characteristics of a healthy society are built and strengthened.

Neglect of the Local-level Community Development

It is certainly not the case that the local level of social development has been ignored in conceptual presentations of social development, for it is in fact quite frequently stressed. Nor is it the case that it has been completely neglected in the field, in that many, if not most, of the agencies involved at the international level have devised, encouraged, funded and participated in development programmes and projects that are located, at least in part, at the local level. In our opinion, however, two tendencies have contributed to the comparative neglect of the local level. First, major development agencies at the international level tend, understandably, to place a strong emphasis on the international (i.e. relations between nations in terms, for example, of donor aid) level and on the national level. The activities they do support at the local level have tended to be those initiated by development contractors, NGOs and others with a concern for the local level across a specified region, but the resulting projects have been all too frequently one-dimensional and so restricted in scope, either when viewed against the concept of comprehensive social development or in terms of the extent of existing needs. Moreover, at times, some of these agencies able and willing to operate at the local level feel it necessary to select the more promising local situations located within those countries that are already making some progress. To do otherwise seems to be perceived as likely to court failure by not achieving the goals accepted by the donor and, hence, to experience difficulty in raising further funding. Thus, internationally initiated development work undertaken at the local level has often been criticized as being largely project-based, one-dimensional, sometimes unsustainable and, even when successful, desperately requiring replication on a greatly expanded basis. Seldom does one locate a relatively comprehensive local-level development programme addressing any of the world's most needy areas and peoples and undertaken on an extensive basis.

Second, there appears to be a significant focus on national-level development by both significant players within the international development community and by national governments themselves. This approach is consistent with the strong focus throughout the post–World War II period on macroeconomic development. National governments were seen as needing to modernize, largely through focusing on urbanization, industrialization and associated infrastructure development, essentially to undertake all steps seen as necessary to achieve economic growth. Players at the international level were keen to support such developments through promoting global trade, especially on a free trade basis, grants for large-scale development projects and expanding global investment markets. For some time, major donors encouraged large-scale infrastructure and other developments along with macro fiscal, educational and health initiatives that would initially favour the better-off members of elite or majority groups within the country. If and when the local level was considered, it was commonly assumed that the flow-on effects of macroeconomic growth-oriented development would ultimately benefit all levels and dimensions of development and all peoples but that this first step of economic growth was critical if any significant progress was to be made.

There is, however, ample evidence suggesting that the assumed trickle-down or flow-on effects of macroeconomic development often did not occur, largely because the theory implied certain prerequisites that were often not present. It implied a cohesive country and population where those in power would exhibit a national and inclusive concern, whereas in reality many elite or upwardly mobile groups who gained power had little or no sympathy with other sections of the population or country. It implied also a stable, non-corrupt and efficient system of governance, which in reality did not prevail in many countries. Hence, many governments essentially failed to tax growth and redistribute the fruits of growth through social services, income support and other programmes. Instead, many countries became increasingly unequal and often politically unstable as a result. Finally, the theory implied a receptive local level, whereas in fact many local levels were suffering from such entrenched poverty and the absence of capacity-building opportunities that their ability to participate in whatever national-level development occurred was extremely limited, even if they were able to migrate to the urban centres of growth as many of them were inclined to do.

In recent times, the international community has increasingly recognized both the importance of enhancing good governance and addressing local-level poverty alleviation and so on as part of all national-level economic and other development initiatives. This is particularly the case with the World Bank and International Monetary Fund (IMF) following now strongly along the more balanced path long emphasized by the United Nations Development Programme (UNDP) and others (UN, 1995; Millennium Development Goals,

UNDP, 2003), and these emphases have also increasingly become a focus of the overseas aid programmes of Western governments. What is now in fact the widely accepted approach to social development is that development work should ideally be a combination of complementary top-down and bottom-up approaches to development.

Linkages between National Level and Local Levels

This focus on a combination of top-down and bottom-up development initiatives raises the question of whether a significant degree of local-level community development, or bottom-up development as this in effect is, is feasible if national-level development is virtually non-existent, at a very low level, or the victim of corrupt and biased development processes. In other words, is it inevitable that a degree of national-level development, and especially of national-level economic development, is a prerequisite for a reasonable level of local-level community development to be achieved? If this proposition is correct then one might well conclude that there is little point in addressing local-level community development, especially within the numerically significant number in total of least developed countries, failed states and states generally suffering from poor governance. The question is thus an extremely important one regarding the global scope for local-level community development in its own right.

This question of whether significant national-level development is a prerequisite for local-level community development cannot be answered abstractly or with any degree of certainty or generality, and the following attempt at an answer represents largely our own opinions, being based on little strong evidence. However, it should be noted that the UN's 1995 Summit on Social Development emphasized, as its first commitment, the creation of "an economic, political, social, cultural and legal environment that will enable people to achieve social development"—the so-called enabling environment (UN, 1995, p. 11). We would stress, first, that it needs to be made clear that a significant level of appropriate national-level social development will almost certainly increase the chances of successful work at the local level. This will be especially true if that national-level development has been comprehensive in nature, covering all dimensions. Our concern here, however, is how far can local-level community development progress without significant national-level development. Our second point is that the precise nature of the link between the national-level and the local-level developments will be extremely important, and several possible scenarios are evident. Some local levels are simply neglected by other levels of development; other local levels and their development are viewed antagonistically by central governments, usually for cultural, ethnic or political reasons; while other local levels again are victims of national level instability, civil war or a central inability to respond effectively to natural disasters. The precise circumstances surrounding a failure of national-level development to translate into progress at local levels will vary, but it will be these precise circumstances that will become an important factor in determining the outcomes of efforts to achieve local-level community development.

Both points will affect local-level community development at every step. We would argue, however, that whatever the extent and nature of national-level social development and whatever the precise nature of the relationship between a local level and its national level, some local-level community development will always be possible if the necessary resources are available, and action to bring it about will always be worthwhile. Even among extreme local situations, such as gatherings of displaced persons, marginalized indigenous minority populations or communities, populations in extremely remote areas and communities with very high levels of poverty, something can be achieved if the will is there at some level and personnel available to implement a programme. These are crucial prerequisites. Ideally some resources beyond personnel will be helpful, but even that is not crucial, especially if the available personnel are well trained and able to identify and draw on existing local resources. It should always be possible, for example, for workers to enable the local people themselves to operate a basic literacy course, basic primary health care facilities and basic primary schools or income generation schemes that draw initially almost entirely on local resources. Any such measures will be beneficial to local-level community development to some degree, however minimally, and can be implemented with no significant external resources and no dependence on national-level developments. However, clearly, some amount of external resources and some level of ability to link up local level with national-level developments will enhance the potential success of even these basic programmes.

In considering the significance of the nature of the linkages between national-level and local-level development, we would further argue that any success achieved at the local level will carry with it the potential of either contributing indirectly to, or of increasing the pressure for, national-level social development. Local-level community development inevitably enhances capacities among individuals, families, communities and local organizations, strengthens social capital and begins the important process of building civil society. Each of these developments will, within a cumulative and interactive process, build national resources and result in some degree of pressure for national-level development in terms of good governance, equitable redistribution of nation's wealth, expansion of nation's infrastructure and extension of nation's social services provision. As we shall argue later, local-level community development constitutes an essential building block in national development. Indeed, it can be argued that developments at the local level constitute the only foundations on which a strong and secure nation as a total and unified entity can ultimately be built.

Rationale and Goals of Local-level Community Development

In general terms, local-level community development is development that takes place at the local level and is ideally initiated by the local level. It is not essentially or ideally action that occurs at the local level as a result or flow-on of central-level planning and decision-making (UN Centre for Regional Development, 1988, p. 14). As Midgley (1992a, p. 4) puts it, in what he refers to as the populist understanding of social development, "[Local level] social development is said to occur when local people collaborate to strengthen community bonds and take concerted action to improve their social and economic conditions." We would argue that the philosophical base of local-level social development is that local people, through their community structures, are enabled to assume responsibility for their own development.

Rationale

The rationale for focusing directly on local-level community development, as set out in the above discussion, is threefold. Development at this level is designed essentially for three purposes:

1. To address years of neglect of development at the local level, usually reflected in extreme poverty and deprivation;
2. To compensate for failures in development at the national level; and
3. To prepare the local level for participation in further national-level development, especially in terms of the local level being able to take advantage of opportunities that are opening up.

It is not unusual for local-level development to have all the three purposes in mind; however, differentiation between local-level situations in terms of which of these purposes is predominant is also important. Undoubtedly, the most difficult situation is reflected in the first purpose, in that initiatives to overcome years of development neglect will invariably be confronted with the realities of extreme poverty, low levels of personal self-esteem and confidence and very little local organizational development. The second most difficult situation will tend to be where there is minimal national-level development of which the local level can take advantage, restricting local development to those areas for which local resources are relatively adequate, with perhaps minimal levels of essential external assistance in the form of aid of some kind. This situation is rendered much worse if the national level in effect circumscribes or opposes local-level development in significant ways, essentially by presenting barriers to it, which it may do if, for example, it perceives local development as a threat to its dominance. The third situation put forward, namely that of enabling a local level to take appropriate and significant advantage of potentially beneficial national-level developments, is the easiest to respond to, especially if it is possible to work simultaneously at the national level to ensure that it does understand and respond appropriately to local-level development needs. In some situations, all three purposes are relevant reasons for engaging in local-level community development, and these are often both complex and extremely difficult situations for intervention.

Goals

As we see it, there are three broad goals behind local-level community development initiatives, the specific relevance of each being determined by the prevailing circumstances. These three goals are as follows:

1. To assist individuals and other social entities at the local level to overcome significant problems that represent a specific barrier to these individuals' or entities' social functioning and further development;
2. To strengthen the local level as a whole by strengthening individuals, families, specific population groupings and local organizations wherever possible and appropriate; and
3. To promote local-level community development within all dimensions where further development is clearly essential to achieving overall local-level community development.

Local-level Community Development through the Social Development Approach

The social development approach has been presented in Chapter 1 (see Figure 1.1 and Box 1.4). It includes the understanding of existing conditions of local-level communities, setting goals by engaging local people and employing specific strategies by following values, principles and processes appropriate to all levels and dimensions. Here the focus is at the local-level community. It would not be incorrect to surmise that the majority of local-level communities, villages and groups in rural and remote areas in India and Asia are yet to experience the work of professionally trained social and community development workers. Wherever they are working, it is common to see many social work students, social workers, community development workers, social development workers, NGOs, gram panchayats and other government agencies and people's organizations working on one aspect of the community or on one or two issues/needs of the community. Such issues or needs may relate to health, education, employment and income generation, village infrastructure (e.g. roads, sanitation, community centres) and so on. This is often project based and often dictated by funding agencies or opportunities, need priority or crisis situations, and government programmes. Provided that these specific projects adopt an appropriate process, consistent with certain principles, they may in themselves be highly beneficial. At the same time, however, each can have only a limited impact on overall local-level community development because they are tackling but one dimension of the local reality, and therefore, they will exert only a limited, although often significant, impact on the prevailing situation. They may even ultimately fail because they are not integrated within the prevailing local situation— a not uncommon outcome.

As part of such projects, social work student placements are often organized by communities themselves, resulting in discontinuities and disruptions, usually due to the nature of training and educational requirements. However, social work schools and students can choose a particular village or community and work consistently and continuously for a long period to demonstrate the application of social development approach to bring about qualitative improvements in the selected community. Although a single agency or social worker is not expected to work at all dimensions of social development, the planned application of social development approach by them is important and needed to achieve local-level community development. To achieve good results in the application of social development at the local community level, the following six steps may be followed. The first three steps provide knowledge, skills and competencies, and the other three steps demonstrate their use at the local level.

1. Understanding the Social Development Approach

As discussed in the first chapter, many people and professionals understand social development in their own ways, as social development has many definitions and meanings. It is, therefore, important to understand the social development approach presented in Chapter 1. Anyone interested in practising local-level community development, including social workers and social and community development workers, should understand the philosophy, spirit and functionality of the social development approach. Such understanding can be gained by self-reading; attending training programmes such as relevant university courses, seminars and workshops; and by visiting and observing local villages and communities. Such an understanding needs to be developed in villages, communities and groups, local-level leaders, gram panchayat members, people's organizations and workers of NGOs and other government organizations. Fundamental to enhancing their understanding is removing the common misunderstanding that social development is different from economic development. The discussion should broadly focus on the current state of their communities; the goals they want to achieve for their families and communities; how certain values, principles and processes need to guide action; and how the conscious use of a range of strategies can help make progress across all dimensions of communities.

2. Sticking to Values, Principles and Processes

Dean (2010, p. 185) rightly states, "Social development is an ethical project in its own right. . . ."; hence, following certain values and principles and processes is crucial. These are briefly stated in Box 1.4 in Chapter 1, and the four basic values and principles are elaborated in Chapter 3. There is today virtually universal agreement, at least in principle, among those concerned with local-level social development, as to the process that it should adopt. The process is in effect the application of an agreed set of principles to the development process. The five key elements of the process discussed here are that it be participatory, empowering, equitable, based on human rights and sustainable or ecologically sensitive and sound. (These five principles do not represent an exclusive list, and some of those listed may be seen as embracing others, such as self-reliance.)

Taken together, these five aspects of the development process are very far-reaching and in practice quite difficult to implement, which explains why much local-level community development in practice fails to live up to these ideals. It is much easier to do things to and for people without their participation; empowering people can backfire and lead to some people making inappropriate or difficult demands on other levels, such as the nation, to such an extent that some people are wary of an empowering approach. Thus, rationalizing the long-term benefits for everyone of favouring an elite group within the development processes is often much easier than adopting an equitable approach from the beginning within an already unequal situation.

Recognizing all people's human rights can be profoundly unpopular politically, especially if it is seen as likely to undermine an elite or majority group's power base or standard of living, and ecological sustainability can readily be presented as either unnecessary or a highly contentious and dangerous approach, making it easier for the power centre to constantly defer difficult ecological decisions. Although we have reasonable consensus globally on all of these principles as such, the problem lies, albeit understandably, in procrastination regarding their application in the field, certainly by governments and at times even by NGOs and people's organizations. We have a great ability as human beings to rationalize and skirt around principles, even those that we readily endorse 'in principle', when we find them difficult or costly to implement.

This is why all the elements of this process must be strongly emphasized at all the local-level social development initiatives, such as education, training and practice. People, communities, workers and organizations need to develop an uncompromising commitment to achieving the goals of promoting people's well-being or quality of life and empowering people to gain freedom in order to satisfy their aspiration and realize their potential. While working with individuals, families, groups, communities and organizations, workers need to demonstrate respect for people and belief in their capacity and a holistic understanding of human existence, nature and ecology and support pluralism, non-discrimination and human rights. By enabling and engaging people, they need to follow empowering and participatory processes. As pointed above, practising such values, principles and processes may appear challenging, at least initially, perhaps due to vested interests and dynamics of the community power structure, but in the long term it will prove effective and useful.

3. Developing Competencies to Use Strategies

In Box 1.4 of Chapter 1, 10 strategies have been suggested for social development practice. Awareness of these strategies, though important, is not adequate unless effective skills are developed to employ them. They are specific and broad-based strategies that cut across all dimensions. Individual workers are not expected to use all these strategies at the same time. Collective and partnership efforts among individual workers, local people and communities, NGOs and government organizations are needed to implement these strategies. While working with individuals, families and groups, many of the strategies can be used by workers and agencies.

The four most basic requirements for local-level community development are first, where necessary, building of self-confidence and self-esteem and awareness raising; second, capacity building with individuals, families and local organizations; third, income generation; and fourth, developing community resources. The balance and interaction between these in intervention at the local level is crucial. In those situations where self-confidence and self-esteem are at a low level, it is imperative to address this need. At the same time, it may be difficult to address it directly and in isolation from other needs, largely because the need may not be even recognized by many people. Indeed, building self-confidence may sometimes best be addressed indirectly by, for example, focusing on capacity building while carefully building self-confidence in the process. In any event, it is imperative that workers do not overlook the importance of building self-confidence, regardless of how they choose to tackle it.

Box 2.1:
An example of building self-confidence

In one programme involving female-headed households in Bangladesh, workers recognized the need to work with very small groups of women, who already knew each other, over periods of several months if necessary. The overt initial aim was to encourage the women to discuss their life and family situations, needs and aspirations, identify areas ideally requiring change and, where possible, engage in some very basic capacity building within identified areas of life. However, given the extent to which these women had been shunned by society over a long period and made to feel that they were worthless, the crucial indirect aim was to slowly build self-confidence and a healthier self-image. Workers often said that it could take months before some women reached the point of being even able to speak about their situations, let alone begin to see that they might be able to initiate action to change them. It was in some cases only after several months that specific programmes of capacity building could be undertaken.

Where necessary, it is important to stress awareness raising and empowerment, particularly in situations where oppression has commonly been experienced over a long period. Some communities can become so accustomed to oppression that they accept it in a fatalistic way and see no point in striving against it. In such situations, a perceived critical initial strategy is to seek to change the situation by challenging people's basic perception and acceptance of reality. This needs to be done with great care so that it does not further endanger people or leave them with only a heightened level of frustration. The approach adopted by the worker must be undertaken with sensitivity and in a manner that offers constantly available and ongoing support. The two strategies most commonly adopted are awareness raising through dialogue taking place in informal settings and social learning, that is, posing problems and seeking their resolution through action. The assumption in such situations, and there are in effect a wide variety of such, is that

> An awareness of reality is an essential prerequisite to people participating fully in their own development process, in that awareness will frequently lead to a determination to initiate changes and efforts to do just that. (Cox and Pawar, 2013, pp. 203–204)

Workers and organizations need to develop skills to use capacity-building strategies to enhance capacities of individuals, families, small groups, local organizations, or other entities. The strategies may range from a very informal approach to a reasonably formal one. For example, in small cell formations in outreach programmes directed towards female-headed households in Bangladesh discussed above, significant capacity building took place in weekly group meetings. The topics included basic literacy or numeracy, how to approach government agencies to present a request, household sanitation and hygiene, or small plot food production. At the reasonably formal level, examples include the establishment of basic primary schools, health clinics and adult education centres and any other activity considered feasible in such a scenario. And if a food-for-work approach was adopted in the construction of such centres, which has often been the case in India, the Philippines and elsewhere, capacity building would include instruction in handling timber, cement and so on within a basic construction context. In other words, capacity building in a particular situation might be the objective of a programme, or it might occur spontaneously and incidentally within the course of implementing another programme.

The third strategy revolves around income generation. Where necessary and people are willing, workers and organizations with people need to develop local credit schemes, local people's banks and local micro-enterprise developments. There are many examples of all these in India and many parts of the world, and their importance is self-evident. People require capital, no matter how small the sum, to undertake projects or make changes that will enable them to move ahead, and often they will also require access to already established broader micro-enterprise programmes in which they can participate. This type of programme may be initiated by the local people within a locality with a small grant of capital and some external training but without external personnel other than a middle-level facilitator. Alternatively, the programme may be initiated by a national-level agency and involve thousands of participants at many local levels and perhaps hundreds of workers (e.g. see Cox and Pawar, 2006, pp. 150–151, 206–207; Chapter 8 in Midgley, 2014).

The fourth strategy relates to developing a range of needed community resources. Workers and organizations need to focus on local leadership development, local organizational development or strengthening and the linking of local organizations with external sources of support, together with more comprehensive community development programmes. Indeed, the ideal local-level community development through social development approach would encompass also the first three strategies, with the emphases of course being dependent on local circumstances and other prevailing factors.

Workers and organizations first need to develop their own self-confidence and self-esteem, awareness of these and similar strategies, and capacities and skills to effectively use them at appropriate levels within the local-level community. Most important, they need to focus on cultivating the virtues of courage, confidence, commitment, honesty, selflessness, love and hope.

4. Observing and Understanding the Local-level Community

The main objective of this exercise is to understand the current conditions of community and causes of it (see Chapter 1). As stated earlier, the above three steps provide knowledge and competency bases for workers and organizations and the next three steps focus on practice. By consciously using the knowledge, values, principles, processes, skills and strategies, it is important to identify the target local-level community or village or group. Workers and organizations need to immerse themselves within the community to understand it. Workers can employ research, observation and interview and analytical skills in a nonjudgmental manner. Some understanding of the community can be gained by using secondary data such as census reports and historical records, if available. The sense of the community needs to be gained from its people and their belief, faith, conditions and aspirations, geography and topography, demography, sociocultural norms, religious and spiritual practices, politics and power structure, exploitative-dependency-discriminatory structures, groups and sub-groups, source of livelihood and economy and the needs and issues relating to health, education, housing, infrastructure, current community resources, linkages to other communities and urban centres and so on. Several techniques and methods are available to develop community profiling, but it should not be a theoretical documentary exercise, as the focus is on practice. Rapid and participatory village appraisal methods may be important and needed but certainly not adequate. Social workers are not there to evaluate or judge anything, and there is nothing to be gained from moving rapidly into community development work without adequate preparation. While observing the community and people, it is important to understand their past, present and where they want to go in terms of their hopes and aspirations (goal setting, see Figure 1.1 in Chapter 1). While understanding the current conditions of the community, it is important to visualize links to such conditions from other social development levels in terms of globalization processes and the role of international- and national-level institutions. Further details of working in the community are discussed in Chapter 4.

5. Organizing People, Agencies and Resources

Organizing is the essence of community development. It is important and often necessary to organize and mobilize individuals, families, groups, people's organizations, government organizations and NGOs, leadership and material resources to progress work in all the dimensions discussed as follows. Depending on the need, the strategies discussed previously, such as confidence and self-esteem building, awareness raising, capacity building and community resource building at individual to organizational levels can be employed to organize people, agencies and resources by engaging local-level people. All this needs to be done in such way that organized work focuses on the needs, issues and specific tasks and goals as identified by the people and communities. This should result in functional leadership development, youth and youth group development, formation of people's organizations for a range of purposes as needed by the community, capacity building of government and non-government organizations and appropriate linkages and coordination among them to facilitate the local-level community development.

6. Focusing on the Dimensions of the Community

The culmination of the work done in the previous five steps is the sixth step where it is important to focus on all the dimensions of the community (see Box 1.4 in Chapter 1), not just one or two. Sometimes, initially, it may not be possible to make equal progress in all the dimensions at the same time. When it is difficult to address all at once, in a planned and phased manner the focus has to be on all the dimensions, and there is no particular order to work on them as that process will be determined by the people and community.

One way of initiating local-level community development is to build on the cultural dimension of the community (Figure 2.2). The understanding gained about the culture of people and community needs to be consciously used to further build cultural practices and use such practices as the founding base for other community development tasks, where applicable. Workers need to draw on people's beliefs, faith, religious and spiritual practices, art, music, plays, annual fairs, festivals and so on. As many of the cultural practices are gradually eroding, by introducing appropriate programmes and activities it is important to build and retain such activities. Activities such as recreational events, sports, music and spiritual songs, religious practices of different communities according to their faith and traditional plays for children, youth and elderly need to be organized and community resources used to pass on such traditional knowledge and skills to the younger generation.

Figure 2.2:
Local-level community development through social development approach

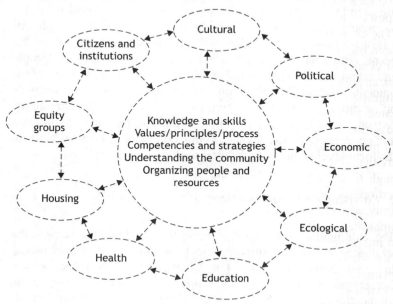

On one hand, such practices build the cultural dimension of the community, and, on the other, they should be geared towards building values, character, virtues and commitment in people. Such positive values and strengths are embedded in almost every culture. Therefore, building such culture and channelling it for community development activities are practical as has frequently been found.

Developing the political dimension of the community is as crucial as developing the cultural dimension, and they are closely connected. Practising within the political dimension has a few core elements that relate to making the community power structure work for community development, appropriate leadership development at all levels and raising awareness of people and empowering them to participate in decision-making that affects their lives. Politically elected representatives at the local governance level, though important, are only one aspect of the political dimension. Community leaders need to be trained and developed at various levels in all dimensions. People's organizations and government organizations and NGOs can help develop such leadership in communities by following participatory and empowering processes.

The economic dimension of the community is vital, as it is the source of livelihood and employment opportunities depend on it. The economic dimension is indeed often the dominating dimension, as people need regular work and income so that they can lead a dignified life. Work and employment opportunities need to be created by translating central and state government programmes into action at the local level. Through such programmes and their own provisions, gram panchayats have initiated such employment activities (e.g. a range of infrastructure development activities, though their nature and the quality of implementation may be in question), which may not be adequate. Depending on the local community, knowledge and skill development, agriculture extension, animal husbandry, dairy farming, irrigation, micro-credit schemes and micro-enterprises, self-help groups and similar initiatives can be the focus under the economic dimension. In local communities, if primary industry is the main focus it is also important to work on marketing and fair pricing for farmers' products. Sometimes, the economic dimension dominates to such an extent that some of the other dimensions do not receive any attention. Such a situation needs to be consciously avoided.

Closely connected to the economic dimension is the ecological dimension. The economy of the local community needs to be developed in such a way that it does not cause any harm to the local ecology. On the other hand, the maintenance and development of the local ecology contribute to the local economy. There has been increasing awareness of ecological issues and green gas emissions in recent years. Several aspects of the ecological approach can be practised in local-level communities, for example, the creation of seed banks to protect original seeds, rain water harvesting and the use of water-saving technologies, producing biogas and using the same, producing and using solar energy, tree planting, growth and protection of forests, soil conservation and so on. In fact, the economic dimension and the 'green economy' go hand in hand.

The next three dimensions relate to education, health and housing. In the interest of brevity and because there is much experience that comes under these dimensions, they have been discussed together, though each one of them is equally important. It is necessary to provide educational facilities and services to offer both formal and informal education. Although primary education is free and compulsory, its quality and retention rate need to be significantly enhanced in local-level communities. Good housing and health are closely connected. As many local communities do not have access to basic health services, it is important to work on providing basic health services to people, both in a targeted and a general way. Affordable good housing is an important issue in local communities, as many people live in thatched or mud-wall houses and often in unhygienic conditions. The housing dimension is closely connected to the economic dimension, as housing often represents a huge financial investment by families and people. It is important to work on low-interest lending provisions and the development of basic sanitation infrastructure that is an accord with local practices.

The next dimension concerns equity groups. Under this dimension the focus is on working with the disadvantaged and weaker sections of the community, such as children, women, elderly, physically challenged, victims of disasters and the sick. Depending on the need, it is necessary to provide community- and institution-based services and, where possible, self-reliance through social and economic rehabilitation needs to be encouraged. Often social workers' practice in the community begins and ends with such equity groups, though many social workers are yet to enter such communities, but it is only one of the dimensions of local-level community development.

The practice focus in the final dimension is the development of good citizenship and local institutions. Simultaneous practice in the other dimensions should lead to the development of good citizens and their institutions. Capacity building of local governing institutions, including gram panchayats, people's organizations, local NGOs, self-help groups, micro-enterprises, cooperatives and similar institutions, needs to be strengthened by providing appropriate capacity-building programmes in such a way that they allow for people's participation and decision-making. For that to occur, good citizenship needs to be developed, consistent with the local culture and by providing education regarding rights and responsibilities. The conscious practice of this dimension will ensure development of local-level communities.

Conclusion

To show how social development approach can be employed for local-level community development, this chapter has first discussed the meaning of local level, community and community development. Furthermore, it has elaborated the significance of and rationale for focusing on local-level communities. In the final section, it has demonstrated how the six steps can be used to practise social development approach in local communities, villages and groups. The six steps cover social development knowledge, skills, strategies, values and processes and the practice dimensions. While bearing in mind that all the levels of development are important and are ideally integrated, the specific focus on the local level of communities is needed in the 21st century because it has been the level most neglected to date. The scope of local-level community development is huge and the suggested social development approach is promising and practical for bringing about qualitative change in the lives of people and their communities. However, as stated earlier, little attention has been paid to the local level, given the scale of action the current situation demands. Partly, the reason for this include an unwillingness to allocate the resources to this level that are clearly required and the absence of adequate numbers of appropriately trained personnel able and willing to work as enablers of development at this often difficult level. The world is changing fast with globalization forces and technological innovations are increasingly helping us to reach out to villages relatively easily. With such changes, it is hoped that the discussion in this chapter will motivate social workers and the social work profession and relevant agencies to take local-level community development through the social development approach seriously.

3

Values and Principles

Introduction

While writing this chapter, I reflected on how communities exist, power dynamics and poverty that prevail in various communities, life of the disadvantaged and marginalized groups, my reading of the values and principles discussed in the community development literature and my experience and observation of community organization and development. Such reflections made me wonder whether values and principles make any sense at the community level, given the way communities operate and how people live within them. Although values and principles can be separately discussed, I have merged them together and decided to choose four values and principles for discussion. The four values and principles that appear essential for community development practice are human rights, self-reliance, self-determination and participation. I do not often find these apparent within communities, although they are often talked about. All the four concepts are difficult and challenging, and yet seemingly useful and effective, as they provide the moral and ethical legitimacy for practice while empowering people, communities and workers. Therefore, it seemed important to endeavour to apply the four values and principles as constituting the core of community development practice.

Human rights in essence encompass all the four values and principles as well as others. However, talking about human rights for community development practice in a composite way may not be so helpful, as considerable controversy surrounds human rights, both in general and when it is used, for example, as a benchmark for approving trade and aid and applying sanctions. Thus, it is important to examine each value and principle separately. As stated earlier, across the field of community development practice, the application of human rights, self-reliance, self-determination and participation is not often found or found present to only a limited degree. The discussion of these values and principles does not necessarily suggest that they emanate from or are linked to all community development practice dimensions as already discussed. Rather, the chapter argues that community development practice ought or needs to follow the four basic values and principles suggested. The reason for such an argument is partly the author's value bias, albeit shared by many others, respect for people and the belief that these values provide ethical legitimacy for sustainable community development practice and are also closely linked to social development values and principles. Furthermore, the following discussion will show how these values and principles are linked to each other and flow from one to another in the sequence they are presented.

It is clearly important to raise the questions of why only four values and principles and what are the justifications for choosing these specific ones? According to the *Oxford Dictionary*, values mean "moral or professional standards of behaviour" and principles mean "guiding rules for personal behaviour" (Hornby, 1993). The four chosen values and principles uniquely combine both moral and professional standards while guiding action. In the various community development texts, several principles have been discussed. For example, Kenny (2007, pp. 22–31) discusses principles in terms of community workers' eight commitments,[1] and Schuler (1996) suggests six core values[2] of community development. Similarly, Ife (2013) has listed 30 community development principles in Chapter 12 of his book, *Community Development*. Although such a long list of principles is helpful for they do provide useful insights for practice, if principles are too numerous they may lose their importance as principles. The chosen four principles are conceptualized here as essential and the basic foundation pillars of community development practice. In other words, without the application of these principles, sound community development practice may not be possible.

Of course, there are examples where community development is practised by not following, or indeed violating, these values and principles. Adherence to these principles in practice is not easy, is often controversial and can challenge the current power structure. However, disregarding such principles in practice has also often resulted in unsuitable community development activities—ones that do not meet the needs of people and result in people's indifference and lack of ownership of such activities. A rights-based, self-reliance and self-determination focus and participatory processes are anti-charity, anti-dependency and anti-oppressive. They are also logically and sequentially linked to one another, and indeed many other community development principles can be constructively linked to these core values and principles. Needless to say, they are comprehensive, focus on the local level and are people centred. They do not favour interventions by external and/or top-down agents. Thus, they are anti-prescriptive. The four values and principles have the potential to bring about a balance between the extremities of state versus individual and rights versus duties or obligations, and both are equally important. These and similar justifications may suffice to warrant the focus on the four values and principles discussed as follows in detail.

Human Rights

Meaning of Human Rights

Human rights constitute both values and principles with both moral standards and guidelines for action inherent in them. According to the United Nations (1992),

> Human rights could be generally defined as those rights which are inherent in our nature and without which we cannot live as human beings. Human rights and fundamental freedoms allow us to fully develop and use our human qualities, our intelligence, our talents and our conscience and satisfy our spiritual and other needs. They are basic for mankind's increasing demand for a life in which the inherent dignity and worth of each human being will receive respect and protection.

The main source of Human Rights is the United Nations Universal Declaration of Human Rights (UNUDHR), though further elaboration and extension are provided in the International Covenant on Civil and Political Rights and the International Covenant on Economic, Social and Cultural Rights. In addition, there are other human rights–related conventions, such as the conventions on the Elimination of All Forms of Racial Discrimination (1965), the Elimination of All Forms of Discrimination Against Rights of Women (1979), the Rights of the Child, the Protection of the Rights of All Migrant Workers and Members of Their Families (1990) and the Declaration on the Rights of Indigenous Peoples (2007). These additional human rights conventions and declarations cover specific areas and target marginalized and vulnerable populations.

Human rights have been categorized into three types: civil and political rights; economic, social and cultural rights; and collective rights. They are also referred to, respectively, as first-, second- and third-generation rights. Labelling them as first- to third-generation rights has been sometimes interpreted as reflecting high to low importance, with some even doubting that third-generation rights are human rights (see Ife, 2001; Uvin, 2004). As such labelling and its interpretation mislead and undermine the importance of human rights, I prefer to abandon such labels and refer to them as three types of human rights that are equally important for the well-being of individuals and communities.

The first type of human rights, civil and political rights (Articles 2–21 of the UNUDHR), are known as 'negative rights'. These include everyone's entitlement to all the rights and freedoms set forth in the declaration, without distinction of any kind (race, colour, sex, language, religion etc.); the right to life, liberty and security of the person; prohibition of slavery and torture and arbitrary arrest, detention, or exile; the right to a fair trial and equality before the law; the right to freedom of movement; the right to seek asylum; the right to a nationality; the right to property; the right to freedom of thought, opinion and expression; the right to freedom of assembly and association; the right to freedom of religion; and the right to participate in one's own government and civic life. These first-generation rights are individually based and mostly legalistic, and it is assumed that every individual possesses these rights and needs to be protected against their violation or abuse. Thus, these are called 'negative rights'.

The second type of human rights, namely, economic, social and cultural rights (Articles 22–27 of the UNUDHR), are treated as 'positive rights'. These include the right to adequate food and clothing, the right to housing, the right to education, the right to employment, the right to an adequate wage, the right to adequate health care, the right to social security, the right to be treated with dignity in old age, and the right to rest and leisure from work. Although these second-generation rights do not have universal acceptance, they suggest active roles and responsibilities for governments in achieving these rights. Thus, they are referred to as 'positive rights'. The main aim of the second-generation rights are social justice, freedom from want and participation in the social, economic and cultural aspects of life (see United Nations, 1992; also Ife, 2001). Ife's (2001, p. 26) analysis suggests, "These are rights of the individual or group to receive various forms of social provision or services in order to realize their full potential as human beings."

The third type of human rights is known as 'collective rights', which are mostly captured in Article 28 of the UNUDHR in embryonic form. Article 28 states, "Everyone is entitled to a social and international order in which the rights and freedoms set forth in this declaration can be fully realized." Ife (2001, p. 27) observes that the third type of human rights, such as the right to economic development, the right to benefit from world trade and economic growth, the right to live in a cohesive and harmonious society, the right to breathe unpolluted air, the right to clean water and the right to experience 'nature' and "belong to a community, population, society or nation rather than being readily applicable to an individual, though individuals can clearly benefit from their realization." In contemporary times, particularly in the context of climate change issues, collective rights are gaining increasing recognition as human rights, though they do not have universal acceptance, and the socio-legal measures required for their realization and protection have yet to be developed.

Human rights have four unique and contentious features—universal, indivisible, inalienable and unable to be abrogated. The universality of human rights suggests that they are applicable to all human beings irrespective of their socio-economic and political background, religion, culture, place of origin, or geographic location. The second feature of human rights is that they are indivisible. That means that human rights cannot be separated from one another; rather they belong together, must be consistent and cannot conflict with each other. It also suggests that all rights are equally important, so that one cannot prioritize them or rank them in any order (see Ife, 2001). The third feature, that human rights are inalienable, suggests that they cannot be taken away from someone and remain with the person as long as she or he lives. Finally, human rights cannot be given up voluntarily and traded for additional privileges; that is, human rights are inabrogable (Ife, 2001).

Critiques of and Obstacles to Human Rights

Although human rights and the values and principles inherent in them appeal to many people and are relevant to community development practice, they have been critiqued and questioned on several counts, and various types of responses have been developed to those critiques (see Uvin, 2004). Critiquing and questioning human rights appear to have more to do with politics and political manipulation than with the inherent nature or appropriateness of human rights. "Even Western governments, which claim to be the foremost champions of human rights, attach greater importance to their national interests than to the realization of human rights" (Ghai, 2001). However, it is important for community development practitioners to be aware of these criticisms and responses to them. The major attack on human rights comes from their universal applicability. The core critique and argument here is that human rights emanate from Western political, cultural, or religious values and are, therefore, not universally valid for and appropriate to different cultures. Many African and Asian countries do not concur with the universality of human rights on the grounds that they have originated in the West with its dominant ideology of individualism, are culturally inappropriate to themselves and that meeting basic human needs is more important than political rights (Ghai, 2001; Mapp, 2008). Uvin's analysis shows six paths to addressing the charge of 'Western-centrism'. First, since a majority of states have ratified the Declaration and Covenants, and are therefore obliged to follow them, there is little doubt about their universality (legalistic path). Second, as the implementation of human rights allows for adaptations to local cultural contexts, they are not Eurocentric (soft relativist path). The third path affirms that it does not matter where human rights originate as long as they are inherently good, objective and important. Fourth, many researchers have tried to find evidence of similar human rights in different cultures, religions and values and their success in doing so suggests their universality (empiricist path). Fifth, a philosophical path contends that human nature everywhere demands, or automatically leads to, human rights and development. Finally, incrementalists argue that people can be gradually brought to uncover the importance of human rights and development in their lives and to act on this realization (see Uvin, 2004, pp. 20–37). Regarding the universal acceptance of human rights, Ife and Fiske (2006) clarify that "universality does not mean 'sameness'; rather it is a principle that emphasizes the essential worth of every human being without the need to reach a certain status or fit a certain model of desirable citizen." The United Nations states that human rights are minimum standards and that each culture can choose the most appropriate manner by which to realize those rights (cited from Mapp, 2008).

In regard to the indivisibility feature, there is no consensus on this, as some governments do not agree with it and some are of the view that social and economic rights are more important than civil and political rights (Ghai, 2001; Mapp, 2008). However, most of the human rights work, campaigning and advocacy have concentrated on the first type of human rights, civil and political rights, to the neglect of the remaining two types as it may be convenient for governments to claim a 'good human rights record', accuse other governments who do not have a good record and accordingly apply sanctions. It is also convenient to legal professions to focus on the first type of rights, which are often dominated by them. Despite such concentration, civil and political rights are limited to the public sphere. A lot more needs to be done in the private sphere, where these rights are denied to women, children, the physically challenged and the elderly. Ife (2001) contends that civil and political "rights are a necessary prerequisite for a just society, but they do not of themselves produce social equality or social justice."

On the human rights critique, Uvin (2004, p. 31) concludes:

Human rights standards being normative aims rather than descriptive facts, it is impossible to ground them with uncontested certainty in a universal manner. Human rights are about dreams, about visions for a better world, about political aspirations, and these will be always contested and to some extent unprovable. They are not a matter of universal fact but rather constitute a language to make claims with, to conceive of and fight for social change.

These concluding remarks begin to show how human rights as values and principles are important for community development practice. The values and principles and legitimacy embedded in rights and claims open up new avenues and strategies for community development workers.

Strategies for Human Rights-based Community Development Practice

Human rights values and principles may be followed in several ways in community development practice. In seeking to achieve social change, equality and social justice, it is necessary and important to include and address all the three types of rights—civil and political; economic, social and cultural; and collective rights—in an interdependent and integrated way, for in community development practice all human rights are closely connected (Ghai, 2001). The conscious use of human rights values and principles helps to shift the focus from individual and community needs to individual and community rights. Such a value orientation and the application of associated principles help to focus on claims and invoke the duties and responsibilities of the state and other social and economic institutions to address claims of their people and communities. It also helps to move from charity, philanthropy and state benevolence approaches to structural change to serve rights-holders rather than passive beneficiaries.

The application of such values and principles helps to analyze community problems and needs from new perspectives. A document prepared by the Committee of Economic, Social and Cultural Rights states:

> The real potential of human rights lies in its ability to change the way people perceive themselves vis-à-vis the government and other actors. A rights framework provides a mechanism for reanalyzing and renaming a "problem" like contaminated water or malnutrition as "violation" and, as such, something that need not and should not be tolerated. . . . Rights

make it clear that violations are neither inevitable nor natural, but arise from deliberate decisions and policies. By demanding explanations and accountability, human rights expose the hidden priorities and structures behind violations and challenge the conditions that create and tolerate poverty. (CESCR, 1998)

In similar vein, The Human Rights Council of Australia states, "Looking at poverty through the human rights lens—as a denial of human rights—enables a richer understanding of the different dimensions of poverty and encourages a more comprehensive policy response to the structural causes of poverty" (Frankovits and Patrick, 2000, p. 7).

The shift from needs and charity to claims helps to focus on accountability, which is key to the protection and promotion of human rights (HRCA, 2001). Human rights values and principles focus on social structures, loci of power, rule of law, empowerment and structural change in favour of the poorest and most deprived (Uvin, 2004, p. 131).

Most important, they also help to follow just and fair processes in community development practice, as often community development or development projects are implemented in such a way that some people's and communities' rights are violated (e.g. development-induced displacement of people without adequate rehabilitation support). On the whole, human rights values and principles direct the focus from needs to rights and claims, invoke duties, help analyze problems in new ways and ensure accountability and proper processes.

The human rights values and principles have been discussed in terms of their main sources, the three types of human rights and their main features, contestation and critiques of human rights and how human rights can be employed in community development practice. Human rights have moral and ethical connotations that invoke our conscience and obligation to act individually and collectively in dealing with issues of livelihood, hunger, poverty, health, education, housing, natural resources (right to water, land, clean air etc.), freedom of thought and expression and so on. All actions of community development practice must ensure that community members' human rights are not violated in the name of development or otherwise but are in practice achieved and protected.

Self-reliance

The Meaning of Self-reliance

The realization and protection of human rights, particularly food, clothing and shelter, and access to education, health and employment facilitate self-reliance on the part of individuals and communities. Self-reliance in turn facilitates the realization of human rights. Self-reliance is a value, principle, philosophy and way of life. To explore the conceptual discussion on self-reliance, I surveyed the subject indexes in more than 10 community development books, but surprisingly none of them indicated the term 'self-reliance' in the list. I just wondered, in the culture of consumerism and globalization, whether self-reliance has become outdated in community development practice. Why have many authors of community development overlooked such an important value and principle? Is it not practical in the contemporary world? Like human rights, the meaning of the value or principle of self-reliance is complex and controversial and connected to other concepts such as independence and sustainability.

In several dictionaries, the meaning of self-reliance is stated as capacity or ability to rely on one's own capabilities (power, resources, judgement, or ability to generate an outcome) and manage one's own affairs. It also means autonomy and independence.

Self-reliance is both means as well as end (goal). It means not being dependent on others for day-to-day living. Self-reliance is not limited to individuals but extends to families, communities and societies. It is not limited to production and consumption in the economic sense and includes social, political and cultural dimensions in a comprehensive way. It may be linked to some elements of individualism and invoke obligations and duties, but that is not the meaning I wish to convey. Self-reliance does not mean individualism and individualistic self-centredness. It also does not mean interdependency; these two are different but not antithetical and can coexist in harmony. Does self-reliance mean an ability to borrow and return, as is done in microfinance schemes? Can any society that thrives on (over)borrowed money (home and material mortgages, credit cards and high interest rates) be considered a self-reliant society? The US sub-prime mortgage[3] crisis and its impact on families is a case in point. Thus, the value and the principle of self-reliance is a complex one. Self-reliance means leading life and building communities in such a way that individuals, families and communities do not unnecessarily depend on others for their meaningful coexistence. Dependency results in unsustainability, but self-reliance gives rise to hope for sustainability (Rees, 2006).

The UN High Commissioner for Refugees (UNHCR, 2005), in its publication, *Handbook for Self-reliance*, defines self-reliance as follows:

> Self-reliance is the social and economic ability of an individual, a household or a community to meet essential needs (including protection, food, water, shelter, personal safety, health and education) in a sustainable manner and with dignity. Self-reliance, as a programme approach, refers to developing and strengthening livelihoods of persons of concern, and reducing their vulnerability and long-term reliance on humanitarian/external assistance.

Self-reliance is also based on the assumption that, everything being equal, no individual and community should have to beg, be at the mercy of others, or be dependent; on the contrary, everyone should lead a self-reliant and self-dignified life. Thus, leading a self-reliant life is innate to everyone, whereas leading a dependent life is a learned behaviour brought about by various mechanisms (colonization, nation building and politicization, state intervention and vested interests). Applying the value and the principle of self-reliance and achieving it in community development practice empowers individuals and communities and enhances their dignity. In the context of refugees, the UNHCR (2005) has argued that self-reliance helps people to

> claim their rights and provide a basis for equality, equity, empowerment and participation. It promotes collaboration, trust, and social and economic interaction between communities, and strengthens coexistence. It can prevent human suffering and social unrest. It can motivate and attract governments, NGOs and donors to provide support and strengthen their partnership. It can reduce dependency, offset demand for handouts and subsidised services and reduce the impact of budget constraints.

These arguments hold ground for community development practice in any general context. All of this suggests that self-reliance is highly relevant today. Self-reliant communities are those that are able to produce and consume all goods, not just economic, according to their requirements, and to share surplus production with other communities. In this sense, self-reliance means individuals and communities are not dependent on others for their day-to-day living. Such individuals and communities enjoy the sense of self-respect and dignity, although that does not preclude them from interdependency. Thus, the whole purpose of community development is to make communities self-reliant and resilient, so that they develop the capacity to meet their needs and effectively address issues.

A Critique of Self-reliance

Despite such promising outcomes for individuals and communities, the value and the principle of self-reliance have been criticized from several perspectives. First, for some, self-reliance appears too ideal, not practical and hypocritical. It appears ideal because it is difficult to practise self-reliance if it is not practised from the beginning, and some people advertently or inadvertently tend to depend on others. In the globalized world, where lopsided free trade agreements and practices prevail, the focus on self-reliance is a problematic one. If nations and states are not self-reliant and if they try to acquire resources either through cooperative means or through any other methods ranging from covert manipulation to open war, how can we expect individuals and communities to be self-reliant? In this sense, talking of self-reliance appears hypocritical, inconsistent, contradictory and not practical. One also cannot aspire to become self-reliant by making others deprived and dependent.

Second, it appears that self-reliance has been only partially embraced, as its application is often limited to economic activities in terms of self-sufficiency in rural or village communities. Looking at cottage industries that were established to create local employment opportunities in India and other countries, Brokensha and Hodge (1969, p. 189) observe:

> Such an attempt ignores the powerful market forces and other economic elements which inexorably link villages more and more to the wider world. This policy generally represents a misguided paternalism and a

reactionary refusal to recognise the rights of rural population in the national economy. A more rational approach would be the encouragement of even greater participation in the national economy, trying to understand and to some extent direct the channels which provide links with the wider world.

Although villages and rural communities are now linked to the wider world through market forces and globalization processes, they tend to become more dependent on the market and are mostly excluded from benefits derived from such processes. Thus, self-reliance should not be limited to economic activities and rural communities. It is a comprehensive concept and needs to be comprehensively applied at social, cultural, political and economic dimensions and at local, regional, national and international levels. Third, some aspects of self-reliance such as ability, mental status, attitude and proclivity seem to be intangible, for, although outcomes can be seen, some processes remain invisible. Finally, although self-reliance is a good thing to practise, one wonders whether it is ethical to expect long-term-deprived people to demonstrate self-reliance without providing them, at least initially, with the necessary support.

Obstacles to Self-reliance

There are several obstacles to practising self-reliance. First, there are different understandings and perceptions of self-reliance, which may inhibit practising it. For example, those who relate it to individualism and do not appreciate the downside of individualism may avoid following self-reliance. Second, in the world sometimes characterized by indulgence, unremorseful consumption and finite resources, which tend to be accumulated in one corner of the world and the country, are manipulated and not shared on an egalitarian basis with all community members. It then becomes very hard for people and their communities to become self-reliant. This also suggests that, instead of depriving communities of basic human rights but recognizing the interdependent nature of the world, resources have to be shared so as to achieve self-reliance. Third, those individuals and communities, which are hungry, sick, suppressed, oppressed, subjugated, exploited, deprived of basic human rights and needs and powerless over a long time, will continue to be dependent and unable to be self-reliant for themselves in the short term. Fourth, some people and communities have been made (at times inadvertently) dependent for years. That has led to asking external agents to give, and then receiving from such agents becoming a way of life. Changing this learned dependency is an important obstacle and challenging task for community development practitioners. Fifth, in some communities, especially at the local level, existing power structures seem to sustain dependency of people, perhaps with myopic views, to retain their feudal patron–client relationship. This can be an important hurdle in at least the initial stages of community development work. Sixth, a lack of trained personnel who are well prepared and available to guide or facilitate the practice of self-reliance in local communities can also be an important obstacle.

Strategies for Self-reliance

It is important to demonstrate that self-reliance is a practical idea, though for many it has remained an ideal yet to be achieved. It may be understood as a gradual process and a continuum with communities' self-reliance seen as ranging from lowest to highest. In a simplistic sense and as stated earlier, self-reliance means that people and communities do not unnecessarily depend on others for livelihood and survival. In community development practice, the process of non-dependency must be initiated from the beginning and begin from where the peoples' levels are. If we accept the assumption that every human being has an inherent drive to be self-reliant and self-dignified, our community development practice should focus on rekindling that innate ability to be self-reliant and unlearning what it is to be dependent. When necessary, individuals and communities need to be appropriately supported in reducing dependency and achieving self-reliance. This appropriate support, as Uphoff (1986) calls it, is 'assisted self-reliance'. According to Uphoff,

> the assisted self-reliance strategy involves using external resources such as advice, funds, training, and material assistance to strengthen local capacities to initiate, manage, modify, and sustain activities that obtain benefits for which the poor are responsible. Continuing assistance may be

provided from outside as long as it is given in such a manner as to not displace people's efforts to generate income, manage natural resources, enhance the quality of life, or create infrastructure.

The formation of people's or community-based organizations is an important step towards achieving self-reliance (Nyoni, 1987). As part of the community development process, such organizations should be informed about their rights and claims and ways of progressively realizing them in a self-reliant manner, with the emphasis on using local knowledge and human and material resources for capacity-building and community development activities. As stated earlier, self-reliance is about power and resources, but those power and resources need to be developed by employing capacity-building approaches.

Such capacities may be directed towards producing and consuming social, cultural, political and economic goods that enhance the quality of life of individuals, families and communities. If the community development process is led by external agents, it is important that they systematically phase themselves out at an appropriate time so as to ensure the self-reliance of communities.

These strategies are only indicative rather than detailed, as the main purpose is to discuss self-reliance as a value and principle and its significance in community development practice. Accordingly, this section has explored the concept of and critique on self-reliance, some obstacles to practising it and some possible strategies.

Self-determination

Meaning of Self-determination

Self-determination is an important value and principle and a subject of analysis in many disciplines, including international law, political science, psychology and social work and community development. The International Court of Justice has defined self-determination (in the West-Saharan case) as the need to pay regard to the freely expressed will of peoples (IWGIA, 2009). It is a right held by people rather than a right held by governments alone. In terms of international law, the principle of self-determination applies to all. The principle of right to self-determination is enshrined in the Charter of the United Nations, the International Covenants on Civil and Political Rights and on Economic, Social and Cultural Rights. Common Article 1, paragraph 1 of these Covenants states:

> All peoples have the right of self-determination. By virtue of that right they freely determine their political status and freely pursue their economic, social and cultural development.

The UNUDHR Article 21(3) states:

> The will of the people shall be the basis of the authority of government; this will be expressed in periodic and genuine elections which shall be by universal and equal suffrage and shall be held by secret vote or by equivalent free voting procedures.

Drawing on United Nations studies, Parker (2000) points out two trends: (1) a history of independence or self-rule in an identifiable territory, a distinct culture, and (2) a will and capability to regain self-governance, which have given rise to possession of the right to self-determination. The use of the self-determination principle to claim independence and sovereignty from the existing government and to form a new state and government are referred to as self-determination at the national level, and this principle is a subject of international law, politics and political science. However, this is beyond the scope of this chapter and this volume.

The other levels in which the value and the principle of self-determination apply are at the individual, group and indigenous peoples' levels (Clements, 2004), which are pertinent for community development practice. Durlak (1992, cited from Clements, 2004) states that, at the individual level, "the term self-determination refers to the extent to which a person assumes responsibility for his or her own goals, accomplishments and setbacks, and includes such characteristics as assertiveness, self-advocacy, creativity and independence." Self-determination at the group level refers to groups as communities coming together to determine for themselves how to address their issues or realize their legitimate aspirations. Finally, as the term explicitly indicates, self-determination is extensively used in indigenous peoples' contexts as they have been suppressed and marginalized in many nation-states. Article 3 of the UN (2008) Declaration on the Rights of the Indigenous Peoples states:

> Indigenous peoples have the right to self-determination. By virtue of that right they freely determine their political status and freely pursue their economic, social and cultural development.

According to IWGIA (2009), "Self-determination is the right to participate in the democratic process of governance and to influence one's future politically, socially and culturally."

In psychology, what motivates individuals to self-determine has been researched (Deci and Ryan, 2002, 2008; Lepper et al., 1973). From the perspective of psychology, self-determination is a choice of behaviour with free will and without any influence of external factors or interference. Although people make choices or decisions on the basis of several internal and external factors, Deci and Ryan (2002) have identified three intrinsic factors that seem to motivate people to self-determine. These are (1) need for competence (refers to the need to experience oneself as capable and competent in controlling the environment and being able to reliably predict outcomes), (2) need for autonomy (refers to the need to actively participate in determining one's own behaviour and includes the need to experience one's actions as a result of autonomous choice without external interference), and (3) need for relatedness (refers to need to care for and be related to others and to experience satisfaction in participation and involvement with social world).

In social work, self-determination implies facilitating individuals, groups and communities to make decisions or choices for themselves from available alternatives or opportunities (Compton and Galaway, 1999, pp. 110–111), often with the enabling assistance of social workers. From a community development perspective, Kenny (2007, p. 26) discusses self-determination as follows:

> People must have control over knowledge and information, social relationships, decision making and their own resources. Communities must be able to do things in their own way. While a community development worker's job is to work with communities to determine goals, issues and strategies, the ultimate power to accept or reject these lies with community members. In the final analysis, it must be the community's views or interests that prevail.

In community development practice, these conceptual developments in international law and politics, psychology and social work and at the three levels—individuals, groups and indigenous peoples—may be creatively employed. Self-determination as a human right, democratic governance in micro-level activities and motivating and enabling people to self-determine are very pertinent for practice.

Critique of Self-determination

Although self-determination is a laudable value and principle, some people and communities cannot determine for themselves due to historical, health, or cultural factors. Many a time, peoples' and communities' self-determination is claimed without their genuine self-determination. For example, in the democratic election of members votes are purchased or manipulated on caste or class bases or people are violently pressurized to vote in a particular way or abstain from voting. Sometimes communities are persuaded to co-opt decisions made under duress or by outsiders. Self-determination is simply not acceptable and not allowed if the determination is harmful to individuals and communities. As self-determination involves making choices and decisions, if choices or alternatives are not available, self-determination has little meaning. Self-determination may also be significantly compromised if adequate time is not provided to consider and think over issues. Self-determination is constrained when people believe that they cannot influence events around them. Spicker (1990) argues that self-determination ignores cases or contexts where direction is legitimate and desirable. The issue of self-determination may be contested and argued in a court of law, and it is difficult for common people to follow such complex court proceedings. Webley-Smith (2007, p. 204) argues that the idea of self-determination promises much more than it can deliver in a global era. This argument suggests that a lot more needs to be accomplished to realize the promises of the value and principle of self-determination.

Obstacles to Self-determination

Long and persistent experience of deprivation, disempowerment and learned helplessness make it difficult for people to self-determine. Local elites and vested interests dominate decision-making processes, if a process has indeed been followed, or they decide themselves on behalf of the people, often without any due consultation. Indeed consultation processes are often conveniently manipulated to endorse decisions already made. As self-determination essentially involves decision-making, it has political, power and resource implications. Although we would like people and communities to decide for themselves in regard to what they want and do not want, many a time the concentration of the three elements—politics, power and resources—works against communities self-determining for themselves, as it often involves elites sharing power and resources with people and communities immediately or in due course. Sometimes government organizations', NGOs', INGOs' and donor agencies' funding or programme requirements create a situation where programmes are implemented irrespective of peoples' needs and self-determination. In some situations, legal and institutional structures and cultural practices do not allow for the self-determination of people. The self-determination of people and communities is significantly affected when programme implementers and community workers do not value local people and their views. Clements (2004, p. 73), a community development worker from New Zealand, reports that, in her work, it was difficult to achieve a group's self-determination when the group's only common bond was oppressive treatment, people labelled as oppressed, people polarized into 'haves' and 'have nots' and more layers of oppression created while addressing one layer. Lack of information and communication also affects the ability to self-determine. Uvin (2004, p. 170) argues that aid conditionality is a form of intervention that affects the poor due to actions of outsiders and violates people's right to self-determination; that is, unreasonable and arbitrary conditionality stalls any progress made towards people's self-determination. Instead of treating all human rights equally, the right to self-determination has been treated as one among the third generation of collective human rights and considered not as important as civil and political rights. This kind of branding and categorization disadvantages the application of the right to self-determination principle.

Strategies for Self-determination

The first step to facilitate self-determination is recognizing and valuing people and communities and whatever is there with them. One of the core elements of self-determination is decision-making and decision-making involves thinking. Thus, an important strategy for community workers is to facilitate people's thinking about themselves and their communities. It is much easier for self-reliant people and communities to determine for themselves than it is for those who are not self-reliant. As dependents, the latter have to adhere to conditions prescribed by others, with little choice. However, it does not necessarily follow that all self-reliant communities are able to self-determine for themselves or that communities that are not self-reliant cannot self-determine for themselves. Peoples' and communities' awareness need to be raised in regard to their right to self-determination. Towards this end, popular education can play an important role. Cadena (1984, p. 334, cited from Clements, 2004) suggests that popular education needs to increase people's ability "to consciously appropriate their own reality, influence and control the processes in their daily lives, including equalization of distribution of goods and services, defend their own interest and define the type of society that would serve them best and to make the society less hegemonic and more responsive to them."

In community development practice, it is important to develop a genuine commitment to self-determination, not just lip service. The use of self-determination principle helps to hold people and communities accountable and responsible (governance) for their decisions and consequences. If external agents decide for communities, accountability for such decisions by the community may be significantly reduced. This is one of the reasons for failure of development programmes in communities. Since politics and power are involved in decision-making, 'who decides' becomes a vexing question in community development practice. If a small number of elites within the community determine what is to be done and not done in the community, and community people become apathetic about such decisions, then all members of the community are unlikely to be beneficiaries of such decisions, and at times the community may not benefit at all due to vested interests involved in self-determination. Thus, the basis of self-determination should be democratic values and the un-manipulated and unbridled free participation of people and communities in all decision-making.

Self-determination may be increased by efforts to increase opportunities in the environment—both by removing blockages within the environment and by helping individuals to remove blockages within themselves that limit their abilities to utilize environmental opportunities (Compton and Galaway, 1999). Based on her firsthand experience as a community development worker, Clements (2004, p. 73) has identified some factors that helped her to enable groups to make progress towards their self-determination. These are: as a common person, interact with people and communities; identify and build on current constructive community groups; listen carefully and respectfully to all involved; change oneself in give-and-take relationships as community members change; and recognize and respect all parties involved in a situation. Broadly, the community organization and development process can be consciously employed as a strategy to enable people to determine for themselves.

On the whole, the value and principle of self-determination contributes significantly to community development practice with a difference. Despite the critique and several obstacles, by employing systematic strategies people and communities may be enabled to determine for themselves.

Participation

Meaning of Participation

The values and principles of self-determination and participation go hand in hand. Self-determination is an important element of participation, as people need to determine to participate in community development activities. Participation is a value, principle, method and strategy and, thus, both means and end or the whole process and outcome of community development. Participation is also very much embedded in human rights. People have the right to participate in matters that affect their lives, communities and environment. In that sense participation is both a right and responsibility.

The essence of various familiar phrases in community development such as 'bottom-up development', 'people-centred development', 'participatory development' and 'community-driven development' is participation. The concept of participation has social, political, economic, developmental and cultural connotations. It means that, instead of being dictated to or imposed upon by someone, some structure or authority from the top, people—particularly, at the grassroots level, including the marginalized and disadvantaged—should get involved, participate, plan and decide for themselves in social, political and economic affairs that affect their lives. This is a basic expectation from the humanistic and human rights perspectives and also a civilized desire to protect the marginalized and disadvantaged from the imposition of structures by authorities above and the consequent harm that might befall them as a result. It is an empowering process that will enhance their well-being. Thus, the concept and spirit of participation has become popular in community development practice and in establishing democratic systems. Without the participation of people, it is difficult to achieve sustainable community development.

According to the *Oxford Dictionary*, 'participation' as a noun means the action of participating in something, and 'participate' as a verb means to take part or become involved (in an activity; Hornby, 1993). However, in the real world the meaning is not so simple as it is underpinned by value and power dimensions and other complex factors.

The *Blackwell Dictionary of Social Policy* has constructed the meaning of participation as follows:

> Participation is the involvement and incorporation of users and citizens more generally in service planning and delivery, providing an opportunity to voice their concerns and contribute to policy formation. In terms of welfare services, it is part of a broader shift in the processes of public policy making towards *empowerment* and inclusive *citizenship*, intended to increase *accountability* and secure more responsive, sensitive provision. The concept itself however, remains both elusive and contested. At practical level many commentators argue it reflects consumer models based on clearly defined *rights* and starting with the experiences of service *users* themselves, rather than from the interests and concerns of providers. This points to the need for more radical approaches, based not only on understanding how *citizens* might be able to play a more active part in policy-making processes, but the issues on which they might want to have a say and what these imply for the practice of service professionals. (Maltby, 2002)

In the fourth edition of the *Social Work Dictionary*, the term 'participation' does not appear, but it has included participative management, which means

> A decision making strategy used by some social agency administrators to involve all those who are likely to be affected by desired organizational

change. This strategy includes building voluntary consensus and commitment among the organization's personnel, clientele, sponsors, and other
interested groups to achieve organizational goals. (Barker, 1999)

The *Blackwell Encyclopaedia of Social Work* has discussed the
concept of participation from the service users' perspective:

> User participation implies active involvement in the social sphere and re-
> fers to a range of involvements which individuals and groups may have in
> organizations, institutions and decisions affecting them and others. These
> extend from having control to being a source of information or legitima-
> tion. Participation is crucially judged by the extent to which people can
> exert influence and bring about change. (Beresford and Croft, 2000)

While discussing the concept of participation from social policy
and politics perspectives, Richardson (1983, p. 9) includes the collective dimension in it:

> Participation entails more than taking individual responsibility for some
> action. It implies sharing in an activity, undertaking activity with other
> people.

As the collective dimension of participation, that is, undertaking
activity with other people, appears too general in Richardson's concept, it may be clarified as "a flow of influence upward from the
masses" (Verba et al., 1978) so that it emphasizes the involvement of
grassroots-level people in participation.

The UN's concept of participation is broad. It defines participation as

> the creation of opportunities to enable all members of a community and
> the larger society to actively contribute to and influence the development
> process and to share equitably in the fruits of development. (UN, 1981, p. 5)

Furthermore, the UN Economic and Social Council resolution
1929 (LVIII) states:

> Participation requires the voluntary and democratic involvement of peo-
> ple in '(a) contributing to the development effort, (b) sharing equitably
> in the benefits derived there from and (c) decision-making in respect of
> setting goals, formulating policies and planning and implementing eco-
> nomic and social development programs'. (cited from Midgley, 1986)

The analysis of the nature of participation suggests different variants of participation such as authentic, pseudo, unreal, spontaneous, induced, coerced, indirect, direct, full, partial, consumerist-oriented and democratic-oriented participation (see Pawar, 2005; for similar other typologies, see Cornwall, 2008). Common sense seems to suggest that authentic, full and democratic participation should be encouraged and practised rather than its other variants. According to the UN Research Institute for Social Development (1980), authentic participation (1) is not imposed from above but arises from the grassroots, (2) is focused on distribution becoming a means of obtaining a larger share in the fruits of development and (3) involves a heightening of the participants' awareness of their own capabilities to make choices and influence outcomes (cited in Midgley, 1986, p. 26). These three criteria also appear to help distinguish authentic from pseudo-participation. Pateman (1970, pp. 70–71) defines full participation as "a process where each individual member of a decision-making body has equal power to determine the outcome of decisions." Democratic-oriented participation starts with people's lives and not systems. It is committed to people speaking for themselves, to human and civil rights and to empowerment. It emanates from powerful and influential movements of disabled people, psychiatric system survivors, older people and other welfare recipients (see Beresford and Croft, 2000).

The common theme that emerges from the analysis of these definitions and descriptions is that all people, including the marginalized and the disadvantaged, need to participate in planning and implementing matters that affect their lives, with the necessary enabling opportunities provided to do so. Thus, it has connotations of power and politics, in contrast to some potential participants' disempowered circumstances.

Critique of Participation

If practised and promoted appropriately, few will deny the essential goodness of participation for people and society as a whole. However, some of its variants as indicated above may be seen as causing more harm than good. Cornwall (2008) comments,

"The term, 'participation', has become mired in a morass of competing referents." It is important to caution against potential negative outcomes of participation. Beresford and Croft (2000, p. 357) warn that some participatory actions "may serve to obstruct rather than increase people's involvement, may be used to tokenise and co-opt people, delay decisions and legitimate predetermined agendas and decisions." Similarly, De Kadt (1982, p. 574) has observed that the concept of community participation "has popularity without clarity and is subject to growing faddishness and a lot of lip service." Furthermore, Midgley (1986) points out that participation may be perceived as being or potentially being paternalistic. Indicators such as the number of people attended the meeting and number of people who cast their votes are only beginning phases of participation and do not suggest full participation. Moreover, since many disadvantaged and marginalized communities and people are completely occupied in meeting their basic needs, their continuous participation in society may not be practical. Often participation does not occur naturally, and it calls for creating enabling conditions for participation. The genuineness of the support of capitalist states for participation is questioned. Berner and Phillips (2005) argue that participation, a radical concept, has been co-opted into mainstream theory and diluted in potential. Finally, whether participation at the grassroots level can achieve real improvements is debatable.

Obstacles to Participation

Although participation is one of the core values and principles of community development practice, ensuring the participation of all people in communities is a challenging task. Participation patterns suggest that only a small proportion of people actively participate in communities. This raises a basic question, why do people not participate in matters that concern them, their communities and environment? Obstacles to participation may be found in the environment and the individual, though both are closely connected. The main factors in the environment are non-participatory and non-democratic institutional structures that create significant hurdles for people's involvement in community activities. Dictatorial or dominant leadership styles at various levels discourage people's participation. For example, feudal leaders and class structures in varied ways suppress common people's participation. Oakley (1995, p. 4) rightly states:

> Participation . . . cannot merely be proclaimed or wished upon rural people in the Third World; it must begin by recognising the powerful, multi-dimensional and, in many instances, anti-participatory forces which dominate the lives of rural people. Centuries of domination and subservience will not disappear overnight just because we have "discovered" the concept of participation.

Another important reason for non-participation, particularly in relation to gender, is discriminatory cultural practices in which women are directly or indirectly held back both within the family and outside family matters. Discriminatory social stratifications inhibit the participation of all diverse groups. A culture of non-participatory programme implementation by NGOs and government organizations makes it difficult to change the habit of non-participation. At the individual level, long-term deprived and suppressed conditions disempower people to such an extent that the possibility of participation remains beyond their imagination. This is not to suggest that such people cannot participate. By employing systematic strategies, they can be enabled to participate, but it is a long-term process, and that in itself may be construed as a hurdle. Lack of cohesion in the community, distrust among people and officials, perception of lack of immediate gain, lack of confidence, lack of belongingness to the community and negative experiences of previous participation significantly reduce people's participation (see Cornwall, 2008).

Strategies for Participation

Participation requires people to think critically about their situation and the causes of that situation and to explore ways of addressing their needs and issues, take individual and collective decisions, consistently work to implement those decisions and consume and share the fruits of their work. Thus, the well-known phrase of 'of, by and for' applies. That is, participation in community development should be of the people, by the people and for the people (UNDP, 1992).

Midgley (1986, citing from UN, 1981; Pearse and Stiefel, 1979, 1981) points out that authentic participation requires (1) 'profound social structural change', (2) a 'massive redistribution of power', (3) change in domestic political institutions and international economic order so as to involve the poor and (4) emphasis placed on autonomy and self-reliance.

Although these four requirements may be necessary, they alone may not result in people's participation. At the practical level, many disadvantaged, marginalized and weak groups need access and support provisions. Beresford and Croft (2000) are of the view that

> without support only the most confident, well-resourced and advantaged people and groups are likely to become involved, while without access, efforts to become involved are likely to be arduous and ineffective. (p. 356)

To them,

> access includes equal access to the political structure at both central and local state levels and to other organisations and institutions which affect people's lives; support includes increasing people's expectations and confidence, extending their skills, offering practical support like child care, information, advocacy and transport enabling people to meet together in groups; and ensuring that minority ethnic groups and others facing discrimination can be involved on equal terms. (pp. 356–363)

By understanding the heterogeneous life of the community, it is important to ensure that participation is representative of the diversity of the community (Ledwith, 2005, p. 35). Along with measures to enhance the clarity and specificity of participation (see Cornwall, 2008), it is important to include appropriate participation methods in design and planning; initiate dialogue, discussion and negotiation; and, if necessary, mobilize support of government organizations and NGOs for new initiatives.

On the whole, participation may lead to positive outcomes, depending on the type of participation. Among the positive spin-offs is the fact that participation is both a means and an end in itself. It is a strategy as well as a value that underpins dignity and worth, self-reliance and respect and empowerment. Drawing from relevant literature (Hollnsteiner, 1977, 1982; Majeres, 1977; UN, 1975,

1981; White, 1982), Midgley (1986) has listed several outcomes of participation, including the strengthening of interpersonal relationships, fostering self-confidence, improving material conditions and reducing feelings of powerlessness and alienation. Such outcomes would significantly contribute to community development practice.

Conclusion

Any value or principle is often contested from moral, ethical, legal, social, cultural, or professional perspectives. The four values and principles for community development practice presented in this chapter are not exceptions and can be contested, critiqued and questioned. However, in my view, community development practice in any context needs to follow the values and principles of human rights, self-reliance, self-determination and participation, which are interconnected. Faced with various values and principles, I have provided justification for suggesting these four as core, as they capture the essence of many other values and principles or systematically link to them. These values and principles are not only controversial but are also challenging in terms of applying them to community development practice. Each value and principle has been presented in terms of conceptual discussion, critique of it, obstacles to applying them in practice and some strategies to do so. I hope community development students and practitioners find this analysis useful. Dynamics of and challenges for community development practice mainly emerge from adherence to or departure from these core values and principles. The next chapters will look at these dynamics and challenges.

Notes

1. The eight commitments are commitment to powerless people and social justice, citizenship and human rights, empowerment and self-determination, collective action, diversity, change and involvement in conflict, liberation, open societies and participatory democracy, and fighting and practising the power of example.

2. Schuler's (1996) six core values of the new community are conviviality and culture, education, strong democracy, health and well-being, economic equity, opportunity and sustainability, and information and communication.

3. "Sub-prime mortgage loans have higher (interest and repayment) rates than equivalent prime loans. Lenders consider many factors in a process called 'risk-based pricing' when they come up with mortgage rates and terms. This makes it impossible to generalize about sub-prime rates. Their rates are higher, but how much higher depend on factors such as credit score, size of downpayment and what types of delinquencies the borrower had in the recent past. From a mortgage lender's standpoint, late mortgage or rent payments are worse than late credit card payments.

   A sub-prime mortgage loan also is more likely to have a prepayment penalty, a balloon payment, or both. A prepayment penalty is a fee assessed against the borrower for paying off the mortgage loan early, either because the borrower sells the house or refinances the high-rate loan. A mortgage with a balloon payment requires the borrower to pay off the entire outstanding amount in a lump sum after a certain period has passed, often five years.

   If the borrower can't pay the entire amount when the balloon payment is due, he has to refinance the loan or sell the house. And that's exactly what happened" (The University of Queensland, 2009).

4

Dynamics of Community Development Practice

Introduction

As a community development practitioner and observer, I have seen a range of dynamics in community development practice. In this chapter, such dynamics are presented as critical aspects for the practitioner. Although community development practice has many dimensions (see Chapter 2) and involves many complex and challenging dynamics, depending on one's perceptions and experiences, drawing on the available data and my own analysis, I have categorized the dynamics into four areas, which are very common in any community development endeavour. These are the application of the values and principles of community development; entry into the community (if an outsider) or beginning community development work (if an insider) and acceptance by the community; awareness raising and capacity building that include leadership development, institution building, developing community-based or people's organizations and strengthening existing local institutions; and sustainability of community development programmes or projects or activities in terms of continuity and self-governance and management. The dynamics involved in achieving each of the four areas can then be analyzed.

It may be clarified that, in addition to professionally trained social workers and community development workers, several other professionals such as community workers, welfare workers, health and allied professionals, lawyers, architects, engineers and managers and non-professionals such as local community leaders contribute significantly to community development. Thus, the discussion here is not limited to community development practised by trained professional social workers, though their work is important, for they are but one of the many types of players in the overall community development field in India and the South Asian region. By expanding the scope of analysis in this way, it is possible to look at broad community development practices in the region, irrespective of who has contributed to them.

The Application of the Values and Principles of Community Development

As discussed in the previous chapter, the application of values and principles—human rights, self-reliance, self-determination and participation—is one of the basic and crucial aspects of community development. As much importance is attached to them, they need to be properly understood and recognized before community development activity begins and also during the process and in assessing the outcome of community development. In essence, the application of the values and principles of community development involves upholding or practising human rights and encouraging people to be self-reliant, to think, to make decisions and own them and to participate in the whole process. As argued earlier, human rights embody all the other values and principles as well as social goals such as social justice and social development. Those who lead or are engaged in community development need to be aware of these values and principles with a view to applying them in communities. Whether all those who are engaged in community development are applying the values and principles in their work or not is an open question, as this is difficult to determine. Assuming, however, that some do not, why do some apply them and others not? Many community development activities may result in the realization of some human rights. However, what is important is that such realization should occur through the philosophy and practice of self-reliance, self-determination and participation.

At the macro level, it appears that the language of these values and principles has been incorporated by international organizations such as the World Bank, the United Nations, INGOs, DFID and some GOs, and NGOs irrespective of what community development approaches they follow. Reading their policy documents suggests that they follow bottom-up, participatory and people-centred community development approaches and that they do at least intend to apply the values and principles. However, at the micro or community levels, it is not clear whether these values and principles are applied in letter or spirit. When we critically examine the written policies and field practices in terms of these values and principles, we see a huge hiatus between the two. Field realities suggest that often these values and principles are blatantly violated in communities, by communities (though not all people) themselves and sometimes by external community development agents. Difficulties in applying the values and principles emanate from interconnected dynamics at several levels.

For example, at the macro level, there appears to be near-universal consensus regarding human rights and the obligation to realize and protect them. However, the moment human rights are used as a controlling and sanctioning (a kind of punishment) tool to grant or withhold trade and aid to countries, particularly Asian countries, the validity of universal human rights is questioned and cultural elements stemming from diversity introduced, implying that the meaning and application of human rights is seen as culture specific. Furthermore, counter accusations of a violation of human rights are made against the accuser. This common tendency dilutes the realization of human rights in local communities. If there is a genuine commitment to achieving human rights, we should not be witnessing situations where millions of people remain hungry every day. The target set to eliminate extreme poverty by 2015 appears within our reach, but the evaluation of the progress made so far shows that we are far from it, and many are speculating that we shall fail to keep that commitment, especially given the impact of the current global credit and economic crisis. Without removing extreme poverty in communities, it is hard to see how human rights can be realized. It is only through the application of self-reliance, self-determination and participation approaches that extreme poverty can be eradicated and various community development activities initiated on a sustainable basis. Perhaps the implementation of values and principles at the macro level calls for an enabling approach rather than imposing sanctions.

Uvin (2004, p. 59) has convincingly argued that sanctions or political conditionality presents four types of difficulties:

(1) conditionality is unethical (it ought as a matter of principle not be employed); (2) conditionality is never fully implemented (even if it were ethical, it is never really employed); (3) conditionality does not produce the results it aims for (even if it is employed, it does not work); and (4) conditionality destroys that which it seeks to achieve (not only does it not work, but it causes more harm). (see also Schimmelfennig, 2007)

Box 4.1:
Sanctions on Burma

Since 1998, the military has been subject to growing censure for its denial of democratic and other human rights, reinforced by diplomatic and economic sanctions to weaken the regime. Most western governments have suspended non-humanitarian bilateral aid, imposed an arms embargo, and denied tariff preferences to import from Burma as well as preferential financing for trade and investments. Washington has further banned new investments by US firms and blocked all imports and financial services, making it one of the tightest unilateral US sanctions regimes against any country. Western governments have failed to get agreements within the UN on mandatory measures against Burma. They have, however, blocked all support from the international financial institutions, except minimum technical assistance, and restricted funding for the UN specialized agencies and INGOs to humanitarian programs. (Pedersen, 2008, p. 3)

It may be noted that since the progress towards the civilian government in 2011 and the parliamentary by-election in 2012, many countries have been gradually lifting such sanctions on Burma.

Source: Pedersen (2008, p. 3).

In regard to Burma, despite the application of sanctions for more than a decade, the human rights situation there did not improve. Indeed, this kind of approach at the macro level diminishes the possibility of realizing human rights in local-level communities. Such an external carrot–stick interventionist approach is likely to have an impact on the self-reliance and self-determination of people and their communities, and thus, their participation in their own development. Based on his research, Pedersen (2008) argues that sanctions on Burma have not supplied any solutions, and he suggests an alternative model of critical engagement that emphasizes socio-economic development of the country on a long-term basis. Recognizing this dilemma, the international community has cautiously shifted its conditionality to a positive support policy that focuses on creating democratic structures and processes, organizing elections, opening up the media and improving and implementing laws and quality of justice. It appears that about 10 per cent of aid is directed to this positive support policy (see Uvin, 2004, pp. 83–86). Compared to the policy of conditionality, the positive support approach appears good. In 2011, civil government was put in place, and in 2012, by-elections were held, and the democratic reform appears to be in progress. But has it made any change at the micro level in communities?

Grassroots-level communities in the Asian region, particularly in rural areas, have been experiencing extreme deprivation and discrimination for a long time. Irrespective of political structures, democratic or otherwise, the current social, economic and political arrangements are advantageous largely to local elites and feudal leaders. Existing government bureaucracies often tend to please or comply with the requirements of these leaders. Although some NGOs have done some good work, they have not reached out to all communities. However, it is clear that any change that aims to alter the current status quo is likely to be resisted by some elements within these grassroots-level communities. The nature of such resistance can be extreme, including violence and deaths, thus causing further violations of human rights. Poor and marginalized people who have been suppressed and weakened over a long period are not in a position to see beyond their current situation (involving apathy, indifference, helplessness and powerlessness), and changing that situation is likely to take a long time. To deal with such complex issues and dynamics in grassroots-level communities, talking about only civil and political rights, though necessary, is not sufficient to be effective in bringing about change.

First, as suggested in Chapter 3, it is important to alter the hierarchal articulation of human rights in terms of civil and political rights; economic, social and cultural rights; and collective rights.

At the community level, all these rights are equally important, and prioritizing them one against the other makes little sense. It is essential for people to experience freedom—freedom of thought, expression, speech, association, participation and from want—and equal protection under the law. It is also essential for them to access and experience good education, health, housing, employment and living in a good environment that has adequate and clean water, air and nature. All these are interconnected and contribute significantly to community development. It may be relatively easier to convince the local community about their total significance than the international community, which appears to be still preoccupied with civil and political rights.

Second, at local levels and connected higher levels, education and training in the values and principles of community development need to be provided in such a way that they not only raise awareness of all human rights, self-reliance, self-determination and participation but also translate that awareness into action. Particularly, such training is needed for government officials at all levels, relevant NGO personnel, local political leaders, community leaders and youth, with a strong emphasis on women's participation in such educational programmes. Appropriate methods should be employed to disseminate this information, as new information is received or resisted in different ways by different people. This education and training should be provided with cultural sensitivity, as there is much cultural diversity in the region.

Third, experience of working with long-term deprived people and communities shows that, irrespective of whether the agency or community worker is an insider or outsider, in any community development activity the people's initial tendency is to ask, 'What do I get from it, and what is there in it for me?' If their own observations and assessment suggest that there is nothing or little for them, they may not return for the next meeting. Talking to such deprived and marginalized groups about their human rights, self-reliance, self-determination and participation may not make much sense to them or capture their attention. Their immediate concern is all too often, 'What do I do for my next meal, how am I going to feed my children and is there any work for me tomorrow?' Attending to and addressing their immediate concerns, while at the same time preparing them to focus on how they can become self-reliant, make decisions and participate in day-to-day affairs that affect them, is a balancing task, and no readymade solutions are available, as each context is so different. However, the value and principle of self-reliance should be followed from the beginning. Initially, this may appear very hard and even discourage people from participating. On the other hand, delivering services by compromising this value and principle in the long term does more harm than good to people and communities. Enabling them to realize that the cause of their situation lies elsewhere in socio-economic and political structures and that they can change that situation by redefining their conditions and taking responsibility to change that situation is a long-term process. Renaming their needs as rights and claiming services as a matter of right and not seeking charity or help call for empowering people based on their own strengths and resources (local knowledge, culture, skills, emerging leaders and other resources). Understanding that the state has the responsibility to meet the basic needs of people empowers people and their communities. This in turn enables people to participate productively in community life in a self-reliant manner.

It is not uncommon to see how undemocratic decisions are taken in community meetings. Sometimes advantaged groups dominate decisions. On a number of critical issues decisions are made in the name of community, even though few people own and support such decisions. Self-determination has to be a genuine democratic process, where people from all diverse groups together make decisions and participate in implementing those decisions. This suggests that people and communities have both rights and responsibilities and that to assume those responsibilities they need to be adequately supported and provided access to resources and institutions. At every stage of community development, people need to determine what they themselves will give to the community and receive from it. Both are equally important. Community development calls for an element of sacrifice, and people's determination to make sacrifices is a first step. People need to contribute creatively to communities to ensure that everybody's rights to clean and safe water, unpolluted air and access to nature are met.

Finally, adhering to and practising the values and principles of community development call for strong and undivided commitment to them throughout the process. Such a commitment inevitably leads to both favourable and unfavourable dynamics. Whereas favourable dynamics are heartening for all those who are engaged in community development, it is important to be conscious of unfavourable dynamics and prepare to deal with them. First, local-level leaders and power structures may resist the application of these values and principles or may try to manipulate them in their favour. Second, some people who are deeply rooted in cultural discriminatory practices may not support these values and principles. Third, due to such complex dynamics, whatever progress is made in community development work may come to a halt or revert back to almost the original situation. Fourth, resources that were committed to the work may not be forthcoming due to situations beyond anyone's control. Fifth, important personnel engaged in the work may decide to discontinue due to whatever pressures or factors. Sixth, people who are seeking immediate results may become disappointed and reduce their support for the activity. Such dynamics in the field can often be frustrating. To deal with these dynamics, it is important to remain unperturbed, patient and unshaken about the values and principles and have a long-term vision for community development. Fortunately, these dynamics are often relatively short term and short-lived. It is also important to learn from such dynamics and experiences and to appreciate that community development is a long-term process, the gains of which are often sustainable.

Box 4.2:
Human rights, self-reliance, self-determination and participation in Ralegan Siddhi

> Ralegan Siddhi, a rural village in India, was once afflicted by extreme poverty, drought, unemployment, indebtedness, alcoholism and related problems. People felt helpless with no hope for the future. So-called panchayat (village council) democratic elections caused major conflicts and disunity. People had little trust in the government's development schemes. This clearly shows that many human rights were not enjoyed by the people.
>
> Mr Anna Hazare, from the same village, emerged as a leader who transformed the village from poverty to prosperity. People

(Box 4.2 Contd.)

(Box 4.2 Contd.)

were mobilized to participate in cultural development, political development that involved the nomination of panchayat and committee members by consensus, the formulation of norms (laws) and penalties, natural resource management through watershed development, economic development through agriculture and dairy, sacrifice in the form of voluntary labour, health and hygiene initiatives, the removal of discriminatory practices and the banning of alcohol and tobacco consumption. These participatory reforms have resulted in overall socio-economic and political developments that have resulted in demonstrable and measurable outcomes in the areas of education, health, income, self-sufficiency, cultural practices, removal of discrimination, participation of women and sustainable natural resource management. Except for the government's development schemes, no aid was sought or used for development of the village. Although the leader and the village people never explicitly referred to human rights, the development of this village epitomizes the realization of civil and political rights; economic, social and cultural rights and collective rights; and the achievement of self-reliance, self-determination and participation to a great extent on a sustainable basis (Hazare, 2003; Lokur, undated).

Source: Hazare (2003); Lokur (undated).

Note: Non-election of panchayat members and some punitive practices to introduce discipline in the village may be debated and perceived as contrary to some human rights. However, in my view, the harm caused by them would be probably less than the consequences of political conditionality.

Entry into the Community, Beginning Community Development Work and Acceptance by the Community

As in the old adage 'A good beginning is a job half done', in any community development endeavour, a good entry to or a good beginning in the community lays a strong foundation for community development. In community development practice, this is the basic phase, and without successfully or effectively completing this phase, it is hard to achieve anything in community development. Before discussing this crucial phase, a distinction may be made between entry into the community and beginning community development work. Entry into the community refers to the involvement of an 'outsider'—who may be a development worker/community worker/social worker/ NGO or its representative, INGO, corporate personnel, or any other interested person—who enters a community to undertake community development work. Beginning community development work refers to an 'insider', who may be any person from the same community who assumes some responsibility for community development and so begins community development work. How does an outsider enter the community to begin community development work? How does an insider begin community development work? Then, irrespective of whether one is an outsider or insider, how do they gain acceptance in the community and the acceptance of their community development agenda? Addressing and understanding these questions are important as this beginning part of community development is surrounded by a lot of issues and dynamics, which have to be amicably dealt with or settled by genuinely engaging community members before there can be any progress in community development. The time required to complete this initial part depends on the community, the issue to be addressed and the community worker. However, if it is not completed successfully and effectively, community development work is likely to falter.

Generally, an outsider, a trained professional or otherwise, adopts a range of different approaches to enter the community, depending on what information is available about the target community and access to it. These approaches may include reading a profile of the community, if available, developing a profile of the community by employing a range of research methods (observation, survey, meetings, discussions, rapid rural appraisal and so on, see understanding community in Chapters 1 and 2) or undertaking a needs analysis. Alternatively, a worker may decide to immerse in the community without any background information and learn from the community. How the worker is introduced to the community, with whom she or he interacts, with which groups she or he engages and the introducer, all significantly affect successful entry into the community. If the community worker is replacing a previous worker in an ongoing community development project, people's response and receptivity would be different depending on their previous experience with the worker and the project. An outside community worker is keenly observed, tested and judged by the people against their hopes and individual and collective expectations. People's perceptions and conclusions about the worker may hinder (at least initially) or facilitate her or his actions depending on what those perceptions and conclusions are. Understanding communities based on figures and profiles is important, but it may not be enough to understand people and their culture, beliefs, politics and power structures and vested interests and other dynamics. The community worker needs to devote a significant amount of quality time in the community and with people to gain deeper insights.

A community development worker or initiator from inside the community does not need to undergo this community-knowledge-gaining and community-testing process. It is assumed that the worker knows the people and the community and vice versa. However, both have preconceived notions of each other, and that has to be cleared up if it is unfavourable. In both cases, whether 'outsider' or 'insider', it is important to gain acceptance from the community and people so as to work effectively with them for their community development. Several factors may result in the non-acceptance of the worker. One of the main factors is a mismatch between the expectations of people and the worker's community development agenda. Second, if the worker identifies and interacts frequently with members or a group who are dominant and have tended to disadvantage and marginalize poorer people, the latter may look at the worker with suspicion. Third, if the worker is perceived as a threat to the existing power structure, powerful groups may impose hurdles to initiating any community development work. Fourth, if commitment and skills on the worker's part are lacking, people may find it difficult to support the worker. Fifth, false or unrealistic promises and hopes may result in community disappointment and distrust. Finally, instead of sacrificing, recognizing people and giving credit to them, if the worker engages in promoting self-recognition and taking the credit for others' work, people may gradually distance themselves and begin criticizing the worker.

Hazare's (2003, p. 18) village development experience suggests that:

> At the start of the village development program, one does not get suffi-cient cooperation from the villagers or the authorities of the village. The same is the case with members of your own household.

> The villagers suspect that the organizers have an ulterior motive. Some think that the social workers do their work for their own benefit. Unless they get to know the person and are convinced about her/him, they do not cooperate with her/him.

One of the effective ways to make a successful entry and gain acceptance is to put aside one's own community development agenda and focus on the people's most desperate and felt needs and those that are close to the heart of the culture or the community. This com-monly leads community members to join hands with the worker to do something to meet those needs. In each community, the issue and the needs that are focused on may be different, but whatever it is it opens a gateway for further community development work.

Although these three brief case studies are different, they all show the dynamics and difficulties of entering a community, beginning

Box 4.3:
Beginning community development in Ralegan Siddhi

Mr Anna Hazare, following his retirement from the Indian Army, returned to his village that was afflicted by several social problems (see the previous case study). Among other things, he noticed the dilapidated condition of the temple from where wood had been taken (stolen) by some members of the village to fuel liquor dens.

By contributing his own provident fund (pension) of ₹20,000 (in 1975–1976), Mr Hazare began renovating and rebuilding the temple to demonstrate his unselfish motives and to attract people and create an interest in community development activi-ties. The temple represented the cultural heart of the community

(Box 4.3 Contd.)

(Box 4.3 Contd.)

and enhanced the faith of people in god and their spirituality. Mr Hazare (2003) states:

> Most people are selfish. When they see something they can benefit from, they are ready to cooperate! As everybody was going to gain from temple renovation, one by one they started coming to help. They did whatever they were told to do because they were now confident. Within six or seven months, people had come up in large numbers and joined the work. Some offered whatever financial help they could, while the majority helped with the manual labour. A year and half later the temple renovation, costing Rupees 200,000, was completed. This was the beginning of community voluntary labour. A sense of concern for community was created.

This community development bud has blossomed into several successful integrated community development programmes, resulting in building a self-reliant village and a model for others to emulate.

Box 4.4:
Entry of Sarvodaya's Gramadana workers in Sri Lankan villages

Sarvodaya is a well-known NGO in Sri Lanka, committed to empowerment and poverty alleviation. It works mostly through its key staff members known as Gramadana workers, who enter the village only on village people's request and invitation. It is assumed that such a request indicates motivation and awareness level of the villagers. In exceptional situations, they can reach out to villages, but the village people still need to make a request to Sarvodaya in due course. Based on such an invitation, Gramadana workers begin their work through establishing a group of people interested in development and in assuming lead roles in achieving it (ESCAP, 1996b, p. 93).

Source: ESCAP (1996b, p. 93).

Box 4.5:
Entry through the social work and research centre/the barefoot college in villages of Rajasthan in India

Mr Bunker Roy was educated in prestigious educational institutions and groomed for a career in civil or diplomatic service. Having been deeply affected by famine in Bihar, Mr Roy, as an outsider, founded the Social Work and Research Centre in 1972, now known as the Barefoot College at Tilonia in Rajasthan, India, to work with the most disadvantaged, marginalized and poor people in villages. The centre began its work with a groundwater survey of 110 villages of Silora Block for the Rural Electrification Corporation and it took two years to complete it. The college had no ideological orientation. Roy (1997) states:

> The college wanted to break away from the "social work tradition", which in India had acquired an urban, middle-class, academic colour, and there could not have been a better way to do this than using a professional groundwater survey as an entry point.

When Roy's centre began work at the village level it faced several questions such as: 'Is it pro-government? Is it a scheme started by the rural rich? Who sponsors the scheme? Who provides financial support? Which political party does it support?' Most of the initial years were used to address such questions and appropriately inform village people. This process affected the centre's staff members as well. Based on his firsthand experience, Roy narrates the dynamics at play while making an entry and gaining acceptance.

> Depending on how convincing the answers are, and depending on how aligned the project and its workers are to parties, ideologies, personalities in the area and to government, the peasants will respond accordingly. Ironically, there is a sense of security in exploitation, and the poorest peasants believe the word of the very individuals who exploit them the most. When any project starts, it needs time to settle down; but, simultaneously, it must also win

(Box 4.5 Contd.)

(Box 4.5 Contd.)

> over the confidence of the very people whom the project's agents will hopefully be fighting against in years to come.
>
> The first visible objectives of the project must be harmless to the people having vested interests in the village. Hence services are to be provided to the whole village, including the rich, and the project's agents have to mix less with the poor and more with the rich. The agents have to pamper the latter's wishes and requests and thus establish contact with the poor through protocol. The college had to go through this exercise in order to acquire an image and gain access to the villages it wanted to work with; it had to respond to "the felt needs of the rural population," which were actually the needs of a few. These were years of preparation with villages at large favouring the college's action.
>
> Perhaps this experience made Roy identify with what Mahatma Gandhi once said:
>
> First they ignore you, then they laugh at you, then they fight you, then you win.
>
> **Source:** Milnes (2007); Roy (1997).

community development work and gaining acceptance. Irrespective of whether the community worker is an insider or outsider, they all face similar acceptance and cooperation issues, which emerge often during the initial stages and must be overcome. They all appear to be initial hiccups and meant to go away, if dealt with appropriately. Mr Hazare was an insider in Ralegan Siddhi village, Mr Roy was an outsider in Rajasthan villages in India, and the Gramadana workers were representatives of a well-established NGO in Sri Lanka. Their communities and contexts were significantly different. The first one used people's faith and cultural aspects of the community, the second one entered on request and invitation from the community, and the third one tried to balance engagement with vested interests and the poor, ultimately to gain access to the latter. The time taken to gain acceptance and the nature of dynamics too varied significantly.

What were most common among them were their efforts to build trust and gain the confidence of communities and people. Needless to say, trust and confidence building is a long-term process that calls for commitment and consistency between words and action. Community workers need to nurture their commitment and be realistic and open. When people and communities become convinced and begin trusting, they can confidently cooperate and participate in their own development. Experiences briefly narrated in these cases are not those of ordinary workers. These workers have worked for decades with great devotion and commitment, and their community development work has become exemplary. Both professionals and non-professionals need to learn and gain inspiration from such experiences, and thus, to prepare better to enter deprived communities in the region, most of which are untouched by any community development workers and are badly in need of community development initiatives. Depending on the needs and contexts of communities, entries may be made to begin community development work with members of the community by dialoguing, combining basic service delivery and development work, introducing health and education initiatives, or by community infrastructure provisions, all ultimately geared towards people-centred and integrated or comprehensive community development.

Awareness Raising and Capacity Building

Making a successful entry, starting appropriate community development activities and gaining acceptance may naturally draw community development workers into the strategy of awareness raising and capacity building as they together constitute a crucial force in community development work. Both these activities should go hand in hand and result in empowerment of people. As the process and outcome of awareness raising have many elements of empowerment, though it may be distinguished from empowerment, only the term awareness raising is used for discussion. The trust and confidence of people that has been built up over a period and the hopes created have to be carefully channelled to raising the awareness of people beyond the initial community development activity, cutting across a range of issues that are important for both individual and community development. Raising awareness is not just limited to passing new information to or educating community people. In the process of raising awareness, the impression is created, usually inadvertently, of 'You do not know anything and I know everything.' The creation of such an impression should be consciously prevented, as it undermines people's dignity and devalues them. On the contrary, a message such as, 'You know certain things I do not know and I am willing to learn from and with you,' enables people to look at themselves more positively and build on their strengths. Culturally appropriate, respectful and powerful methods may be employed to raise the awareness of people. In fact, the state of awareness itself in a sense encompasses everything one wants to do. It is a very powerful tool, and that tool should be appropriately and timely employed by showing, directing, or creating concrete opportunities. Otherwise, it may result in frustration and disappointment and even diminish further cooperation in some contexts.

According to ESCAP (1996a, p. 19),

> Awareness-raising is a strategy by which people in a depressed or oppressed situation are helped to become aware of the nature of that situation. There can be many aspects of that awareness including: (a) what is their precise situation; (b) what is giving rise to that situation; (c) how are they responding to that situation; (d) what are the consequences of the situation; and (e) what might be done to change the situation.

These and similar questions essentially lead to what Freire (1972) calls raising critical consciousness or 'conscientization'. Raising awareness for awareness sake is of no use if it does not translate into action. It should help develop people's faith in themselves and their ability to think and act and to transform despair to hope and dependence to independence. How do you raise that kind of awareness? It cannot be achieved through one-way communication or spoon-feeding or blaming people for their situation. It is important to initiate dialogue with people on an equal footing, engage in dialogue that explores and interprets their understandings of the world and in critical reflection on it and to maintain two-way communication to ensure action (see Freire, 1972, pp. 75–118).

Box 4.6:
Awareness raising to strengthen village organizations in Bangladesh

The Bangladesh Rural Advancement Committee (BRAC) is a private sector development organization that aims to work for poverty alleviation and empowerment of the poor through establishing village organizations. One of the main strategies employed to develop members of village organizations is the Social Awareness Education Course. ESCAP (1996b, p. 4) states:

> This month long course, conducted by one of BRAC's trainers, is designed to assist village organization members to become aware of their hidden potential and find possible solutions to everyday problems. This awareness-raising course continues informally through the weekly village organization meetings, and particularly the issue-based bimonthly meetings held to discuss various local social and economic issues.

Source: ESCAP (1996b, p. 4).

Box 4.7:
Awareness raising through moral cleansing at Ralegan Siddhi

Using the renovated temple as a platform for meeting and chatting during leisure time, people began informally interacting in groups and discussed issues affecting village and common concerns. This informal process opened up a pathway for friendship, cooperation and communication. The leader of the village, Mr Anna Hazare, followed the Gandhian approach of self-practising rather than only preaching.

During informal chats, Mr Hazare

> started quoting the sayings of great men like Swami Vivekanand, Mahatma Gandhi, Vinoba Bhave etc. He also used the ideals of Sant Yadav Baba whose memories were still alive in the minds of the people. Bhajans (hymns) and religious discourses etc., in the early hours of the day through a public address system from the

(Box 4.7 Contd.)

(Box 4.7 Contd.)

temple, were used to enlighten the people. Thus a change in the general attitude of the people was brought about by moral cleansing. (Mishra, 1996)

This awareness was effectively used to engage people in their own and the community's development (Mishra, 1996).

Source: Mishra (1996).
Note: Awareness-raising strategies are not explicitly discussed in Anna Hazare's writings. The above case is developed on the basis of observations and secondary literature.

Box 4.8:
Awareness raising for community-led total sanitation

Defecation in open areas is one of the major environmental and health issues in the Asian region, particularly South Asia. To put an end to this practice, a facilitator raises the critical consciousness of people in communities by walking with them along tracks of open defecation and raising critical questions without offering any solutions. Kar (2005) states the following demonstrations as one of the approaches to raising people's awareness of open defecation and its consequences and to change their behaviour.

Ask for a glass of drinking water. When the glass of water is brought, offer it to someone and ask if they could drink it. If they say yes, then ask others until everyone agrees that they could drink the water. Next, pull a hair from your head and ask what is in your hand. Ask if they can see it. Then touch it on some shit on the ground so that all can see. Now dip the hair in the glass of water and ask if they can see anything in the glass of water. Next, offer the glass of water to anyone standing near to you and ask them to drink it. Immediately they will refuse. Pass the glass on to others and ask if they could drink. No one will want to drink that water. Ask why they refuse it. They will answer that it contains shit. Now

(Box 4.8 Contd.)

(Box 4.8 Contd.)

ask how many feet a fly has. Inform them it has six feet and they are all serrated. Ask if flies could pick up more shit than your hair could pick up. The answer should be "yes." Now ask them what happens when flies sit on theirs or their children's food and plate: what are they bringing with them from places where open defecation is practised? Finally ask them what are they eating with their food? The bottom line is, everyone in the village is ingesting each other's shit. Ask them to try to calculate the amount of shit ingested every day. Ask how they feel about ingesting each others' shit because of open defecation? Don't suggest anything at this point. Just leave the thought with them for now and remind them of it when you summarize at the end of the community analysis.

Source: Kar (2005).

The three brief case studies presented in Boxes 4.6 to 4.8 show different approaches to awareness raising. In the case of BRAC, a well-established private development organization has developed a month-long course and trained its own personnel as facilitators to conduct awareness-raising classes for village organization groups. These training inputs are further discussed and reinforced in subsequent meetings. In case of Ralegan Siddhi, sacrifice and self-demonstration by the leader accompanied by moral cleansing were employed to raise awareness and mobilize people, particularly among the youth. In the third case, the impact of defecation in open areas was directly demonstrated to people to raise their critical consciousness. The context of each case presented is very different, and so is the respective awareness-raising method employed. What is common among all of them is that they were effective in raising awareness, changing behaviour of and producing action by people, and thereby achieving, respectively, objectives of poverty alleviation, integrated village development and community-led total sanitation.

Generally, practice aspects of awareness raising may include formal and informal discussion and dialogue with people; formation of a range of groups (youth, the elderly, women, extremely poor, unemployed and local community leaders), depending on the need and issue; identifying competent facilitators or volunteers from the community; holding 'train the trainer' workshops or sessions, providing exposure to model community development projects and to people engaged in such projects; and drawing maximum resources from the community (local cultural and religious aspects that can make the point quickly and to which people can relate). Dynamics during awareness raising generally differ from one community context to another. Homogeneity and heterogeneity of groups, mismatch between awareness raising and community members' expectations, people joining and dropping from groups, inadequate number of volunteers, looking for immediate results, interference by vested interests, opposition from some community members and lack of personnel, leadership, or other necessary supports for basic survival may contribute to challenging dynamics in practice.

Capacity Building

As stated earlier, awareness raising and capacity building often go together. The consequences of awareness raising without capacity building and capacity building without awareness raising would frustrate people and community development workers and may not help to make significant progress in community development. The raising of awareness of people in many respects (confidence, critical analysis of the situation, hope and ways to realize the hope) should build the capacity of people generally to some extent and further motivate them to strengthen their capacity in specific needed areas. Like many other development phrases, 'capacity building' is an overused phrase in the field of development. Capacity building is used or referred to in wide ranging contexts from local to international, individuals to groups and GOs to NGOs. Thus, the meaning and scope of capacity building can be highly focused or highly diffused. For the purpose of this book, the meaning and scope of capacity building is limited to the context of local-level community development. Capacity building is a means, process and goal of community development. According to UNDP (1997, p. 3), capacity building is "the process by which individuals, organizations, institutions and societies develop abilities (individually and collectively) to perform functions, solve problems and set and achieve objectives." While the UNDP emphasizes the development of abilities, Hussein (2006, p. 374) slightly modifies it to emphasize improvement of abilities—capacity building is "the search for improvements in the ability of institutions, individuals or groups to efficiently and effectively fulfill their responsibilities." Keeping with the values and principles of community development, capacity building is developing and/or improving the abilities of individuals, groups, organizations and institutions to realize the human rights of people, particularly of the disadvantaged and marginalized groups, on a sustainable basis.

The capacity building of individuals, groups, organizations, institutions and infrastructure is essential to ensure social, cultural, economic and political development in communities on a sustainable basis. Towards this end, specific groups or categories in local-level communities need to be identified for capacity building. Generally, these will include individuals and groups, particularly marginalized and disadvantaged people, functional leaders, facilitators or catalysts, volunteers, community-based organizations (CBOs) or people's organizations (POs), existing or new youth groups, NGOs and local institutions and infrastructure. Depending on the issues, needs and objectives set, capacity building calls for knowledge and skill development or improvement. It is also important to raise the question of what and whose knowledge and skills we are talking about and imparting. Often a 'clean slate' is assumed on the part of people and communities, and capacity-building recipients are bombarded with so-called new knowledge, information and skills. This is probably the most inappropriate approach to capacity building in local-level communities. People in local-level communities have the knowledge and skills and strengths required to implement development programmes. It is important to recognize and understand local knowledge, local skills, richness in local culture (refer to the value and principle of self-reliance) and to try to build further on what is already there. Roy (1997), based on the experience of the Barefoot College, argues, "Just because someone cannot read or write does not mean he or she is uneducated" (Milnes, 2007). Eade (2007, p. 663) also argues along similar lines, stating, "Most development aid has precious little to do with building the capacities of 'the poor' to transform their societies . . . the tendency of development industry is to ignore, misinterpret, displace, supplant, or undermine the capacities that people already have" (see also Girgis, 2007). Roy further states:

> The biggest threat to development and changes in the rural areas is what in the urban areas is called Educated Man. He usually is conservative, inflexible, conceited, arrogant and not open to new ideas; he refuses to work with his hands and he considers anyone less qualified on paper inferior and shows it; he has preconceived notions of development and how to solve problems; he uses knowledge as a tool for exploitation and power; he disseminates information on schemes and subsidies in the form of patronage. Tilonia (Barefoot College) has never faced any problem in communicating and working with the poorer peasant. But it is the Educated Man who has persistently sabotaged the introduction of innovative and progressive ideas.

Roy's above argument is based on the following evidence.

Box 4.9:
Capacity building from local knowledge and skills

The Barefoot College (BC) has set an example by delinking qualification from experience. For instance, the Centre's Health Programme is run by a village-level health worker who has a degree in an arts subject from a Kishangarh school. Kishangarh, Silora Block's only town, is a small rural centre, but this health worker has—in BC's terms—more relevant knowledge in preventive health and village participation than most physicians, even those who have graduated from the country's leading universities. At BC, physicians have to work under him. Likewise, BC's educational programme, which involves the running of 30 night schools for 1,500 dropout children in 30 villages, is run by a priest who has no degree, and he has trained teachers with bachelors' degrees in education working under him. The Agricultural Extension Programme is looked after by a youth from the village who has no qualification in agriculture but has produced tremendous results. The Tradition Media Section, where puppetry is the most prominent means of communicating messages, is run by a one-time sheep farmer who has received no training in this art; he just picked it up. The same holds true for the Rural Orientation Programme; it is run by an individual from the village. The new 60,000 sq. ft. campus has been built by a village youth who is illiterate. (Roy, 1997)

Source: Roy (1997).

Keeping in mind that people's capacities can be developed based on their existing knowledge and skills, additional knowledge and skills may be required and transferred in such a way that these dovetail with existing knowledge and skills. At the individual and group level, capacity building may focus on developing confidence and faith in oneself, needed knowledge and skills and interest in participation in whatever identified project or task. Such capacity building at individual and group level may be geared towards forming CBOs/POs, goal setting, task performance plans and implementation. By identifying voluntary functional leaders and catalysts/facilitators, their capacities may be developed for better communication, coordination and facilitation. It is also important to develop skills of participatory group norm development and a proper process of following such norms and performing tasks to achieve set goals. Local NGOs and similar organizations' capacities need to be developed, consistent with the values and principles of community development and how to be responsive to people's human rights, issues and needs and how to work with people and other organizations. It is also important to make them conscious that they can be easily trapped into or preoccupied with management tasks of monitoring, evaluation and producing funding proposals that meet the requirements of donors or external agents. Similarly, local institutions' capacities need to be developed to ensure good governance and coordination, cooperation and equip them with non-bureaucratic skills so as to promote self-determination and participation of people. Their capacities need to be developed to remain transparent, open and honest, and thus, able to maintain the lasting trust of and respect for people and communities. In most rural communities, basic infrastructure is very poor or non-existent. Hence, social and physical infrastructure (schools, roads, health centres, bridges, water and sanitation etc.) needs to be developed by engaging and expanding their capacities. The motivation levels of people to develop their capacities, available opportunities or lack of them to use those capacities, resource constraints and power inequalities may all pose difficulties in capacity development activities. In addition, who drives the capacity development agenda, who resources capacity development activities, what roles NGOs play and who controls them are important questions, and deeper dynamics are embedded in these issues (see Eade, 2007; Girgis, 2007; Smillie, 2001).

On the whole, awareness raising and capacity building together, and as means and process, can be employed for political activism when necessary and in social, cultural, economic, political, educational and health development in local-level communities in the Asia-Pacific region. Although some limited efforts have been made in this direction, in many parts of the region a lot more needs to be done on a sustainable basis.

Sustainable Community Development: Continuity and Self-governance/Management

Awareness raising and capacity building together lay a sound foundation for sustainable community development, which is the fourth aspect of community development practice discussed here. Sustainable community development is vital in the contemporary context, and it is also the important goal that everyone wishes to see achieved. Sustainable development has two meanings. First, in view of finite natural resources, population pressures, pollution, exploitation and abuse of resources and climate change issues, all natural and environmental resources, such as water, air, land, minerals, fossil fuels/energy and biodiversity, need to be managed in such a way that people and nature live together in harmony to ensure equal distribution of these resources, particularly to the poor and the most disadvantaged and, thereby, ensure the well-being of all people and future generations. Second, the phrase 'sustainable community development' is used in a limited sense to connote need-based community development activities that can be planned, developed and continued by communities and people themselves without depending on external support or with minimum external support. Both meanings are important and need to be employed in this aspect of practice.

This is a crucial and critical phase because sustainability has emerged as a core issue in development, and unsustainable industrial activities and human behaviours associated with them must be modified to ensure sustainability. Many community development projects are initiated with great enthusiasm with or without external aid but do not continue, particularly when the funding stops, the project period ends or they fail to achieve set objectives. More often than not, externally aided community development is time bound and aid is offered on an unsustainable basis, based on several factors beyond the actual need, and is going to end one day. The World Bank (2005, p. xiv) states:

> Infrastructure and other activities supported by the Bank's CBD/CDD projects have been difficult to sustain beyond the Bank presence because of a lack of needed resources from the government and communities to ensure their operation and maintenance. More broadly, Bank projects have often failed to provide consistent long-term support for an activity to become sustainable.

With whatever reasons or justifications aid is offered, all aid providers and development enterprises would like to see their activities continue in communities beyond the project funding period, and it is frustrating to see that this often does not happen. They also would like to extend their work to hitherto untouched areas. Sustainable community development is inherent in the values/principles of self-reliance, self-determination and participation. Although this is a difficult area of practice, given the nature, scope and vastness of community development work in the Asian region, it appears to be the most practical and desirable aspect to focus on and aim for.

Sustainable community development calls for participatory planning and implementation of community development programmes and activities incorporating climate change and biodiversity concerns. It may include conserving and protecting community natural resources, such as land, water, forestry and natural energy, and developing mechanisms to share and have equal access to these resources. It is also important to include the most poor and the marginalized in the process. Many rural communities have their own indigenous methods of reusing and recycling their natural resources, and such methods need to be consciously employed. It is also important to reinforce the link between natural resource management and good quality of life in terms of economically sustainable productive activities, education, health, housing, culture and spirituality. For example, water and sanitation issues are closely linked to time spent in accessing them, pollution, spread of diseases and the consequent impact on the health of people. Conserving land and water brings about better agricultural production. In addition to food and fodder production, which is vital for living, agricultural activities create employment and income for people. In the Asian region, agriculture is the core aspect of rural communities and is closely connected to natural resource management, and these need to be squarely focused on in community development.

Sustainable community development also calls for both utilizing the existing capacities and extending the capacities of individuals, groups, leaders, organizations and institutions in relation to developing participatory mechanisms for self-governance and management without unnecessary external dependence and interference. The main vehicles for self-governance and management are CBOs/POs, local NGOs and other associations and local institutions (councils). By meaningfully networking among these groups, flexible structures and processes need to be developed for self-governance and management of a range of community development activities in the areas of health, education, employment, housing, culture, natural resource management and economic production. In both China and India, decentralizing governance systems to local-level democratic institutions—Villagers' Committees in China and Panchayati Raj in India—has been introduced. Instead of developing parallel governing systems, people in local communities, through CBOs/POs, NGOs and other associations, in coordination and cooperation with these local institutions, plan and implement village/community development programmes and activities. Although these institutions have democratic structures (theoretically) and are thus avenues for people's participation, their governance systems need to be radically changed and transformed by becoming transparent, honest, open, responsive and accountable to people and themselves. They need to be inclusive of common people and responsive to their voices. Sustainable community development practice should essentially focus on translating these local-level institutions and their written commitments into appropriate practice. This may call for amicable dialogue, building trust, cooperation, collaboration, communication and understanding (Clarke and Stewart, 1998) and, at times, political activism on the part of people and communities to make these institutions work along the lines intended. Under the current conditions and functioning patterns of these institutions, this may appear to be a tall order for community development practice. However, since these institutions have substantial resources, legitimacy and responsibility, their resources must be optimally employed for need-based community development activities that lead to the realization of people's human rights as well as the goals set for these local institutions. Making and enabling local institutions to be responsible for sustainable community development is not intended to undermine or overlook important community development activities undertaken by NGOs and other civil society organizations. Undoubtedly, these also contribute to local-level community development, although their quality, quantity, consistency and active working duration vary significantly. Whatever work they do is important, but if they do the same as local institutions, regarding coordination and collaboration, while remaining independent, such collaboration may improve the practice of both and help them contribute significantly as local institutions to sustainable community development. They can mobilize and motivate people to engage constructively with local-level institutions so as to make those institutions work for community development without undue politicization. On the whole, sustainable community development is not just an ideal. The following brief cases demonstrate that it is feasible and that committed people, communities and leaders have developed sustainable communities that are worth emulating elsewhere.

Box 4.10:
Sustainable community development at Ralegan Siddhi

Mr Anna Hazare, then a common man committed to village development, on the one hand initially sacrificed his own resources to renovate a temple, and that renovation resulted in mobilizing people and youth and their voluntary labour, and, on the other, accessed government institutions at taluka (the government's administrative office base between the village and district) and district levels to understand and disseminate the government's schemes for the development of villages. By engaging local people, several community-based organizations were formed (e.g. The Sant Yadav Baba Education Society, the Yadav Baba Milk Producers' Association, several women's

(Box 4.10 Contd.)

(Box 4.10 Contd.)

groups, a credit society and several committees). All important issues were discussed and decisions were/are taken at the village assembly (Gram Sabha) and tasks assigned to members and groups on a consensus basis. By combining the villagers' voluntary labour and government schemes, several watersheds were developed to conserve water, soil and vegetation (see Chapter 3). This participatory natural resource management significantly improved agricultural production. Earlier water was not sufficient for 150 acres of land, but now more than 1,500 acres of land receives sufficient water for cultivating two crops. The produce increased six- to eight-fold. Earlier 85 per cent of people did not receive sufficient grains. Now there has been an 85 per cent increase in output, ending the necessity of buying grain from outside. Milk production increased from 300 to 3,000 litres per day. The per capita income increased from ₹200 to 2,000. A non-agriculture cooperative bank was established without the help of any financial institution.

Earlier there was a school providing an education up to year four, but now education is available up to year 12. Many girls became able to access education and some have become teachers. Several school classrooms and hostels have been built by mobilizing villagers' voluntary labour and support. By imparting health education and by developing healthy practices (clean house, water, clothes, environment and personal hygiene), the health status of villagers has been significantly improved. "In the last 20 years, two or three doctors have abandoned their practice due to lack of patients." Without any government funding and through community participation, a piped water system was developed for household water consumption. A grain bank operates to help those who are in need of grain. The villagers have also contributed to cultural development by instilling a sense of discipline, celebrating the village birthday and honouring achievers and newcomers, arranging low-cost community marriages, wiping out blind-faith practices and

(Box 4.10 Contd.)

(Box 4.10 Contd.)

almost eliminating many undesired habits (alcohol, tobacco etc.). While Indian governments' schemes contributed, no foreign aid was used. Once a donor's cheque was even returned. All initiated community development activities have been continued, governed and managed by community people themselves, though the success of this village development has been attributed to the committed leadership of Mr Anna Hazare, who has successfully contributed to the realization of human rights, self-reliance, self-determination and participation of villagers for their own and the community's development.

Source: Hazare (2003); the author's observations and interview.

Box 4.11:
Barefoot college's innovative contributions towards sustainable community development

Barefoot College is an NGO founded in 1972 at Tilonia in Rajasthan state of India, by Mr Bunker Roy who, though an outsider, has devoted his life to building the organization and developing innovative capacity-building approaches for sustainable community development. By developing local-level leaders from disadvantaged sections, the college addresses problems of drinking water, girl education, health and sanitation, rural unemployment, income generation, electricity and power as well as social awareness and the conservation of ecological systems in rural communities. The college and its participants have together developed 10 codes of conduct that emphasize having a base in rural communities, non-discrimination, gender equality, democratic political processes, non-partisan political agendas, willingness and ability to learn, law-abiding and social justice, collective traditional knowledge and wisdom, preservation of natural resources, appropriate technology that sustains community and practising what is preached.

(Box 4.11 Contd.)

(Box 4.11 Contd.)

By drawing on local knowledge and skills and engaging the most disadvantaged people, it has built an 80,000 sq. ft. Barefoot college. This runs night schools, has enhanced access to drinking water, has introduced measures to harvest rain water, has trained solar engineers who fabricate and produce solar lanterns and install solar home lighting systems, has improved the health of people through health centres, has introduced wasteland development practices that are implemented and managed by villagers themselves, has built homes for the homeless by employing indigenous architects, has created opportunities for locally based employment and income generation, has effectively employed traditional media methods (puppetry) to raise awareness across a range of issues, has contributed to a right to information movement and has formed participatory women's groups.

The Barefoot College's night school is a basic foundation for all the other programmes. Democratically elected and participatory-based Village Education Committees and Children's Parliament collaborate to run night schools in a self-reliant manner.

The College takes men, women and children who are illiterate and semi-literate from the lowest castes, and from the most remote and inaccessible villages in India, and trains them at their own pace to become 'barefoot' water and solar engineers, architects, teachers, communicators, pathologists, midwives, IT workers, accountants and marketing managers. Once trained, these villagers work within their own communities, thus making them less dependent on 'outside' skills. (Milnes, 2007)

The college's solar energy programme is implemented by developing a CBO known as Energy and Environment Committee, which is responsible for deciding monthly payments, trainees, collecting payments, maintenance and monitoring solar engineers work.

(Box 4.11 Contd.)

(Box 4.11 Contd.)

> Village Energy and Environment Committees have successfully managed the project for the last five years, and the villagers have made monthly contributions towards repair and maintenance totalling $32,372 during this period. This has been paid voluntarily by people who routinely earn less then $1 a day. (The Ashden Awards for Sustainable Energy, 2003)
>
> Many of the college's programmes have been sustained over a long period, and some programmes are being replicated both nationally (14 states in India) and internationally (Afghanistan, Ethiopia, Bhutan, Senegal and Sierra Leone). The college has received funding contributions from communities, GOs and international agencies. To Mr Roy, the real achievement is not the result, but the process—"the fact that the communities have done this on their own, by sharing their own knowledge and skills."
>
> *Source:* Barefoot College (2009); Roy (1997).

Both of the case studies presented in Boxes 4.10 and 4.11 have inspired people to practise sustainable community development. Although their context, leaders and background are different, they have focused on local people, local knowledge and local skills. Particularly they have included the most disadvantaged people, practised non-discrimination and promoted gender equality. By developing the use of people's capacities, they have formed participatory CBOs and engaged them in several community development programmes. They also have emphasized natural resource management issues. Both success stories are leadership driven, though people have contributed significantly to the success. However, Hazare was an insider to the village who fully emphasized self-reliance and refused to receive external funding, whereas Roy was an outsider who mobilized external funding support for some programmes, though people's contribution was maintained. Both have worked with and accessed government resources by both collaborative and adversary approaches. Both also have taken a long time to achieve sustainable change. Those who (particularly donors) expect quick results in a reasonable period may become impatient and wonder whether one needs to wait for such a long period to see sustainable community development. However, these cases suggest that sustainable community development is a long-term process and calls for consistent commitment and patience. In both cases, there appears to be some ideological similarity in terms of the influence of Gandhian ideas.

Although many community development projects/programmes begin with good intentions, they do not result in the end as presented above. Why are many community development projects not sustainable? What are the dynamics that make them unsustainable? There are several seemingly common reasons, such as the following. They compromise on the values/principles of community development. Community development is sometimes project, programme and donor oriented rather than people oriented. The process may be heavily top-down in the approach. Moreover, communities may have got used to the culture of funding dependency. Community development initiators and implementers' commitment may leave much to be desired. Ego issues in collaboration and cooperation among CBOs/POs, NGOs and local institutions may complicate operational dynamics. Partisan politics, unnecessary politicization and vested interests may subvert the process of community development. Colonization and globalization factors may also adversely contribute to community development dynamics. Despite such likely dynamics, the above cases demonstrate that sustainable community development is a practical goal and well worth pursuing.

Conclusion

The main aim of this chapter was to examine briefly various practice dynamics of community development. Depending on how one looks at community development, its dynamics can be many and varied. However, for the purpose of the present analysis, four areas of dynamics were identified: the application of values/principles, entry into the community, awareness raising and capacity building and sustainable community development. They seem to follow a more or less similar sequence in practice, though with some overlap. Each area of dynamics has been briefly discussed in conceptual terms along with some important practical aspects and issues surrounding them. To make a point or substantiate the discussion, brief case inserts from different parts of the region would have been good. However, many of the cases presented are from India. There may be many good examples from across the region, but they could not be presented here because of the author's limitation of not having direct access to them. The discussion on these dynamics may not be comprehensive. It is expected that readers may relate to the issues raised differently, or raise other issues, as everyone's community development experience and understanding varies depending on the context of practice. Despite these limitations, I trust that the chapter has captured the essence of community development practice dynamics and the analysis is useful for practitioners to engage in social and community development work with more vigour.

Section II

Education for Social Policy and International SCD

To bring about much-needed local-level development by using the social development approach presented in Chapters 1 and 2 and to facilitate community development practice according to the values, principles and processes discussed in Chapters 3 and 4, we believe that workers' knowledge, capacity and skill need to be developed in two important areas, namely, social policy and international social and community development or international social work. This second section of the book, consisting of two chapters, focuses on these two areas. The first chapter, that is, Chapter 5, looks at providing a social policy education for social and community development workers, and the second chapter, Chapter 6, discusses international social and community development education for social workers. In some ways, the two chapters are closely connected. Understanding social polices is highly relevant for social development practice, and garnering international social and community support for local-level social development is crucial.

To what extent and how social policy education is provided to social and community development students and how that knowledge is integrated into the social work theory and practice component are not clear and will differ from one social work school to another. Recognizing this issue, the first chapter of this section discusses the significance of studying social policy for social and community development workers. The purpose is not just the study of social policy but also exploring how social workers can contribute to the policy-making process. The chapter shows how the content of social policy curricula can be analyzed in terms of objectives, subject content and teaching and assessment methods. More important, it identifies a range of factors that are likely to influence the development of the social policy curriculum, and an awareness of such factors is important to the development of a high-quality social policy curricula. Towards that end, the chapter suggests a model for developing a balanced curriculum in accordance with the social work school's context.

The second chapter in this section focuses on international social and community development education for social workers. To engage in local-level development, both local and international actions are needed. The way that social, economic, political and technological developments are occurring in India and the Asian region suggests that international activities will significantly increase, with India and China playing important roles, not only in trade and commerce but also in international social and community development. Already both countries are active in the Asian and African regions, and many commentators are calling this century the Asian century. In view of such developments and social workers' interest in international social work, the chapter develops some ideas as to training and preparation of social workers for international social and community development. In particular, it discusses the meaning of international social work, provides a framework and guidelines for developing curricula for training social workers for international social work and points out some opportunities and challenges for social workers to engage in international social and community development with passion, commitment and vision. We hope both social and community development students and educators will find this section useful.

5

Social Policy Education for SCD Workers

Introduction

The focus of this chapter, as the title suggests, is to discuss the need for social policy education and knowledge for social and community development workers and how best that can be developed and imparted so that they can effectively contribute to social and community development practice that we have discussed in the previous chapters in Section I. It may be clarified that social and community development workers also include professionally trained social workers, and I would like many of them to significantly engage in social development practice preferably in local-level communities.

I have been teaching social policy–related subjects for more than three decades now. In the early 1990s, I taught several subjects in the field of criminal justice, which constitutes an important segment within the social policy arena. My reflections on crime and development or a lack of development and correctional policies naturally drew me towards social policies that focus on overall social development, not just remedial and reactive. I realized the close connection between social policies and social and community development work and was attracted more towards it. For nearly two decades I have been teaching social policy subjects to social work students in Australia. Initially the social policy subject I taught was known as *Social Policy and Social Theory*. One of my interesting tasks was to rewrite this subject as many students were not appreciative of its curriculum content, particularly theory part of it. Recognizing this important feedback, I was curious to know what was taught in social policy subjects for social work students and what resources were used to teach social policy subjects. To quell my curiosity, I conducted a national survey of social policy subject outlines and analyzed the curriculum content. Drawing on such an analysis, I developed the *Social Work and Social Policy* subject in two parts and offered it to social work students. Later, again I revised the subject to make it more relevant to social work and social development practice. The revised subject is renamed as *Social Work and Social Policy Practice* to bring in practice perspectives in social policy. In this chapter, I share relevant part of my social policy teaching experience for the wider benefit of social and community development students, workers and educators in India and in the Asian region generally.

The first part of this chapter looks at the significance of social policy education and knowledge for social and community development workers. In other words, I address a simple question: Why should social and community development workers study social policy? Second, it looks at the content and teaching methods of social policy subjects; third, it identifies a number of factors that affect the development of social policy curricula; and finally, it suggests a model for developing the social policy curriculum for training social and community development workers.

Significance of Social Policy Education for Social and Community Development Workers

What Is Social Policy?

Social policy as a field of study is of recent origin, and it has not yet emerged as an independent discipline. Essentially, social policy is an interdisciplinary subject, as its content is drawn from various social sciences. Social policy deals with day-to-day, practical, complex, contested, personal and political issues, and it directly or indirectly affects everyone. Social policy is about enhancing the well-being or quality of life rather than welfare alone (Dean, 2012; Fawcett et al., 2010). Thus, social policy is close to the heart of social and community development practice. According to the proponent of social policy discipline, Richard Titmuss (1974), social policy is seen to be beneficent, redistributive and concerned with economic as well as noneconomic objectives. Like many of the other definitions, social policy (as with economic policy) is all about 'what is and what might be.' It is thus involved in making 'choices in the ordering of social change' (p. 30). The Department of Social Policy, London School of Economics (2012) states:

> Social policy is an interdisciplinary and applied subject concerned with the analysis of societies' responses to social need. Social policy is focused on those aspects of the economy, society and polity that are necessary to human existence and the means by which they can be provided. These basic human needs include: food and shelter, a sustainable and safe environment, the promotion of health and treatment of the sick, the care and support of those unable to live a fully independent life, and the education and training of individuals to a level that enables them fully to participate in their society.

Due to paucity of space other social definitions have not been discussed here. As you start reading about social policy you will come across a number of definitions with different perspectives. Social policy in the field is in a constant state of flux, but it is important to understand the nature of social policy from both theoretical and practical points of view.

The meaning and the purpose of social policy imply so much significance of it for social and community development practice. Its significance has been further elaborated by looking at the constitutional provisions, spending on social policies, magnitude of social problems, the linkage of the dimensions of social development to social policies, how it constitutes part of social work theory and practice (this includes all methods of social work) and the potential roles social and community development workers can play in the implementation of social policies and thereby contribute to policy change and refinement.

Constitutional Provisions

Social and community development workers can gain legitimacy for their practice from the relevant constitutional provisions. For example, in the Indian Constitution, the directive principles of state policy, Article 38, 'State to secure a social order for the promotion of welfare of the people', states as follows:

> The State shall strive to promote the welfare of the people by securing and protecting as effectively as it may a social order in which justice, social, economic and political, shall inform the institutions of the national life. The State shall, in particular, strive to minimise the inequalities in income, and endeavour to eliminate inequalities in status, facilities and opportunities, not only amongst individuals but also amongst groups of people residing in different areas or engaged in different vocations.

Further Articles such as 39, 41 and 45 focus on adequate means of livelihood, distribution of community resources, prevention of the concentration of wealth, right to work, education, public assistance, rights of children and compulsory and free education for children. Without developing good social policies and without effective implementation such constitutional provisions cannot be realized. To uphold such constitutional and similar provisions social and community workers can play crucial roles.

Spending on Social Policies

Social policies tend to give an impression that or there appears to be a perception that they are not economic policies or that they have little to do with economic policies. In fact, all social policies are economic policies. They are very important because significant proportion of national income is allocated to social policies. Since it is a significant proportion of the government budget, it needs to be taken seriously. For example, in India nearly 20 per cent of the central government expenditure and about 25 per cent of the central and state government expenditure was allocated to social services and rural development in 2012–2013. The Union Budget and Economic Survey (Government of India [GOI], 2013, pp. 271–272) shows that as a proportion of total expenditure, Central government expenditure on social services and rural development (plan and non-plan) has increased from 14.77 per cent in 2007–2008 to 17.39 per cent in 2012–2013 (Budget Estimates [BE]). Expenditure on social services by the general government (centre and states combined) has increased from 22.4 per cent in

2007–2008 to 24.7 per cent in 2010–2011 and further to 25.1 per cent in 2012–2013 (BE). On health alone, in 2010, India spent 4.1 per cent of gross domestic product, though more may be needed (for details visit: http://indiabudget.nic.in/es2012-13/echap-13.pdf).

Magnitude of Social Problems

The magnitude of social problems in India and Asia generally is such that a clear focus on social policies is needed. South Asia is the major concentration of poverty in the world. In India alone there are more than 440 million people below the poverty line. Although India is achieving a good growth rate (5–9 per cent) and poverty is declining, concomitant growing inequality is a major challenge. The situation of women, children, elderly, socially and economically disadvantaged populations, indigenous groups and other vulnerable populations need sound social policies. A large number of people are displaced due to development projects or disasters. Demographic trends in South Asia, in terms of the high proportion of youth, pose both challenge and great opportunity. Communal harmony and social integration is also very much needed. Rural and urban disparities are extreme. On the whole, India's overall Human Development Index in 2011 was low (0.547) as it ranks 134 out of 187 countries in the world.

The Link between the Dimensions of Social Development and Social Policies

Social policies are significant to social and community development workers because the social development strategies, levels and dimensions (see Box 1.4 and Figure 2.1) in which they work are closely linked to social policies. The formulation of social policies at international, national, regional, state, district, taluka and gram panchayat levels and their application for the cultural, political, economic, ecological, health, education, housing, vulnerable groups' and citizens' and their institutions' development are directly relevant for social and community development practitioners.

Integral Part of Social Work Theory and Practice

Social policy subjects constitute a significant part of social work training. In fact, teaching of social policy is one of the requirements for course accreditation bodies, where they exist and implement accreditation standards (e.g. in Australia and the USA). Both Social Work Education Review Committees 1 (pp. 77 and 89) and 2 (p. 95) (University Grants Commission, 1965, 1980) and the National Consultation on National Network of Schools of Social Work for quality enhancement of social work education in India (Nadkarni and Desai, 2012) present social policy as a core component of social work courses. Several social work educators have also emphasized the need for the increasing involvement of social workers in social policy practice (see Figueira-McDonough, 1993; Gal and Weiss-Gal, 2013; Ife, 1997a, 1997b; Popple and Leighninger, 2001; Weiss et al., 2002).

Contribution to Implementation and Innovation of Social Policies

Social and community workers are significantly involved in implementing social policies in various ways in the field. The effective implementation of social policies calls for understanding social policies in terms of who gets what provisions, who pays for it and how they are operated (see Gilbert and Terrell, 2012) and how some deserving people end up not getting provisions. Such an understanding also helps raise awareness of policies and provisions in local communities and helps eligible people to gain the benefit of policies that are meant for them. As social and community development workers work at the coalface, they know what the problems are, what works and what does not work. They know what are the needs, gaps and shortcomings in the operation of social policies and what can be done to rectify them. In these days of economic rationalism, efficiency and effectiveness, we cannot afford to waste this valuable practice wisdom. It should flow into the policy-making process. As such, social policies do not begin and end at the parliament. The range of social policy is wide and includes individuals, families, groups, communities, organizations and social, political and economic institutions at local to higher levels. Social policies keep flowing and evolving through this range. Developing and implementing needs-based social policies are challenging and satisfying tasks. Social and community development workers' social policy wisdom is rooted in day-to-day life and practice, and the very nature of their profession and practice places them in a better position to participate in social policy development, implementation and evaluation processes. Their profession's value premise and their commitment to social development goals, social justice, selfless service and anti-discriminatory practice put them in a preeminent position to participate in social policy processes by contributing to policy change and refinement. Such a bottom-up process can lead to innovations in social policy creation and implementation. The above points clearly make a convincing case for social and community workers to gain knowledge of social policy and practise it in communities.

The Content and Teaching Methods of Social Policy Subjects

What is taught in social policy and how the subject is taught seem to significantly differ from one course to another or one social work department to another. The title of the subject is also named differently. For example, it is titled as social welfare administration, social administration, social work and social welfare and administration of social services. An experienced social policy educator states that there are many ways of introducing students to the subject, beginning, for example, with services, with clients, with theories, with dominant themes, with history and with politics. Every approach has its own advantages and disadvantages (Spicker, 1995). According to Ife (1997b), the way social policy is defined within social work courses and the way it is taught could be one of the reasons for the relative ineffectiveness of social workers in the social policy arena. Ife aptly observes the separate treatment given to social policy and social work theory and practice subjects (these are social work methods subjects) in social work courses and argues in favour of integrating the two subjects. Such an involvement may be facilitated by examining and improving social policy curricula.

Although Specht and Courtney (1994) point out that most schools of social work do not provide their students with either sufficient knowledge or professional tools to undertake policy practice, the increasing relevance and significance, as discussed above, of social policy inputs for social workers is axiomatic through recent social policy publications by social work educators (e.g. see Bryson, 1992; Dalton et al., 1996; Ife, 1997b; Pathak, 2012; Rees, 1991; Weeks, 1994; Weeks and Wilson, 1995; Wilson et al., 1996). A few of these publications have been used as textbooks by many schools of social work in the Australian context. Although these developments are heartening, a review of the literature indicated that there is hardly any research done on the social policy curriculum for social work training. Earlier research that looked at various subject titles, including social policy (Cox et al., 1997c; Pawar, 2000b), tried to ascertain social development content in the social work curriculum. One limitation of this study was that it did not look into the details of subject outlines. It is important to examine the existing social policy curriculum and critically review it to develop the revised curriculum. For such purpose, I pose the following questions (see Box 5.1) as guide for their review.

Box 5.1:
Questions for the review of social policy curriculum

- What are the objectives of social policy subjects?
- What is taught in social policy subjects?
- What are the topics covered in social policy subjects?
- What are the common themes in the social policy curriculum?
- Is the curriculum well balanced in terms of theory and practice?
- Is the curriculum regularly revised?
- Whether or not the curriculum relates well to the current issues and needs?
- Does it include or allow for the inclusion of new policies and programmes introduced by governments?
- Whether or not the curriculum is well integrated with social work theory and practice core curriculum?
- What are the reading material/textbooks used?
- What are the teaching methods used?
- What are the assessment methods used?

To analyze the social policy curriculum, in light of the above questions, as I did not have ready access to social policy curricula, particularly social policy subject outlines, developed and followed in social work schools in India and Asia, as an example I will discuss in what follows the analysis of social policy subject outlines used in schools of social work in Australia. Social and community development workers and educators may find it useful to undertake similar analysis according to their learning and teaching needs and requirements. Of the 22 social work schools in Australia I approached to share their social policy subject outlines, 15 schools (68 per cent) responded to the request and mailed their subject outlines. Six schools sent two subject outlines and the remaining sent one subject outline for a total of 21 outlines. Content analysis was carried out in five areas: objectives, topics covered in social policy subjects, reading material, teaching methods and assessment methods. It may be noted that due to multiple responses and selective analysis of subject outlines, the total number of subject outlines varies from variable to variable and table to table.

Social Policy Subjects' Objectives

It is important to develop clear objectives for each social policy subject/curriculum. Just listing topics to be covered is not enough. Clear objectives of the curriculum will help both social and community development learners and teachers to focus on the subject and know what to expect and what outcomes to deliver. Although it is difficult to recommend the optimum number of objectives for the social policy curriculum, objectives should comprehensively cover what the subject aims to address and achieve in the entire semester/year. Needless to say, the objectives should be clear, simple and precise. The number of objectives stated in the subject outlines surveyed ranged from 2 to 8 (see Table 5.1). On the whole, 91 objectives were analyzed to ascertain common themes and areas for social

Table 5.1:
Number of objectives stated in the outlines

No. of objectives	2	3	4	5	6	7	8
Subject outlines frequency	1	3	4	2	3	4	1

Table 5.2:
Social policy subjects' objectives

Objectives	Subject outlines frequency
To acquire a conceptual understanding of social policy	5
To understand the historical development of social policy	5
To discuss politics, political system, state and government	9
To understand the theoretical discourse/social theory	9
To study social values and goals	7
To explore factors influencing social policy processes	8
To develop policy analysis skills	8
To understand the implementation of social policy	1
To discuss evaluation of the impact of the policy	3
To discuss specific issue areas, issues and debates	9
To study the impact of globalization	2
To explore the link between social policy and economic policy	5
To study the link between social policy and social work practice	4
To analyze comparative policy	2
To follow the social change process	1

policy study. The analysis showed 15 different areas, though some may appear overlapping (see Table 5.2). In other words, collectively there were 15 different objectives for the social policy subject.

About half of the objectives aimed to discuss social theories, values and goals; politics, political system, state and government; factors influencing social policy process; policy analysis skills; and specific issue areas such as health, disability, aborigines, children, housing and so on. Five subject outlines' objective was to develop conceptual understanding and historical development of social policy and the connection between social policy and economic policy. Only four outlines had a specific objective of linking social policy with social work practice. A couple of subject outlines had an objective of covering implementation of social policy, impact of globalization, comparative social policy and social change process. Why do the objectives vary to such a great degree from one outline to another? A broad scope of the subject and unlimited topics to be covered in it; limited time, especially in an undergraduate programme; and the coverage of some social policy topics in other social work subjects may influence the choice of objectives. Equally important factors may be social policy educators' perception of students' learning needs and goals and judgement of how best students would develop a grasp of social policy.

Topics and Lectures Covered in Social Policy Subjects

The topics covered in social policy subjects flow from the objectives. Although some common themes emerged from the analysis, each subject outline differed in terms of the sequence and coverage of topics. These were grouped under a number of broad categories (see Table 5.3). Most of the social policy subjects had an introductory topic that delved into conceptual understanding of social policy (e.g. nature, definitions and importance of social policy, social policy and social work and setting the policy context). Fourteen subject outlines included topics on social theories that are important bases for social policy. These theories were drawn from political ideology and economy, philosophy and feminism. However, each subject outline

Table 5.3:
Topics and lectures covered in social policy subjects

Topics/lectures	Frequency in subject outlines
Introductory/conceptual	15
Historical contexts and social policies	7
Theoretical	14
Current reforms (privatization, managerialism, etc.)	5
Comparative policy	3
Economics	7
Issue based topics	12
Policy analysis	8
Policy-making process	13
Policy implementation	4
Policy evaluation	2
Policy practice	4
Local NGOs' work and discussion	1
Conclusion/review	10

differed in choice or preference of these theories and the proportion of their coverage in the subject. It is important to give some thought to how much attention should be devoted to social theories in social policy subjects. How many hours can be devoted to this topic? A judicious decision on these questions is desirable, as these are very broad interdisciplinary topics and can be the matter of a full subject.

Policy-making process as a specific area of study was included in 13 subject outlines. It is important for social and community development workers to understand how the policies are formulated and what is the policy-making process so that they can identify appropriate policy process entry points in which they can participate according to their level of position and influence. Generally, policy-making process topics included basic concepts and models of policy making; role of state institutions, government and bureaucracy; significant players/participants in policy making; and location of social workers in these processes.

It is common to include some issue-based topics such as health, disability, housing, women and children, poverty, unemployment and so on in social policy subjects. Undoubtedly, these are important social policy concerns and they do deserve some place in social policy subjects. Although about half of the social policy subject outlines did not include such issue-based topics, including aboriginal policy and poverty, the remaining 12 subject outlines included a range of topics (see Table 5.4). In addition, the following issues appeared with single frequency: social class, new labour/Thatcherism, privatization and corporatization, personal services, charity, HIV/AIDS, urban and regional planning, transport policy and criminal justice policies. On the whole, 26 issues were discussed in social policy subjects.

Table 5.4:
Issue-based topics included in social policy subjects

Issues	Frequency
Aboriginal policy	8
Poverty	7
Social security system/safety net, work and unemployment, health, housing	5
Race and racism, multiculturalism, gender/feminism, Education	3
The aged/elderly, Child welfare, Disability, Families and communities, Redistributing—wealth/taxation	2

About half of the outlines covered social policy analysis topics in which several policy analysis frameworks were discussed. Seven subject outlines included historical development of welfare state and social policies. Some particularly referred to the Harvester Judgement of 1907, the 1945 White Paper, 1983 Accord, 1994 Working Nation Document and Work for the Dole schemes. Topics relating to economics such as economic schools and theories, economic systems, basic economic concepts and welfare economics were found in seven subject outlines. Current reform topics such as privatization, globalization, reform of the public sector, changing role of the non-government welfare sector and new managerialism were part of five outlines. The remaining topics (comparative policy, policy implementation, evaluation and practice and local NGOs' work), though important, appeared in the outlines with less frequency (four or less than four; see Table 5.3). The analysis further showed that in the last lecture, social policy subjects were concluded in different ways in 10 outlines. Some reviewed what has been covered in the whole semester, others raised futuristic questions and the remaining outlines did not specifically include concluding topics. Since social policy draws from the past, addresses the present and looks at the future, it is interesting to raise a question: how can one conclude social policy subjects?

Reading Material for Studying Social Policy Subjects

The analysis of social policy subject outlines showed that students were directed to reading material through five methods. These are presented in Table 5.5. Recommended reading lists were provided in all the subject outlines. A lecture/topicwise reading list was provided in 13 subject outlines. In nine outlines a general reference list was included at the end. General reference lists included books, articles, journals and Internet addresses. The general reading list ranged from 24 to 306 references, and the number of recommended journals ranged from 3 to 20. Most of the subjects did not have a required reading list and Internet addresses for further reading.

Table 5.5 shows that only nine subject outlines prescribed textbooks to study social policy. The number of textbooks ranged from one to six. Altogether 18 different textbooks were used to teach social

Table 5.5:
Reading resources indicated in the subject outlines

Textbooks		Recommended reading list		Required reading list		Lecture/ topic-wise reading list		Internet addresses		General reference list	
Yes	No	Yes	No	Yes	No	Yes	No	Yes	No	Yes	No
9	6	15	0	4	11	13	2	2	13	9	6

policy subjects, though some were more popular than others. Those textbooks are not listed here as they may not be relevant in the Indian and Asian context.

Teaching Methods

Table 5.6 shows the range of teaching methods employed by social work educators to teach the social policy subject. Lectures, tutorials, presentations by students, workshops/seminars and guest lectures were more frequently stated teaching methods. Research on learning has well demonstrated that student-centred teaching methods such as simulation games, issues-based or solution-focused (SF) learning, case study, free group discussion, field trips, seminars/ workshops and workbook are more effective than teacher-centred teaching methods (lectures, teacher controlled tutorials etc.; see Burns, 2002; Jacobsen et al., 1999; Kauchak and Eggen, 1998). Generally, the lecturing method represents passive one-way communication and helps to provide a lot of information in a short span of time, but it has been often found to be ineffective as it leads to

Table 5.6:
Use of teaching methods as indicated in the outlines

Teaching methods	Lecture and tutorial	Only lecture	Presen- tations	Simula- tion games	Site visits	Issue based/ SF	Work- shop seminar	Guest lectures	Case study	Work book
Subject outlines' frequency	11	5	8	2	1	1	8	7	1	2

boredom, forgetting and so on. Thus, teaching methods that facilitate participation of students in the learning process need to be employed. These methods require careful planning, direction and moderation, and involvement of students in the learning process. Otherwise, they may take more time and become less effective. Although students' effective learning is important, practical considerations such as size of the class, content of the lecture topic, availability of resources (time, teaching aids, tutors etc.) influence the choice of teaching methods. Due to such considerations, teacher-centred teaching methods are more commonly used. However, it is encouraging that, though small in number, some social policy subjects had combined both student-centred and teacher-centred teaching methods. For further research, a few questions may be raised. What are the methods that are more effective in enhancing students' learning? Why are student-centred methods not commonly employed by many social work educators? What can be done to promote the use of effective social policy-teaching methods?

Assessment Methods

Table 5.7 shows a varied combination of five assessment methods employed in social policy subjects. The number of assignments ranged from one to three. In nine subject outlines, only one assignment was given; in eight outlines, two assignments were given; and in one, three assignments were given. The weighting for the assignment ranged from 30 to 100 per cent. In four subjects, it was 100 per cent, and in the remaining there was no discernible trend.

Table 5.7:
Assessment methods employed in social policy subjects

Assessment methods	Only assignments	Assignments and examination	Tutorial presentation in the class	Take home examination	Participation in tutorial/ seminar/debate
Subject outlines' frequency	11	5	9	4	9

Assignments enable students to develop an analytic approach to a problem/need, collect relevant data/information, build an argument in response to the analysis, plan a logical structure and write their reflection and evaluations, reach argued conclusions and test them against wider reality (Burns, 2002). In addition, assessment feedback further enhances student learning. As assignments motivate and involve students in the assignment topic and encourage independent thinking and analysis, they contribute to students' effective learning. Its limitation is that although students thoroughly learn about the assignment topic, some students may not intensively read other topics of the subject.

The weighting for the closed examination ranged between 40 and 60 per cent. In the three subject outlines, it was 40 per cent, and in the remaining it was 50 and 60 per cent, respectively. Four subject outlines had the provision of take-home examination with a weighting of 30, 40 and 50 per cent, respectively. Written examinations motivate students to read and understand most of the topics of the subject and get ready to write answers to questions. However, the written examination approach may often result in rote learning and forgetting, as many students prepare under pressure. To some it appears as a test of memory rather than learning. Thus, it is hardly surprising that many students ask for more weighting for assignments and much less for closed examinations, and some of them would prefer not to have a written examination at all. Although written examinations continue to be used, Burns (2002) suggests that many professional courses are now steering away from them.

Four subject outlines indicated 20 per cent weighting for tutorial presentation, one indicated just 5 per cent and the remaining had no weighting. Of the nine, three subject outlines had given the weighting of 20 per cent for participation in tutorial/seminar/debate. Although it is difficult to assess, tutorial presentations and discussion by students lead to in-depth learning and develop skills of searching, thinking, summarizing and understanding. It is assumed that assigning weighting for these methods would further motivate students and thereby enhance their effective learning.

The data show that as an assessment method, assignments are more popular both in terms of frequency and higher percentage of weighting. However, it appears that varied assessment methods with different proportions of weighting are geared towards encouraging reading, participation and understanding, ultimately to enhance the effectiveness of learning both by students and educators. Social and community development educators need to further research and address the following questions so that some consistency and standards can be attained in the teaching of social policy subjects to social work students.

- What are the appropriate assessment methods for teaching social policy subject?
- What should be the proportion of weighting for different assessment methods?
- What is the rationale or what are the guidelines for addressing the above two questions?

A Model for Developing the Social Policy Curriculum

The above analysis of social policy subject outlines demonstrates that some common themes emerge in the curricula, but the coverage of objectives, topics and their content, depth, breadth and emphasis vary greatly. To address this variation in social policy curricula, the reflective method was employed to identify factors that influence the development of social policy curriculum and to suggest a flexible framework for developing social policy curriculum. The reflective method involved raising critical questions, introspecting teaching experience and observation and obtaining feedback from a few social work educators. Three questions raised for reflection are as follows:

1. What are the probable factors that influence the development of social policy subject?
2. Why does the coverage of topics significantly differ from one subject outline to another?
3. Is it possible to develop a flexible framework for teaching social policy subject to social and community development students?

These questions have been addressed below.

Factors That Influence the Development of Social Policy Subject

Based on the author's teaching experience, observation and reflection, some factors that influence the development of social policy subjects have been identified for further research and analysis. The following factors, from 1 to 8, are classified as common factors. Factors 9 to 17 are classified as positive factors and the remaining as limiting factors. The list is not an exhaustive one; many more factors may be identified and included.

Common Factors

1. Background and interest of the educator
2. One's own ideology, thinking and imagination
3. Tradition of the school/department
4. Objectives of the whole course
5. Inclusion of certain topics in other subjects of the same course
6. Interdisciplinary nature of the subject
7. Broad and many topics
8. Revision of the curriculum

Positive Factors

9. Application of social work profession's mission and objectives
10. Awareness of a clear objective and purpose of the subject
11. Students' learning need and feedback
12. Consultation with interest groups/peer advice
13. Incorporation of local and regional issues that are close to learners' life experiences
14. Periodic and systematic revision of the curriculum
15. Connecting social policy with social work practice

16. Integrating social policy with social work theory and practice subject
17. The use of appropriate teaching and assessment methods

Limiting Factors

18. Blind 'adoption' of subjects developed by other educators
19. Limits of one's own perception and imagination
20. Development of the subject under certain pressures (time, urgency)
21. Learning by trial and error
22. Non-consultation with peers
23. Practical considerations such as number of hours available for the subject
24. Irregular and unsystematic revision of the curriculum
25. Lack of any guideline or yardstick to develop a subject
26. Non-availability of textbooks and resource materials
27. Treating and teaching the social policy subject separate from social work subjects
28. The use of inappropriate and ineffective teaching and assessment methods.

The analysis of the influence of these factors would help to answer the second question: Why does the coverage of topics significantly differ from one subject outline to another?

Reasons for the Variation in the Coverage of Topics

It is assumed that the variation of coverage of topics in social policy subjects depends on the way in which and the extent to which the above-identified common, positive and limiting factors influence the curriculum. The common factors have potential to influence both in a positive and limiting way, depending on each subject's context. Certainly, the educators' background, interest, ideological preference and the departmental context would influence the choice of topics in the social policy curriculum. The nature and scope of the subject itself is very broad and a lot of choice is available in formulating the curriculum. If there are no specific accreditation standards for the subject or broad curriculum guidelines, the coverage of topics in the social policy subject may significantly vary. Further discussion on the second question will be clear when we consider the third question: is it possible to develop a flexible framework for teaching social policy subject to social and community development students?

A Model for Developing the Social Policy Curriculum

Based on the understanding of the influence of the above factors, it is possible to suggest a flexible model for developing the social policy curriculum for training social and community development workers. The model is based on a proposition that an effective social policy curriculum develops when there are constructive elements in common factors, greater influence of positive factors and minimum influence of limiting factors. Conversely, a very weak or ineffective social policy curriculum develops when there are destructive elements in common factors, minimum contribution of positive factors and maximum influence of limiting factors. The variation of topics within the curriculum depends on how these factors operate.

The model is presented in Figure 5.1. The model shows the linkages between common, positive and limiting factors and how these collectively influence the comprehensiveness and effectiveness of the social policy subject curriculum. The common factors have the potential to influence both in a favourable and unfavourable way on the social policy curriculum. For example, an educator's suitable background, keen interest and high motivation in the subject and a good mix of ideologies and creative thinking may favourably influence the curriculum.

On the other hand, an educator's unsuitable background for the subject or less interest and motivation in the subject or strong belief in a particular ideology may unfavourably influence the curriculum. While developing the curriculum, it is difficult to be free from all the limiting factors and to concentrate on only positive factors, though that may be an ideal way. Thus, positive and limiting factors may be viewed as a continuum of factors. At the right end of the axis, positive factors predominate, and at the left end of the axis, limiting

Figure 5.1:
A model for the development of social policy subject

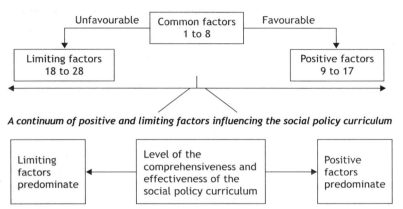

A continuum of positive and limiting factors influencing the social policy curriculum

factors predominate. The mid-point on the axis separates positive and limiting factors, though in reality these factors cannot be separated as they operate in a continuum. A square consisting of both limiting and positive factors positioned, as an example, below the mid-point, rudimentarily suggests that the curriculum is influenced by an equal number of limiting and positive factors. Depending on the extent of the influence of positive and limiting factors on the curriculum, the square changes the position towards the right or left direction of the axis, roughly suggesting the quality of the curriculum. In other words, if a majority of positive factors influence the curriculum, the square moves towards the right, suggesting that the curriculum is relatively free from limiting factors. On the other hand, if a majority of negative factors influence the curriculum, the square moves towards the left, suggesting a weak and ineffective curriculum. Thus, the overall comprehensiveness and effectiveness of the curriculum depend on the influence of the relative mix of positive and limiting factors.

Social policy educators can employ this model by following three steps or exercises to develop relatively effective and comprehensive social policy curricula for training social and community development workers. First, they need to identify favourable or constructive elements in common factors and build the curriculum on those elements. As stated earlier, the common factors have the potential to influence curriculum both in a positive and a limiting way.

For example, social work educators' interest, ideology, imagination and awareness of the course need to be positively cultivated in such a way that these help to develop sound social policy curricula. Otherwise, these factors may operate as limiting factors. Equally important are clear objectives of the course and subject.

Second, social policy educators need to enhance the influence of positive factors on the development of the subject. I have suggested nine positive factors in the model. For example, social policy educators while periodically revising the subject can attend to the positive factors and particularly address students' learning needs and evaluation feedback. New textbooks and reading material and relevant issues need to be included to make the subject contextually relevant, effective and interesting to learners. The curriculum should be planned and developed in such a way that it lends itself to learner-centred teaching and assessment methods as such methods enhance the effectiveness of students' learning.

Third, it is very important to minimize the influence of limiting factors on the curriculum. Although the control of some of the limiting factors may not be in the hands of curriculum designers, it is important to be aware of them and consciously stop their influence. For example, blind adoption of a curriculum developed by someone else should be avoided. It is important to introspect to see whether one's own narrow perceptions, thinking and imagination are affecting the development of the subject. If so, it is necessary to broaden the horizon by getting acquainted with contemporary developments and students' learning needs in the subject. Time pressures, urgency and inadequate resources can greatly affect the development of the subject. These limiting factors may be overcome by organizing/committing adequate time, prioritizing academic tasks, mobilizing available resources (marking assistance, subject/teaching development funds etc.). Well-informed consultations may help overcome the dependence on a trial-and-error approach. Instead of treating the social policy subject separate from social work subjects, one can consciously integrate it with social work theory and practice subjects. Inappropriate and ineffective teaching and assessment methods need to be avoided by employing learner-centred teaching and assessment methods that actively involve learners in the learning process and enhance the effectiveness of their learning.

It may be noted that no social policy subject can be found perfect in its content, depth, breadth and sequence. Several factors influence its making, and the influence occurs in a continuum of limiting factors to positive factors. Ongoing efforts are needed to preserve the most of the continuum in positive factors so that a better social policy curriculum can be developed for training social and community development workers.

Conclusion and Future Directions for Social Policy Education

As was aimed, this chapter has briefly discussed the meaning of social policy and the significance of social policy education for social and community development workers and educators. As an example, it has presented an analysis of social policy curricula, and, based on that analysis and reflection, suggested a model for developing the social policy curriculum. As noted earlier, the example is drawn from the Australian context and that may be a limitation of the chapter, but the purpose was to show a way of researching and analyzing social policy curricula.

Social policy education for social and community development workers is essential, as the very nature of their work demands such professional input and preparation. The analysis of social policy curricula revealed that the subjects had a wide range of objectives and, to accomplish those objectives, the content of the subjects covered several relevant topics and employed a variety of reading material and a combination of different teaching and assessment methods. Common themes did emerge and so did differences and variations. This analysis and reflection resulted in the identification of several factors that influence the development of social policy curriculum and the development of a flexible model for developing the social policy curriculum for training social and community development workers.

For future work in the Indian context, it is important to mention two relevant developments at the time of writing this chapter. These are social work educators' thoughts and concerns as reported by the *National Consultation on National Network of Schools of Social*

Work for Quality Enhancement of Social Work Education in India (Nadkarni and Desai, 2012) and the deepening academic reforms as envisaged in the *Twelfth Five Year Plan, 2012–2017, Social Sectors, Volume III* (Planning Commission, GOI, 2013, p. 108). The Network clearly indicates social welfare administration as one of the core subjects in social work training, and it has deliberated to standardize the curriculum in such a way that it is uniform and at the same time allows for the incorporation of the local context. The Network is also planning to persuade the UGC to appoint the third review committee to review social work education in India. The Twelfth Five Year Plan (Planning Commission, GOI, 2013, p. 108) includes

> regular revision of curricula for making them up-to-date and relevant to contemporary and future needs. To help institutions reform their courses, subject-specific model curricula and packaged, re-usable digitised content (such as packaged lectures and open source textbooks) would be created by instructors with the requisite expertise. This can best be done by subject-based networks such as Network of Social Work Education led by the Tata Institute of Social Sciences.

These are promising developments and offer great opportunities for reviewing social policy curricula. To come up to the expectations of the Twelfth Five Year Plan, both the Network and the social work departments in universities need to assume more active and proactive roles. Often in many universities the curriculum is planned and approved by the Social Work Board of Studies consisting of members from a few universities (this nomenclature may differ from one university to another) and, once it is approved, individual lecturers have little choice in modifying it, though they are aware that changes are needed. This bureaucratic hurdle may be one of the reasons for following the social policy curriculum constructed when the social work courses began first. Instead of ritualistically meeting, Social Work Board of Studies or similar bodies in universities need to take more proactive roles and undertake periodic curriculum revisions. Towards this end, future research may look at the application of this model and its further refinement. It is important to undertake thorough research and review of social policy curricula before developing the new curricula and revising the existing one. In addition, an exploration of professional background and ideologies of social policy subject educators may offer further insights. Many new staff members are often advised to develop subjects and reading material in case of distance education. Without clear direction and information, some staff members may find it difficult to complete such tasks or complete them to meet the minimum requirements. However, we need to underscore that the development of any subject and its content are crucial for both learning and teaching. It is important to offer broad guidelines for developing the social policy curriculum. 'Social work and social policy practice' may be a better title for the subject rather than 'social welfare administration', which appears outdated now. Several steps can be undertaken in this regard: preparing resource materials both in digitized and hardcopy format, including new policies and programmes of both central and respective state governments to keep the currency of the subject and keeping the policy practice focus in the subject so that students are actively engaged in policy issues rather than being passive learners. The Indian democratic structure, a range of policies (Kailash, 2013; Kannan and Breman, 2013; Pawar, 2012; Srivastava, 2004) developed at central and state levels and the scope for implementing them at various levels, particularly at the grassroots level, provide a fertile ground for social and community development practitioners to actively engage in agenda setting, policy formulation/modification, implementation and evaluation, a seamless cycle of the policy process. To meaningfully engage in that policy process, the analysis undertaken and the model developed in this chapter are intended to aid social and community development practitioners and educators, who are interested in developing new subjects or revising the existing ones, and it is hoped that the chapter serves that purpose.

6

International SCD Curricula for Training Social Workers

Introduction

In this chapter, I use the terms 'international social and community development' and 'international social work' interchangeably. When I began studying social work, I did not know that there was a subject called international social or community development or social work, though I used to see a journal titled *International Social Work*. I was attracted to the term 'international social work' without knowing much about it; however, I was properly introduced to this subject only when I was appointed a lecturer in international social work at the Regional Social Development Centre, Department of Social Work and Social Policy, La Trobe University, Melbourne, Australia. At that time, Professor David Cox was the director of the centre and one of the leading scholars in international social work. Although I had not enrolled as a formal student in the Master of International Social Work course, I voluntarily attended most of Professor Cox's lectures on international social work. Since then, I have been teaching the international social work and development subject for nearly two decades. International social development is a very vast and constantly growing and changing field. I often felt that no amount of reading was enough; regular updating was always needed. I also had the opportunity to conduct a few international projects in the Asia-Pacific region. As the president of the Asia-Pacific branch of the International Consortium for Social Development, in collaboration with my international colleagues and organizations, I have organized several international conferences. I also had a rare opportunity to co-author with Professor Cox a textbook entitled *International Social Work: Issues, Strategies and Programs*, which was first published in 2006 by SAGE Publications and its second edition has appeared in 2013. For the South Asian region, this book was reprinted by SAGE Publications, New Delhi. It has been used as a text to teach social work and social and community development students in many countries. International social and community development, as an academic subject and as field of practice, is becoming more popular both in developed and developing countries, and many books have now been published in this field (e.g. Healy, 2008; Healy and Link, 2012; Hugman, 2010; Lyons, 1999; Lyons et al., 2006, 2012) and many social workers are engaging in international social and community development practice.

Is there a need for international social work (ISW) education in Asia? To this simple question, responses of social work educators and practitioners may differ, some perceiving the need and others not so, depending on their own country contexts and perceptions. Although ISW education and teaching it as a full subject or a single unit within another subject is not new in many Western developed countries (Johnson, 1996), such may not be the case in many Asian countries. This does not mean that there is no need for and/or interest in ISW education in Asia. A well-meaning colleague of mine once mentioned to me that he was very much interested in teaching ISW in his school/department, but he did not know how to develop the ISW curriculum and teach it. In their review of *International Social Work: Issues, Strategies and Programs* (Cox and Pawar, 2006), Alphonse and Adsule (2007), social work educators from India, stated that the book "is a welcome effort for many young professionals who seek scholarship as well as commitment in addressing the most burning problems affecting society in different countries today" (p. 36). Such remarks and anecdotal evidence suggest that there is a significant need for and interest in teaching and practising ISW in India and Asia.

My reflections on these experiences and current developments in India and globally suggest that this subject is relevant to social work and social and community development students in India and Asia generally, for several reasons. Many Indian professionals, including social workers, have contributed to international social work and development in varied ways, but that was probably due to their own interest and motivation and opportunities they encountered to work in the international arena. With systematic and purposeful training and preparation, India can contribute more to this field. As India is perceived as an emerging economy, and this century has been declared an Asian century, China and India have been playing dynamic roles in world affairs while international expectations of them have increased. Moreover, India is gradually reducing the receipt of international aid and assuming the role of a donor (Andreas and Vadlamannati, 2012; Banerjiv, 2012; Chanana, 2010; Ramachandran, 2010). For example, DFID has decided to cease foreign aid to India in 2015 (Banerjiv, 2012), and India has plans to offer US$11 billion as international aid in coming years (Andreas and Vadlamannati, 2012). It has pledged nearly US$2 billion in Afghanistan for various capacity- and institution-building purposes. Ayyar (2010, pp. 45–46) has categorized Indian overseas development cooperation into three parts. First, project assistance to neighbouring countries (e.g. Bhutan, Nepal, Afghanistan etc.); second, technical assistance to 156 countries in Asia, East Europe, Central Asia, Africa and Latin America under the Colombo Plan, Indian Technical and Economic Cooperation [ITEC] and Special Commonwealth Assistance for Africa Programme (SCAAP); and third, extending Letters of Credit (LOCs) to developing countries through Export-Import [EXIM] Bank for financing imports of Indian equipment, technology, projects, goods and services on deferred credit terms. More than 70 per cent of ODA is delivered as project assistance. The Government of India's Ministry of Foreign Affairs is planning to set up an international development agency.

In addition to such developments in India, globalization and its ideological underpinnings, such as liberalization, privatization and free market, managerialism and its outcomes such as increasing trade and commerce, and the likely weakening of state borders (Deacon, 2007; Ferguson, 2008; Yuen & Ho, 2007), have made the world an interdependent village. It is very difficult for any country to escape from this globalization process, despite the fact that it is often leading to distorted development (Midgley, 1995, pp. 2–7) in many countries. Several improvements notwithstanding, disparities between the rich and the poor, and women and men, low-level development or neglect of local and grassroots-level villages and communities, particularly of indigenous populations, are glaring. Most important, some of the social problems such as poverty, low human development index, climate change and its consequences, natural disasters and displacement, intra- and inter-country labour migration, refugees, human trafficking and health issues such as HIV/AIDS are global in nature and internationally connected. Like globalization of commerce and trade, there is the potential to develop globalized social protection systems, ensuring food security and minimum standards to everyone across nations (Deacon, 1997, 2007). Similarly, there is also the potential to achieve comprehensive social development at the local level (see Chapter 2). Negative consequences of globalization (Alphonse et al., 2008; Artner, 2004; Deacon, 2007; Lyons et al., 2006; Shari, 2000) call for such a global and regional response. In addition, my own living experience in Asia and observations suggest that the region has the knowledge and ability to teach and practice international social and community development. The region also has a number of innovative and successful social experiments that need to be disseminated and replicated where applicable in other countries for the general good of those societies. These factors underscore the relevance of ISW in the region and lend themselves to ISW education and practice in Asian countries and beyond.

Given the contemporary social, economic, political and technological developments in India and Asia, and 21st-century Asian growth projections, particularly of China and India (Hicks et al., 2010; Moni, 2008), it appears that India needs to better prepare to contribute to international social and community development. Such a need may also be increasingly felt in many Asian countries. To address this need and meet the demand, proper training and skill development is a first step. Many social work schools and educators may already be contemplating teaching international social or community development. Responding to such developments, some social work schools have begun offering an international social work subject in their courses (e.g. Tata Institute of Social Sciences and Indira Gandhi National Open University in India).

Keeping these developments and personnel needs in mind, this chapter discusses how international social and community development may be taught in the globalizing Asian context. Towards this end, it clarifies the concept of international social work, presents a broad curriculum framework and a general guideline for curricula and critically discusses some opportunities and challenges for teaching and practising international social and community development in the region. Drawing on this analysis the chapter argues that the region offers a fertile ground for practising international social and community development, but such practice needs to be squarely focused on least developed countries and least developed pockets within the relatively developed countries in the region.

The Concept of International Social Work (ISW)

The concepts of social development, local level and community development have been already discussed in Chapters 1 and 2 and those concepts are relevant to this chapter. Here we are discussing the concept of international social work because social and community development subjects are often offered as part of social work programmes, and many professionals use the term 'international social work' as a subject as well as a field of practice. Thus, it is important to understand the meaning of international social work.

The concept of international social work is well debated in the social work literature (Ahmadi, 2003; Cox and Pawar, 2006, 2013; Healy, 2001; Hokenstad et al., 1992; Hugman, 2010; Johnson, 1996; Lyons, 1999; Lyons et al., 2006; Moni, 2008; Payne & Askeland, 2008), though there may not be a clear consensus on what it should constitute. In recent ISW textbooks (Cox and Pawar, 2013; Healy, 2001; Hugman, 2010), ISW has been defined as follows. Healy (2001, p. 7) defined international social work as "international professional practice and the capacity for international action by the social work profession and its members. International action has four dimensions: (1) internationally related domestic practice and advocacy, (2) professional exchange, (3) international practice and (4) international policy development and advocacy." Healy's definition emphasizes professional practice in the international context and the social work profession's and social workers' capacity for international action in the four areas. The four areas or dimensions appear somewhat restrictive as they are limited to four specific areas. One of the very interesting aspects of Healy's definition is that to practice international social work one need not go to another country, as some aspects of international social work practice such as international labour migrants, human trafficking, refugee resettlement and international adoption can be undertaken domestically. Cox and Pawar (2013, p. 29) further comment:

> One aspect of international social work that we find missing from Healy's definition is the goal of the profession to see itself established around the world. The current reality is that social work is virtually nonexistent in all of the poorest countries of the world (the UN's least developed countries, or LDCs, of which there are some 49) and is in an embryonic stage in many other developing countries. It is not professional ambition that leads to our desire to see a strong social work profession in all countries. Rather, it is our vision of the roles that social work can play, and should be playing, in the least or lesser developed countries, and our concern as we discuss international social work is that it does not represent a form of neoimperialism, with the Western branches of the profession spearheading its emergence as a truly international profession.

Drawing on Healy's and other definitions, and our own understanding of international social work, Hugman (2010, pp. 18–20) identifies five elements in the concept of international social work: (1) practice in a country outside its own, (2) working with service users who have crossed borders, (3) working with international organizations, (4) exchanges or collaboration between countries and (5) the impact of the global market economy on people's well-being.

Cox and Pawar's (2013) definition slightly differs from the above two. To them,

> international social work is the promotion of social work education and practice globally and locally, with the purpose of building a truly integrated international profession that reflects social work's capacity to respond appropriately and effectively, in education and practice terms, to the various global challenges that are having a significant impact on the well-being of large sections of the world's population. (p. 29)

The three definitions are complementary. Cox and Pawar's ISW concept focuses on social work education and practice both at global and local levels so as to build the social work profession and its capacity internationally in such a way that it is able to address both global and local challenges concerning the well-being of the whole population. By critically examining these and similar definitions, one may question the applicability of these concepts in the Asian context, as they appear to have been defined in the Western contexts reflecting Western concerns. Thus, there may be scope for developing the Asian concept of ISW and there is a great potential to do so. For example, an African trainee mentioned that when she attended a training programme in the UK she was told what to do to develop her country. When she attended a similar training programme in South Korea, trainers shared about how they developed South Korea. Obviously, there is a great difference between telling someone what to do and sharing about how they themselves developed. Thus, India and Asia can develop a distinct approach to international social and community development and social work. For the present purpose, it appears that ISW is about action, about building capacity of the social work profession and social workers by initiating and strengthening social work education and practice so as to attend to both global and local issues and local-level or village-level social development.

Understanding ISW in Asia from this perspective is important because the social work profession, education and practice present a diverse, unbalanced, inconsistent and mixed picture in the region. By and large, in many countries in the region the social work profession appears to be weak and not well established and mostly urban based and biased, as it mainly focuses on urban areas and issues, often with a remedial perspective (Cox et al., 1997a; Pawar, 1999b; Pawar and Tsui, 2012). However, in some countries, for example, China and India, social work schools are growing (Kwok, 2008; Xiong and Wang, 2007) without consistent standards. In many countries of the region, particularly in land-locked and least developed countries, access to quality social work education and practice is minimal. Despite years of development efforts and some improvements, at the local-level villages and grassroots-level communities have remained relatively underdeveloped in many areas such as education, health, housing, economy, infrastructure and political awareness, or in terms of the Millennium Development Goals (UNGA, 2010). Thus, the concept of ISW in Asia must include the capacity building of the social work profession, social work education and social work practice within a diverse context resulting inter alia in a stronger focus on comprehensive local-level social development (see Chapter 2).

A Framework for Teaching International Social Work/ Social and Community Development

ISW education and practice may become lopsided, biased and misdirected if it does not follow a broad comprehensive framework or an approach that adapts to the diverse contexts of the region.

Each regional context or country may develop its own framework to teach and practise ISW, but it must adhere to basic social work values and principles as enunciated in the IASSW/IFSW code of ethics or must be guided by certain norms and values that dovetail with basic social work values. In their text, Cox and Pawar (2013, pp. 35–66) have developed an integrated perspectives approach (see Figure 6.1) for ISW education and practice, and this approach provides a broad

Figure 6.1:
An integrated perspectives approach for international social work education and practice

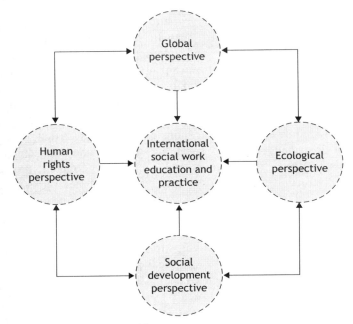

Source: Cox and Pawar (2013, p. 36).

framework for teaching and practising ISW in the region. It consists of a global perspective, an ecological perspective, a human rights perspective and a social development perspective. The teaching and practice of international social work becomes more meaningful when these four perspectives are integrated in a comprehensive manner, as each perspective is closely connected to the other three and together they are mutually reinforcing. Cox and Pawar contend that any of the perspectives alone would constitute an insufficient guide to international social work education and practice. In essence,

- the global perspective represents the overall context,
- the human rights perspective the value base,
- the ecological perspective the essential link between humanity and nature, and
- the social development perspective the overall guide to action or sense of direction underpinning action (p. 37).

These perspectives and the overall framework are broad and flexible enough to adopt in any context and adapt to local situations. The global perspective aims to capture social, economic and political contexts at all levels, and it may be delineated and discussed in terms of unity, diversity and interdependence and localization, globalization and world citizenship. The human rights perspective essentially provides values and rights as a base for practice, and needless to say, these human rights are very close to core social work values. The human rights perspective and rights-based practice need to include all three generations of human rights: first, civil and political; second, economic, social and cultural; and third, collective (rights to peace, development and a clean environment protected from destruction). Although the universality of human rights may be controversial (see Pawar, 2010; Uvin, 2004) in the Asian context, it is generally agreed that they are a real guide for living and behaviour. Like the global perspective, the ecological perspective is a unifying one, but with a difference. It helps to weld humankind with nature both from a spiritual and a practical point of view. Particularly, in the context of unbridled consumerism and climate change and their consequences, it is difficult to practise social work without the ecological perspective. Most important, this perspective helps to emphasize sustainability. The social development perspective helps to focus on the comprehensive development of all individuals, families, communities and society at large and at all levels (local, regional, national and international), with participatory and people-centred values and intervention strategies (for details see Chapters 1 and 2). The integrated perspective approach, consisting of global, human rights, ecological and social development perspectives, provides a sound framework for ISW education and practice in Asia.

The ISW Curriculum Guidelines

Developing the ISW curriculum is a complex and challenging task, and it may not be appropriate to suggest overly specific curriculum content to the social work schools and educators as countries' contexts and interests are so diverse in the region. Thus, the ISW curriculum should be locally developed and contextualized. The curriculum content suggested here should not be taken as given but should be viewed only as a broad guideline to stimulate further thinking on the ISW curriculum development. With this qualification, an attempt has been made to develop broad guidelines to help those who are new to the subject.

ISW curricula should consist of two components. These are knowledge and skills or practice, with the necessary orientation to values in each of them. Under the knowledge component, it may include the concepts of ISW and its critical understanding. At the outset, it is important to clarify what ISW is. Then a brief history of ISW globally and in the Asian context would be in order. It may be possible that some countries in the region may not have any engagement in ISW, and, in such a case, it is good to draw on the region and neighbouring countries. The next topic could be the introduction to professional social work organizations at global and regional levels, their main activities and how they are engaged in ISW. The main organizations/associations are International Association of Schools of Social Work (IASSW), International Federation of Social Workers (IFSW), International Consortium for Social Development (ICSD) and International Council on Social Welfare (ICSW) and regional bodies such as the Asia Pacific Association of Social Work Education (APASWE) and ICSD, Asia-Pacific branch. Generally, information about these organizations is available on their respective websites and it is a good source for teaching. In addition to these professional organizations, other organizations such as the UN and associated agencies such as the Economic and Social Commission for Asia and the Pacific (ESCAP) and United Nations Development Programme (UNDP), regional bodies such as the South Asian Association of Regional Cooperation (SAARC) and the Association of South East Asian Countries (ASEAN) (though these bodies do not cover all Asian countries) and international non-government organizations (INGOs), for example, the Red Cross, Doctors Without Borders and so on, may be introduced as relevant. This background information does provide the necessary orientation for moving into the global and Asian context of ISW that needs to be developed and discussed around the integrated perspectives framework. Relevant topics for inclusion could include the following:

- Contemporary political economies of the region;
- Major issues such as poverty, unemployment, human trafficking, child labour, overall neglect of the local-level development, ecological degradation and sustainability, conflict and building peace, inter- and intra-country labour migration, refugees and displacement of people confronting the region and how these issues are connected at the global and local levels;
- Critical discussion on development, underdevelopment and the least development trajectory of a range of countries in the region;
- Comparative analysis of developed, developing and least developed countries and lessons that can be learned from the five Asian tigers (Hong Kong, Japan, South Korea, Singapore and Taiwan) and the fast-developing economies of China and India; and
- Analysis of successful development projects in the region and how such projects can be replicated in the most disadvantaged areas.

The skill or practice component may include how one needs to orient to the targeted country for ISW practice (see Cox and Pawar, 2013, Chapter 15); cross-cultural communication problems and skills; language; basic strategies for ISW, particularly for the local-level development; safety and self-care issues; avenues and organizations for ISW; facilitating student and staff exchanges; initiating social work training programmes with an emphasis on indigenous content; building professional bodies and connecting them to international organizations; and campaigning and advocacy at local, national and international levels. In addition, a key requirement is to develop skills to use information technology across a range of practice areas.

Opportunities for ISW Education and Practice

The chapter is based on the assumption that there is a sufficient interest in and the opportunities for ISW education and practice in India and Asia, but the degree of interest may differ from one country to another and from school to school within a country. The development of the five Asian tigers and the fast-growing economies of China and India suggest that opportunities for ISW within Asia will grow significantly. For example, like Japan, now South Korea is also looking to initiate new projects in developing countries in Asia.[1] This trend is likely to grow with the growth of economies and globalization processes.

Regarding the concept of ISW, the Asian region needs to focus on building capacity for professional practice in terms of social work education, practice and professional development. The quality, quantity and orientation (in terms of Western influence and remedial and developmental focus) of social work education, practice and professional development significantly vary from country to country and school to school. For example, in some countries of the region, such as Hong Kong, South Korea, Japan and Singapore, social work schools and the profession are relatively well established. In some other countries, for example, India, although some schools are well established, professional development in terms of having a national-level strong professional body seems to be lacking (see Chapter 7). In very big countries such as China and India, social work schools are proliferating both at undergraduate and postgraduate levels, but it is not certain whether such massive expansion is commensurate with minimum expected standards in terms of infrastructure, education and practice. In some countries, such as Afghanistan, Bhutan, Cambodia, East Timor, Laos, Maldives, Nepal and Sri Lanka, professional social work education programmes have been either recently introduced or not offered in a full-fledged form. Within a country, many social work schools are well established, for example, India, Indonesia and the Philippines, but they are mostly urban centred and do not reach out to the most needy rural and remote areas; however, recently rural-based social work schools have emerged and social work distance education programmes have been attempted (see Chapter 8), although their standards remain an open question (see Alphonse et al., 2008; Noble, 2004). On the other hand, some well-established and elite social work schools have played a significant role in the capacity building of social work education by training social work professionals from various countries. For example, the Tata Institute of Social Sciences, Mumbai, India, regularly trains a small number of people from many south Asian countries and beyond.[2] Similarly, social work schools in Hong Kong have acted as a gateway for the spread of social work education in China and have provided social work qualifications to Chinese scholars (Chui et al., 2010, p. 60; Xiong and Wang, 2007, p. 567). A common influencing factor on many schools of social work is their colonial past that has an impact on the culture of social work schools in terms of textbooks, clinical practice and developmental orientation—what Midgley (1981) brands 'professional imperialism'.

This necessarily circumscribed overview of social work education in the Asian region suggests that there is tremendous scope for building capacity of social work education and profession, but such building needs to occur in a planned and purposeful manner rather than serendipitously. Schools and scholars interested in ISW in India and Asia, perhaps by developing a special interest group or an association or coalition of existing regional groups, which are already associated with international bodies such as IASSW, APASWE and IFSW, first need to prepare competent personnel for social work education and practice for all countries of the region and for the neediest areas within a country. These professional bodies need to be more active and effective. Second, by using such personnel, social work training programmes based on needs and issues so as to reach out to rural, remote and disadvantaged areas should be initiated. Third, professional bodies should help build necessary infrastructure in terms of library, classrooms, field agencies or practice areas. Fourth, as far as possible, efforts must be made to indigenize the curriculum content so that it addresses the local needs and issues (see Chapter 7) rather than implanting the content from the West (Beecher et al., 2010). This generally calls for expanding social work education and practice from an individual, curative and remedy-oriented perspective to a community and social development-oriented perspective (see Cox and Pawar, 2013; Pawar and Cox, 2010c; Yuen-Tsang and Wang, 2002, p. 379). Several systematic strategies have been suggested to indigenize social work education (see Chapter 7), but the limited space does not allow for a detailed discussion of them in this chapter. Fifth, as social work personnel are being trained, professional bodies should be established to facilitate quality and standards in social work courses rather than simply monitoring them (see Chapter 7). To individual scholars and schools, all this may seem like a tall order, but collectively and cooperatively, step by step and country by country, it is feasible. For ISW in India and Asia this is the most practical agenda, and opportunities for doing so are almost unlimited. Having developed the capacity of the profession through social work education, training and building strong professional bodies, such capacity needs to be appropriately and effectively used to address key issues that will enhance the well-being of the whole population. Such key issues and needs are many and varied depending on each country's context. However, a few of the most common issues are presented here as examples of opportunities for ISW in the region.

As indicated in the introduction, despite different degrees of (economic) development efforts in the range of countries in the region, one of the most common issues confronting the majority of Asian countries is the almost total neglect or low-level development of villages or grassroots-level communities. The Asian region provides a fertile ground for practising local-level social development, which calls for villages' and communities' comprehensive development, through addressing major dimensions of the community such as culture, politics, economy, ecology, education, health, housing, equity groups and citizens and their institutions (see Chapters 1 and 2). ISW in India and Asia needs to squarely focus on local-level social development along with the suggested framework, as the current development efforts have bypassed thousands of local communities, and unless concerted efforts are made they are less likely to directly gain from the national and international development efforts.

The region is increasingly experiencing climate change-related issues such as natural or human-led disasters, displacement of people, weakening of ecological systems (drying of rivers and wet lands, reduced underground water, water shortage; see Pawar, 2013, 2014) and global warming affecting agriculture and food security. These issues are internationally connected, and ISW can significantly contribute to climate change mitigation and adaptation strategies at global, regional and local levels. In regards to natural disasters, ISW is already contributing through raising funds, sharing training materials and participating in relief, rehabilitation and settlement programmes, though a lot more needs to be done (Laksmono et al., 2008; Pawar, 2008; Rowlands and Tan, 2008; Tan et al., 2006). Climate change adaptation and mitigation is a very broad area that offers a wide range of opportunities for ISW in the region. Other important issues for ISW in the region are refugees, inter- and intra-country labour migrants (Hugo, 2005), human trafficking, child labour, adoption, ageing, and peace building in post-conflict situations, and social workers have significant experience and knowledge in such areas. The nature of these problems lends itself to ISW practice.

The region already has a number of successful social experiments or projects that are worthy of replicating, if relevant, in other parts of the region. For example, a number of street children projects in South Asia, the Grameen Bank's micro-credit work and Kamal Kar's community-led total sanitation in Bangladesh, Anna Hazare's comprehensive village/community development and Bunker Roy's Barefoot College in India, scavenger cooperatives in the Philippines, successful poverty alleviation projects in the region (Pawar, 2010; UNESCAP, 1996a, 1996b; also see Hokenstad and Midgley, 2004) and disaster management strategies are important to understand and carefully apply them in other parts of the region, and this is a fascinating and important task for ISW in India and Asia.

To effectively make use of the above-discussed and similar opportunities, international collaborative research projects, international collaboration among schools and NGOs, and student and staff exchanges or visits with clear outcomes would be in order. When social work educators and practitioners from the West and Asian region visit social work schools or agencies to undertake international social work activities, it is important to constructively and collaboratively engage with them to gain from their ISW projects.

Challenges for Teaching and Practising ISW

Although ISW is fascinating, challenging and rewarding, experience suggests that it is resource intensive. Resources in terms of time, money, material and trained personnel are needed more than usual. Mobilizing such resources in the Asian context is a real challenge. Along with resources, keeping sustained interest and commitment of those who are engaged in ISW is crucial. More often than not ISW activities are initiated on an ad hoc basis, depending on individual professionals and available resources at a given point of time.

Formulating ISW curricula and teaching the subject in social work courses may be somewhat challenging to many social work educators and schools in Asia as they may be new to it. Since ISW subjects are often driven by individual staff members' interest, if social work schools are not supportive of such initiatives, it may be challenging to find a place for the ISW subject in the often-crowded course structure. Even if there is space in the course structure, prevailing school dynamics, if any, may not facilitate the incorporation of the ISW subject in the course either as a compulsory subject or an elective. As part of the ISW teaching framework, introducing a human rights perspective in some countries may be challenging, if they do not support the universality of human rights. It is also important to make sure that there is a demand for the subject and that many students are keen to study it.

Although some aspects of ISW may be practised domestically, those who are interested in moving to another country for ISW practice may find it financially constraining to go overseas. This may be problematic for many Asian countries. Experience also indicates that international exchanges do not work in an egalitarian way, as social work educators and practitioners from developed countries are able to go to developing countries through exchange programmes, but such exchanges are really not working from developing to developed countries and more support needs to be provided for this (Moore and Pawar, 2007).

There may be a perception among some social work professionals and schools in Asia that ISW generally tends to mean social work professionals coming from the Western developed countries to help developing countries. If this preconceived notion exists, it may be challenging for some of them to visualize that they can engage in and contribute to ISW in their neighbouring countries. ISW need not be from West to East and it can occur within the East. So far, by and large, the ISW agenda appears to have originated from the West. In other words, what should occur in ISW is often determined by Western social work professionals. When Asian social work professionals engage in ISW teaching and practice, will they develop their own agenda for ISW in the region? As alluded to under the conceptual discussion of ISW, they should do so.

ISW cannot be taught and practised without cooperation and understanding from various quarters. Collaborative projects, exchanges and inter-country work call for tolerance, a lot of cross-cultural understanding and often embracing the unknown, despite necessary preparation. Gaining local reception and acceptance is crucial for ISW practice. Often these could be serious challenges (for similar other challenges see Midgley, 1992b; Pawar et al., 2004), if they are not forthcoming as envisaged.

The ultimate challenge for ISW in Asia is facilitating the local-level social development of the most neglected regions and most disadvantaged and marginalized groups. Asia is home to eight land-locked and least developed countries and a significant proportion of the world's poor, which means more than half of the world's extreme poor (641 million) live in Asia, and this number could be much higher if the impact of the recent inflation in food prices (ADB, 2008) is considered and if measured according to the Multi-dimensional Poverty index (OPHI, 2010). About half of the region's population (1.7 billion people) is poor, with their income pegged at less than US$2 per day. Extreme levels of poverty and the need for significant poverty reduction, particularly in South Asia, are major challenges for the region. If ISW does not address these core issues (Ahmadi, 2003; Kwok, 2008), it has little meaning.

The above-discussed and similar challenges may appear overwhelming, but they are not insurmountable. If we are conscious of such challenges, systematic strategies may be developed to deal with them.

Conclusion

Teaching and practising ISW in India and Asia appear promising. Towards this end, some thoughts presented in this chapter are modest. They are based on anecdotal evidence and, to a large extent, on the assumption that many schools, if not all, are convinced about the importance and relevance of ISW and are interested in teaching and practising it. The conspicuous features of these schools are their rich diversity, the survival issues they face on a day-to-day basis, their resilience and a sense of solidarity. As discussed in the chapter, contemporary developments in India and Asia and future projections make it one of the most interesting and promising regions, in terms of its peoples, industries, governments and NGOs and other institutions. The world is looking to Asia with purpose, imagination and hope. Thus, it is timely that the region prepares well for and ventures effectively into ISW. It may need to develop its own concept and agenda for ISW rather than adopting one directed by the West, and I believe it has the capacity to do this. Some of the ideas presented in this chapter, particularly the rationale for ISW in Asia, the concept of ISW, a framework for teaching and practising ISW, the curriculum guidelines and opportunities and challenges, may help to build India's and Asia's capacity for social and community development through ISW.

Notes

1. A Korean social work educator and dean of the school consulted with the author about their school's plans to initiate community development projects in developing countries.
2. Annual reports of the Tata Institute of Social Sciences include list of graduates, including those who are from overseas.

Section III

Developing the Social Work Profession for SCD Practice

The broad focus of the third section is the social work profession. In any profession, for example, law, engineering or medicine, professional bodies play important roles in ensuring that an adequate number of personnel are trained with the required minimum standards so as to develop appropriate competencies and skills and that they practise according to the code of ethics developed by the respective professional bodies. In any such endeavour, people's and communities' interest should prevail first rather than arrangements serving the interest of the profession itself. From this perspective, the third section has three chapters (Chapters 7, 8 and 9). First, Chapter 7 looks at some significant professional matters and suggests that the profession focus more than it does on social and community development practice; second, Chapter 8 makes a case for offering social and community development education through distance mode as an option; and third, Chapter 9 discusses the social work code of ethics and the place of virtue ethics in social and community development practice.

The important need and scope for social and community development practice, particularly at the local level, including through social policy practice and international efforts as discussed in Sections I and II, respectively, call for the social work profession to critically examine itself and reflect on the issues and challenges it is facing and what it can do to forcefully address those issues and meet those challenges. The growing number of social work schools in India without any quality control, the continuance of remedial and individual oriented social work education, the forces of globalization, the indigenization of social work education, the current status of professional bodies, the place of labour welfare specialization within social work and a range of related issues, all require critical examination and call for the development of new strategies and approaches. Many of the strategies discussed, such as developmental social work in terms of a social and community development focus, the indigenization of curricula and a strong national-level professional body, are not new.

However, what is required is the implementation of recommendations already made. The subject of Chapter 7 includes these and similar issues and strategies for the profession to consider and act upon.

Despite the growth of new schools with whatever qualities they possess, the growing number of issues and the scope for social and community development practice in thousands of villages suggest that a much larger number of well-trained social and community development workers are needed to meet the demand. Social work through distance education is one option that the social work profession needs to consider if it is to meet this demand. Already several social work distance education programmes are in operation, notwithstanding strong views against them by some social work educators. If the profession does not organize itself to monitor such developments, the existing problems will only be intensified. Thus, Chapter 8 develops some justifications for providing social and community development education through distance mode; analyzes some opportunities, threats and strengths and weaknesses pertaining to such an option; and suggests that current technological developments and the proposed Twelfth Five Year Plan are conducive to the preparation of subject material and its dissemination through distance mode. The appropriate developments of this strategy are up to the social work profession and individual social work educators and practitioners, but the potential of the strategy is significant.

The last chapter of the section, Chapter 9, recognizes the significance of a code of ethics in the social work profession. The chapter shows how different ethics theories can influence codes of ethics and what the limitations of such theories are and how they can impact practice. The analysis shows that most of the codes of ethics in social work are dominated by deontological and consequential approaches and that such domination needs to be balanced by incorporating virtue ethics and related frameworks and by developing certain qualities in social workers to promote virtue-led social and community development practice. The development of certain qualities in social and community development workers will help them to focus on practice with a clear vision and to take appropriate decisions when confronted with complex, difficult and unpredictable situations and, thereby, to improve practice. The ideas presented in the three chapters require that the social work profession establish itself on a stronger footing by recognizing the relevance and importance of these suggestions and acting upon them.

7

Adapting the Social Work Profession: Some Issues and Prospects

Introduction

I am a product of Indian social work education and training, which was mainly the American social work curriculum taught by social work educators who were mostly trained in the USA. Although for nearly two decades I have been a social work educator in Australia, my mind inevitably keeps fluctuating between the Indian and Australian contexts. I have studied and taught in India at the Tata Institute of Social Sciences (TISS) and interacted with students and staff members in many Indian social work schools. I keep raising some critical questions regarding which I often feel uncomfortable. What is social work? What is social work education? What is the social work profession? What is not social work? What kind of social work education, training and profession is needed to achieve social and community development, particularly at the local level? Does contemporary social work education and training help to achieve local-level social and community development? If yes, why cannot we see such development occurring in local communities? If not, what can be done to adapt social work to this reality?

The title of this chapter suggests that we need to change the nature and focus of social work profession to facilitate social and community development practice. Why is there such a need, and am I the only one to think in this way? My conversations with some social work educators and practitioners and my reading of the relevant literature suggest that there are many social work professionals who have views similar to my own. Just before the turn of the 21st century, I critically reflected on professional social work in India, and those thoughts were published in an article in the *Indian Journal of Social Work* (Pawar, 1999a). In this chapter, I aim to revisit those thoughts. By examining nearly 100 years of professional social work in India and by reflecting on my own experiences and observations, I discuss in this chapter some key issues that appear to have hindered the development of Indian social work profession, education and practice. Based on this analysis, the chapter argues for reorienting the social work profession towards addressing a social and community development agenda, and it suggests some strategies to deal with the key issues involved. It should be noted that the social work profession and the education and practice issues discussed and observations made in this chapter are only one aspect of the phenomenon, and other facets of the issues are not examined here. The purpose of the comments and observations is not to generalize or universalize the issues but to stimulate debate and discussion with a view to further developing the social work profession and its education and practice, so as to focus on social and community development practice.

Growth in the Number of Social Work Schools

The social work profession, education and practice (PEP) in India[1] is about 80 years young. The profession made a humble beginning in 1936 by establishing the first school of social work, namely, Sir Dorabji School of Social Work, later renamed the Tata Institute of Social Sciences (TISS). Then, in the 1940s, seven schools were established, in the 1950s 10 schools were established and in the 1960s 12 more schools were established. By 1978, there were 34 schools of social work (UGC, 1980). In the last three decades, the number of schools has increased by some ten-fold. Although an accurate figure of social work schools is not available, a recent report suggests that there are about 300 social work schools in India

(Nadkarni and Desai, 2012). These figures show that social work schools are proliferating and, if we assume that on average each school is graduating about 30 students per year, there may now be 9,000 new social work graduates every year (whether this is as yet an adequate number of social work personnel in relation to social and community development needs in India is a different question). The director of the TISS, Professor Parsuraman notes:

> There is a need to expand and establish more and more institutes of social work in India, especially at the rural level. This is required as there is a need to produce highly qualified social workers who can work in rural areas at the panchayat, taluka and block levels (these are local levels for community development). In addition, there is the need for professionally trained social workers to work in various development programmes. . . . (Nadkarni and Desai, 2012)

Recognizing this 'sudden spurt' in the establishment of schools of social work, periodically national-level social work education review committees were constituted.[2] Generally, these committees are appointed to examine the development of social work schools in terms of their overall status, educational content, fieldwork, required facilities and problems and to suggest measures to improve the quality of social work training and maintain standards. These committees have analyzed the social work education issues and suggested several recommendations and measures befitting the given period of time. These reports are an important source of social work education literature (see UGC, 1965, 1980). However, after the second review committee report of 1980, no formal committee has been constituted to review the current status of social work education in India, as of June 2013. The National Network of Schools of Social Work for Quality Enhancement of Social Work Education in India (NNSSWQESWEI), looking at the unbridled nature of social work schools, is urging the constituting of the UGC Third Review Committee on the Status of Social Work Education in the country. There is an opportunity for such a committee to change the social work profession to enable it to focus on social and community development practice, which is generally missing in most the current social work education in India due to the American social work influence or professional imperialism (Midgley, 1981).

Professional Imperialism

The first distraction that has occurred in developing Indian Social work profession, education and practice (PEP) is the transplantation of the American social work model to India (Bodhi, 2011; Desai, 1991; Mandal, 1989; Nagpaul, 1993; Pawar, 1999a; Singh et al., 2011). I would like to further argue that this is not merely an American transplantation in India. Social work education in India is essentially a victim of modernization. To grow, develop, prosper and modernize developing countries, including India, modernization sees these countries as needing to follow the Western path of development or whatever the Americans do. The waves of this modernization have swept the Indian social work PEP. Modern social work history in India clearly shows this. When Clifford Manshardt initiated the first social work programme, he did it with 10 years work experience in India and he attempted to adapt and develop Indian social work PEP, though a couple of social work educators from the USA assisted him (see Mandal, 1989). These adaptive efforts were overtaken by the modernization waves, when, one by one, almost all the TISS social work educators were trained in the USA and returned with enthusiasm to apply that knowledge and methods and specializations through the premier school of social work, TISS (see Desai, 1991). The early products of this institute were, undoubtedly, the products of the American social work model. They spread the model like a contagious disease wherever new schools of social work were established, as some of them became social work educators in such new schools. As the TISS was the premier social work school and leader in the profession, its social work model, essentially American, was replicated without any hesitation or remorse. In many social work schools there is, therefore, little evidence of efforts to support the development of Indian social work PEP.

Some social work educators, devoid of field realities, can do a lot of damage to the profession, for example, ignoring a reality of poverty next to the schools of social work and mechanically following the traditional/remedial social work curricula that were developed in the early 1950s. In fact, one professor who taught the course in the 1950s in India and then visited in the 1990s commented that he does not see any change in the curricula between the 1950s and now, though American social work education curricula has significantly changed from the 1950s to now. Although the professor's reaction cannot be treated as other than a generalization and may not be true of some schools, the reaction clearly reflects the need for revising curricula. The dated curricula do not dovetail with contemporary social, economic and political field realities and major issues. In addition, American textbooks dominate social work courses' reading lists, and many social work educators are often forced to heavily rely on them as there are very few local textbooks. Surprisingly, some follow American textbooks even in the teaching of Indian social problems (also see Nagpaul, 1993). Thus, I argue that most of the social work educators appear to have perpetuated the American model for many years now and that it is still going on, although there may be some exceptions.

A consequence of this perpetuation and orientation is the dominance of casework practice or remedial social work in Indian social work education. This dominance has helped the profession avoid addressing the major issues and needs of the country, such as poverty, unemployment and rural- and local-level development. The conditions of poverty, unemployment and rural underdevelopment call for multi-pronged and interdisciplinary approaches, and of course, political commitment. Social work alone is not a panacea for these massive problems. However, social work PEP does have a particular role to play in addressing these issues. Has it played its role? Is it addressing these issues now? Except for some very good isolated efforts, such as awareness raising through street plays, developing self-help groups and action research projects, social work PEP seems to have been diverted from addressing these conditions due to the dominance of American influence. As a student social worker, I distinctly remember that I did study Indian social problems, including poverty, unemployment, prostitution, housing and so on, but I cannot recollect relating these issues or their alleviation to the social work methods classes. I studied them like watertight compartments. This overemphasis on casework or the American remedial model has caged social work in India like a caged tiger. This orientation has certainly hampered the development of forms of Indian social work PEP that see the need to focus on social and community development.

Globalization

If the social work schools, their curricula and the profession do not adapt to the current changes and renew themselves, they will be further isolated and will become less relevant as the waves of liberalization and market economy roll on. The trend towards the predominance of individual liberty over state supremacy is emerging. The welfare state in the West is under attack and that which constitutes it will be reconstructed, and such developments are likely to influence India and similar developing countries. The power of control is moving into the hands of multinational companies. As a consequence, some small governments have the potential to become puppets while even strong governments will no longer remain strong. Indian history shows that it was through the East India Company that the country was colonized. Now current trends show that a handful of multinational companies have the potential to colonize the world. These developments have a lot of implications for equality, equity, human rights and social justice, which are very close to the heart of the social work profession. Although some of these issues are discussed in seminars, conferences and other such fora, these issues have not become part of regular social work training. As stated earlier, this neglect will further reduce the relevance of social work training, unless appropriate steps are taken.

Ideological Vacuum

Social work education and training is offered in an ideological vacuum. Neither an ideology of selflessness or Gandhian constructive work (see Gore, 1997), nor an ideology of Western liberalism, individualism, capitalism and democracy strictly operate in Indian social work training. The training is devoid of any ideology and is full of material issues such as profession, agency, methods, skills and employment (Drucker, 1993). This is another factor that has greatly influenced many social work schools, educators and practitioners.

By and large, social work schools have often failed to practise what they preach. Principles of equality, justice, democracy, freedom, participation and a nonjudgemental attitude are taught ritualistically.

Neither social work educators individually (there may be some exceptions) nor social work schools as an institution show any indication of demonstrating them, even in a small way, in their own environment. Double standards are often apparent. Some schools have really suffered due to the non-operation of democratic principles and the continuation of feudal tendencies. Professional differences and conflicts seldom result in democratic and productive conflict resolution. Individual myopic intentions of occupying a chair or a position override the professional and public interest. This has been a major stumbling block in the development of social work profession in this country.

It is indeed frustrating for social work students to see contrary practices emanating from the preachers of the principles. This demoralizes the social work climate and affects trainees and the profession as a whole. A number of students, who join the schools with strong motivation to take up a career in social work when they become graduates, enter practice undecided as to whether to continue with a career in social work.

I am not sure whether or not social work schools demotivate social work students, but the schools do often lack good social work models. Social work in many schools is often taught by reading and not by practising. Practice-based teaching is nearly absent in the schools. If this were there, the social work profession would not have remained as an island in a country that has been plunged in poverty for a long time. Thus, the lack of explicit appropriate ideology affects schools, students, teaching and learning, motivation, practice and the whole profession.

Unholy Alliance

The labour welfare and personnel management stream within the sphere of social work has been acknowledged as an Indian contribution to the social work profession (Desai, 1991; Gore, 1997). However, this labour welfare and personnel management specialization within social work was perhaps appropriate in the 1950s. My own observation suggests that offering this specialization within the social work programme, or offering this as a separate programme on the social work campus, has caused the greatest harm to social work profession. It creates an unhealthy competition and affects social work students' motivation. In my view, social work programmes having labour welfare specialization in fact produce two cadres of personnel who often work to serve opposing ideological interests. Labour welfare and personnel management graduates ultimately work for the exploiter (though originally they were meant to work for the labour), and they often identify with the management rather than labour. On the other hand, social work students work for the exploited. As stated earlier, although the specialization began with good intentions, today its contribution to the social work profession, by consuming its scarce resources and creating competition, is very much against the objectives of the profession. The continuation of this unholy alliance has already greatly hampered the profession and will continue to do so. This issue was also noted in the recent National Network report (Nadkarni and Desai, 2012).

Lack of an Active and Recognizable National-level Professional Body

A reasonably developed and active national-level professional social work body with a particular mandate does not exist in India. There are many professional social work associations, namely, The Indian Conference of Social Work, Association of Schools of Social Work in India (ASSWI), The Indian Society of Professional Social Work (ISPSW, earlier known as Indian Society of Psychiatric Social Work), National Association of Professional Social Workers in India (NAPSWI) and Indian Association of Trained Social Workers. These associations appear to claim national status. There are also some state- or regional-level associations: Bombay Association of Trained Social Workers (BATSW), Maharashtra Association of Social Work Educators (MATSWE), Karnataka Association of Professional Social Workers (KAPSW) and Professional Social Workers Forum, Chennai (PSWFC). The level of their activity differs from year to year. Desai (1994) stated that some of these bodies were defunct and Nagpaul's (1988) explanation brings out that due to their ageing leadership; lack of enthusiasm of professional individuals and groups; lack of identification and commitment by members to the profession of social work, especially by those who were employed in the business and industrial establishments; personality conflicts among the leadership;

and non-availability of adequate financial resources and low public image, the professional bodies are not functioning as well as they should be (see also Nanavatty, 1997a). In fact, there appears to be some confusion about which one is the national-level body that should represent the profession in India at the international level, such as at the International Federation of Social Workers (IFSW), or for that matter provide a professional identity for those trained social workers who become members. The theme—the Social Work Profession in India: Bridging Gaps and Building Bridges—of the first Indian Social Work Congress organized by the NAPSWI between 23 and 25 February 2013, testifies to this confusion and suggests that there are gaps and matters to be bridged.

Perhaps one way of attempting to bridge this gap was the creation of the National Network of Schools of Social Work for Quality Enhancement of Social Work Education in India in 2005. The network is organized into five zones—South, North, North-East, East and West—for regional meeting purposes and articulating issues from each region. The National Network of Schools of Social Work met between 2 and 3 May 2012, with the overall goal of the national consultation being to launch the National Network of Social Work Educational Institutions to Enhance the Quality of Social Work Education in India (Nadkarni and Desai, 2012). The National Council for Social Work Profession/Education Bill has also been pending for a long time. Whether it is the deliberations of the Network or the Congress, these are promising developments that suggest that some social work professionals in India are seriously concerned about the state of affairs of professional social work (see Nadkarni and Desai, 2012) and further strategic steps need to be taken without any further delay.

Simultaneous and parallel development of national-level bodies and the emergence of several local-level bodies seem to suggest that they are not addressing the needs of professional social work and social workers, communities and society at large. Silent frictions seem to be apparent. This state of affairs may be analyzed by looking at social work professionals' talents and their professional leadership. The social work profession in India does not have a dearth of talented, skilful and politically oriented people. In the past 80 years, some social work professionals have reached the highest positions in their career. For example, some have held the positions of Vice-Chancellors, Pro-Vice-Chancellors, Directors, Chairperson of the UGC and United Nations Consultants, and one social worker has become an internationally renowned and recognized environmental activist. All these positions call for a judicious mix of academic, administrative and political acumen, along with leadership qualities. From the profession, undoubtedly, some eminent leaders have emerged, though some of them may not identify with or attribute their work to the social work profession. Then, why is it that the profession has not produced a leader or some leaders who can develop and lead a national-level professional body. This state of affairs reflects, on the one hand, significant achievements in various individuals' personal careers, and, on the other, a minimal contribution to the development of the profession itself or a national professional body. Thus, one may argue that professional social work leaders in India are devoid of both the Indian ideology of selfless social work and the Western ideology of individualism with accountability to democratic institutions. Their only ideology appears to be self-interest, or 'selfishness', which is not good for the East, for India or for the West.

Least and Slow Action

Although the social work profession in India is bedevilled with a number of problems, its periodic reviews (UGC, 1965, 1980) and the national-level consultation in 2012 have made a number of useful recommendations to ensure the quality of social work education and to maintain standards. It may not be possible to implement at least some of these recommendations; however, unfortunately most of the recommendations remain unimplemented. For example, the second review committee states:

> The first Review Committee had also set up certain criteria (relating to minimum standards), but these were not enforced, and probably were even not known to the universities which affiliated the colleges of social work, or established their own teaching departments. (p. 3)

The same was mainly the fate of the second review committee's recommendations. If the recommendations remain unimplemented, for whatsoever reason, the reports and the whole exercise will be perceived as rituals. One can only hope that the third review committee, which has been pending for a long time, will represent a significant departure from this pattern.

Not only have useful recommendations not been implemented but also the changes that have been initiated have occurred at a snail's pace. This is what some social work students and educators experience and what I have observed. The snail's pace argument can be demonstrated to a great extent by a couple of examples. The Social Work Educators' Forum, a voluntary interest group formed within the TISS, began working on a code of ethics for professional social workers in 1991–1992, and the draft code of ethics was published in 1997 (TISS Social Work Educators' Forum, 1997). Although the document itself is well developed, it has taken a long time to deliver. Second, after dragging on the proposal to establish a Social Work Education Council for years, the Council bill was ready for submission in the parliament in 1993. Reportedly, the political climate was conducive at that time and one professional stated that the bill should be either submitted now or never. However, since some social work educators did not agree with some aspects of the bill, due to vested or other interests, the bill has been pending for many years now. Two decades have now elapsed, but the bill has not revisited the parliament. If significant professional activities like these are not completed within a reasonable time, the snail-pace will kill the enthusiasm and weaken the purpose and, in turn, hamper the growth and development of the profession.

Urban Concentration

Due to convenience, access and various other factors, not only are social work schools highly concentrated in urban centres but also in geographical terms they are unevenly spread (see Cox et al., 1997c; UGC, 1990). In the North and North-Eastern states, social work education and training is very scarce, though in the past decade new social work schools have been initiated in the North-Eastern region reflecting their own needs and issues. In our recent international survey of social work schools in the Asia-Pacific region, we found that, of the 100 respondent schools in the region, only four were located in rural areas. Of the 30 Indian respondent schools, only three were located in rural areas. Given that the very large rural population is the neediest in the country, it should be a matter of serious concern to any social work professional that social work education and training has restricted itself to urban centres, though recently some rural-based social work schools have emerged. For the promotion of local-level social and community development, more schools are needed in rural areas whereas schools located in urban areas need to extend their focus on rural areas.

Detached from the Field

Within social work profession, there is no systematic link between social work educators and practitioners, which is so crucial to effective social work practice. Similarly, social work educators and schools do not have necessary and adequate coordination with relevant government planning departments, activities and programmes, except that some schools' and social work educators' services are invited on an ad hoc basis for some specific tasks or programmes. There are massive poverty alleviation programmes such as Integrated Rural Development Programme, Integrated Tribal Development Projects, Integrated Chid Development Services, National Slum Development Programme, Jawahar Gram Samridhi Yojana, Swarn Jayanti Gram Swarozgar Yojana, Sampoorna Grameen Rozgar Yojana and so on. Do social work educators participate in such programme planning, implementing, monitoring and evaluation on an ongoing basis with the government, particularly at local community levels? We are all aware that social workers can represent the voices of the community at the policy and programme planning level. However, their lack of ongoing coordination as a social work profession with government activities has hindered the development of the profession and its contribution towards poverty alleviation and related issues.

Professional 'Crabs'

I have observed intergenerational gaps and conflicts among social work professionals, particularly among social work educators. Emerging young professionals are often suppressed by branding them as young men/women in hurry. This suppression process operates in a vicious circle that many undergo. However, it needs to be underscored that growing young professionals have the potential to achieve breakthroughs and excellence, though everyone will not. Their suppression by senior professionals has often hindered their development as well as that of social work profession.

Heads of School without a Social Work Education

Some senior social work educators have caused significant harm to the profession by facilitating the recruitment of non-social work graduates as heads of social work schools, when they were on the recruitment panel. Such deviation from the norm may be necessary in exceptional circumstances, but it needs to be time bound with a proper plan to eventually recruit professionals qualified in social work. There will be a cost to the profession until such blunders are rectified.

'Sale of the Profession'

In the recent past some new trends have emerged in social work profession. One such trend is opening new schools of social work, irrespective of whether they have adequate resources to offer such a programme. Second, some of these schools seem to admit students into the programme by accepting a donation or capitation fee. The motivation of such schools and students is undoubtedly in question. I think that such schools and graduates will cause significant damage to social work profession in the country. The National Level Network has pointed out this issue (Nadkarni and Desai, 2012), and I think immediate steps need to be taken to cease such practices.

Students' Recruitment

Most of the students join social work programmes without any work experience and have no clear perspective. Their confusion and unemployment pressures are understandable. The present student recruitment procedures are not uniform, are often ad hoc and do not identify right candidates for the profession. Desai (1994) found that students' previous extracurricular activities and leadership qualities were not related to high motivation and commitment to the profession. It appears that, if the opportunities existed, more than one-third of MSW students and about one-fourth of BSW students would prefer to change their profession. Unmotivated and weakly motivated students in social work programmes are not good for the profession. On the other hand, highly motivated students seem to possess diminished motivation by the end of their training programme, which appears to reflect on the quality of training and trainers as well as the way students are socialized into social work profession.

Social Work Degrees without Directions

Although most of the students after their graduation find their own place in their respective career paths, some students seem to lead unsettled professional lives. There is no follow-up or any other such system to provide satisfactory support or direction to such graduates, though a few schools may have placement centres. When the number of such graduates increases, their participation in professional activities and bodies will reduce and in turn affect the development of a sound professional body. This phenomenon operates as a vicious circle, on the whole affecting the whole profession.

Reorientation and Strategies for Social and Community Development Practice

There are real prospects for changing the social work profession to facilitate more social and community development practice. In the recent past, proponents of modernization and modernization theorists have examined their own positions in light of developments in Japan and a few East-Asian countries and have come to accept that, to develop and modernize, developing countries need not follow the Western path of development. They can utilize whatever is useful from the West, but they should follow their own path of development. They have further argued that traditionalism and modernization can go hand in hand, in that to become modern one need not give up traditionalism (So, 1990). That is why, perhaps, Gore (1988) has stated that American social work education, methods and knowledge are applicable in India, 'but with a difference'. Although Gore's (1988) work emphasizes the potential for poverty alleviation, he has not explained what this 'difference' is and left this to the reader's own interpretation.

The processes of the reconciliation of the modernization school and the criticisms of professional imperialism (see Midgley, 1981) are in a way interlinked. These processes have given rise to two connected directions to the social work PEP. The first direction is towards shifting social work PEP from individual or remedial social work to developmental social work, and the second direction is towards the indigenization of social work PEP in India. That is, social work education in India should address the major problems such as local-level social and community development, poverty, unemployment and the large group of marginalized and disadvantaged people. Most of the following discussion on reorientation and strategies flow from this standpoint, and some contemporary issues have been discussed above.

Emphasis on Social and Community Development Practice

As has been argued earlier, the social work education model followed so far has avoided major issues due to historical and contextual reasons (see Gore, 1988, 1997). Recognizing this omission, a number of social work educators and committee reports have reiterated that Indian social work education needs a developmental orientation (Cox, 1994; Desai, 1991, 1994; Drucker, 1993; Gore, 1988; Mandal, 1989; UGC, 1965, 1980).

Social work was born essentially to address the problem of poverty, and its origin is rooted in helping the needy. Helping the poor through charity and later through statutory poor relief in the UK (Midgley, 1984) and through the activities of Theodore Roosevelt's Country Life Commission and The American Country Life Association and Federal Emergency Relief Act in the USA (Martinez-Brawley, 1980) amply supports this view. Those poor law principles that were developed in the UK were perpetuated in most of its colonies, including India (Midgley, 1984). In addition, under the

British rule, Christian missionaries had reached tribal communities, which were neglected by most of the rulers. Historically, social work in India is characterized by religious charity, various social reform movements and the Gandhian approach to poverty alleviation and upliftment of villages. Although professional social work in India mostly concentrated on symptoms of poverty, such as rural poor workers who migrated to cities in search of employment, and on industrial labour welfare, one of its major concerns from the beginning was poverty alleviation and development of local-level communities. For example, the report on Social Work Education in Indian Universities (UGC, 1965) states:

> in the uncertainty prevailing at the present, the task of the rural worker and his training has become difficult. It is a herculean task to grapple with the problem of improving 500,000 of villages scattered far and wide all over India. Indian villages generally suffer from a lack of good drinking water, chronic under-employment, insanitation and lack of sufficient food. (p. 9)

Similarly, the report of the second review committee (UGC, 1980) states:

> It is important to note that a pioneering trust stated that an inquiry into the causes of poverty and the evolution of measures for its elimination was the responsibility of social work (p. 12). The structural changes were required to ensure that social work would reach the lowliest in the social strata. The realisation that the village is not a passing phase, that the industrial society has to be bridled, and that poverty, and not lack of adjustments, is to be the main target of social work intervention, has affirmed that it is the social milieu, and not only the individual, that is a major client of the profession. (p. 15)

The National Network consultation report (Nadkarni and Desai, 2012) states the following:

> Looking at the contemporary times and the context in India the focus of social work should be emancipatory. There should be an effort to focus on the marginalised sections of the country by bringing in anti-oppressive social work practices into social work education to achieve the goal of social justice and empowerment. It is high time that we should look at decolonising social work and do away with the western models of social work practice.

We need to study as to how far is the western model of social work curriculum useful in India. This creates the need to re-examine the methods of social work and their suitability with respect to our context. For example, individualised social work may not hold good in most of our context because of the existence of strong community feeling among people. Methods such as community organisation which rely on western models as developed by people like Murray Ross, Arthur Dunham etc. need to be given up. Instead of that the focus should be on looking at community work with a focus on the empowerment of marginalised sections of the society.

These and similar literature unequivocally indicate that reorientation is clearly needed in social work education, training, practice and the profession. The social development approach presented in Chapter 1 and its practice at local-level communities presented in Chapter 2 designed to address issues such as poverty alleviation, improving the life conditions of the marginalized and disadvantaged sections of the society, together with comprehensive village development, serve to provide directions for reorienting the social work profession and education.

To facilitate such a developmental and poverty alleviation orientation in social work programmes, as stated earlier, first, social work education needs to have a social and community development approach drawing from rural development, health, nutrition, education, family welfare, women children, youth and sports, industry and so on, linking all government's sectorial programmes at the local-level communities and villages. Second, social work education needs to develop an articulated training programme, such as certificate, diplomas and degrees at the levels of 10 + 2 + 3 + 2 to meet the requirements of a large number of trained workers at local-level communities. A pyramid shape may guide the total number of trainees trained at different levels, indicating a large number of training programmes and trainees (10 + 2 level) at the bottom of the pyramid and proportionate BSW-, MSW- and PhD-level training towards the top of the pyramid (see Cox, 1994). More important, social work educators and practitioners need to develop the mechanisms for ongoing technical cooperation with relevant government departments at various levels and NGOs and CBOs (community-based organizations) to facilitate the implementation of their strategies and interventions in panchayat institutions for poverty alleviation and related programmes.

Indigenization of Social Work Education Curricula towards Social and Community Development Practice

Social work PEP in India has to be Indian and not American. The American social work model in India has inevitably had its 'Americanness' diluted over the years as, first, it has been applied by Indians and, second, applied in Indian conditions and contexts. Despite this dilution process, however, a lot of harm might have been caused. In classrooms and fieldwork education sessions my students have questioned me a number of times about the relevance of what I was teaching. They clearly stated and asked, "This is all American, is it relevant to us?" At times I ignored this remark and question and at times I defended what I taught, as my teachers had done. With this experiential reflection, I suggest the following strategies:

1. Accept the fact that social work educators are teaching an American social work model.
2. Question the relevance of the model's various specializations and subjects.
3. Identify what is relevant and not so relevant in the Indian context.
4. Find out why whatever is relevant or irrelevant is in the curriculum.
5. Identify the special factors, conditions and circumstances in India that cause a degree of irrelevance of the model.
6. Find out and identify solutions, perceptions, coping methods and so on that exist in Indian culture, including local culture, tradition and practices.
7. Document and incorporate these into classroom teaching, discussions and field education.
8. Undertake a micro-level series of exercises like these, which will facilitate the development of indigenous curricula.
9. Document and disseminate effective social work practices irrespective of whether they are attempted by professionals or other than professional workers.
10. Revise each subject curricula to incorporate the above strategies.
11. Organize curriculum development workshops at the school level by involving educators and practitioners and student

representatives and later at the inter-school level. Through these processes the entire social work curriculum needs to be revised to dovetail with local contexts.

In revising the curricula, specialization issue may pose a problem, and administrative hurdles may block the whole process of revising the curricula. In relation to the specialization issue, considering the needs of India (Gore, 1988) the offer of a specialization in social work programmes appears inappropriate (see Desai, 1991; UGC, 1980). Thus, by and large social work programmes have to be generic and integrated. However, Desai (1991) in her argument offers scope for specializations if they are based on indigenous needs, methods and knowledge. My own experience and observation suggest some scope for a specialization that deals with relating professional social work intervention to a conservative and cast-ridden society. 'Social Work Intervention in Indian Caste- and Class-Stratified Social Structures' could be a useful specialization within the social work programme. A specialization of this kind has great potential for developing indigenous knowledge, methods and skills in social work education and tackling critical issues in local-level communities by employing anti-discriminatory and anti-oppressive strategies.

To introduce curricular changes in most of the universities, as stated earlier, a kind of technical and administrative approval of the board of studies or other such committees, often represented by a few staff from outside the university, is needed. I have observed that some of these committees work perfunctorily and create deliberate hurdles to new changes. Such technical bodies need to be sincere, cultivate a flexible attitude and facilitate such changes.

Dominance of Western textbooks (Hammoud, 1988; Nagpaul, 1993) is another stumbling block in the indigenization process. It is not practical to totally wipe out at once this phenomenon, but concerted efforts will help reduce their dominance. We need to identify locally available relevant literature and incorporate it in the reading list and make it available to students. Social work educators and practitioners, individually or in a group, can undertake small or large projects which will result in social work textbook material, perhaps, on a particular topic, issue or a subject. Conscious and purposeful exercises by all the schools of social work, in collaboration with practising agencies, will help produce such literature. These and similar approaches have the potential to reduce the dominance of Western literature in social work education (e.g. see Desai et al., 1998; Muzumdar, 1997). Already a few research schemes and funds exist for this purpose. It is also important to note that a number of such programmes do not require a lot of money but rather time, reflection and writing skills in regional or English language; undoubtedly, many social work educators have the necessary knowledge, qualities and skills.

Current trends of liberalization, market economy, globalization and dilution of the welfare state model have to enter social work trainees' classrooms, as these have a lot of implications for social work practice and policies that concern our partners. The way the welfare state has operated in the West has not been the way in India (Pawar, 2012). In the situation of a total absence of universal welfare programmes and the lack of access to existing minimum/residual programmes, many indigenous welfare, care and share systems have been followed at the local levels. They are often cost-effective, personal and humane (Pawar and Cox, 2004). Recognizing, documenting and systematizing such practices not only contribute to indigenous social work knowledge but also have the potential to be used as resource material by policy makers and social and welfare workers in the West as they look for alternative models to cope with the consequences of diminishing welfare states.

The National Network report (Nadkarni and Desai, 2012) has repeatedly raised the issue of and need for the indigenization of social work curricula and teaching methods. Thus, in all social work platforms, small or big, wherever there is an opportunity, we should talk about the indigenization of social work education. This will serve to create a conducive culture for debating the indigenizing of social work education and practice and for revising curricula on a continuing basis so as to begin implementing social and community development practice. The proposed academic reforms in the Twelfth Five Year Plan to develop reusable digitized curriculum and the National Network's leadership in this area (Planning Commission, GOI, 2013, p. 108) present a great opportunity to indigenize curricula for social and community development practice.

An Effective Professional Body

To provide the above-discussed social and community development orientation, to indigenize the social work curricula towards that end, to improve and maintain professional standards and to strengthen the profession, a healthy professional body at the national level is desperately needed. Unsuccessful attempts to revive and nurture an existing national-level body, as stated earlier, appear to have resulted in the formation of several state-level professional associations. Whether such a trend is a good trend for the profession is too early to judge. These bodies have the potential to contribute, both negatively and positively, to the profession. The Association of Schools of Social Work in India (ASSWI) is coming back to centre stage and appears to be active (Thachil and Kumar, 1997). The formation of the National Network and its report and the formation of the NAPSWI and its first congress to build bridges and bridge gaps plus the regular conferences of the ISPSW seem to indicate signs of emerging national bodies. Looking at the future, one can visualize the existence of a number of state-level associations, the NAPSWI, the ISPSW, the National Network and the proposed National Council of Professional Social Workers in India. What kind of role each will perform depends on their objectives and activities. As an example it would be useful to look at the objectives of the NAPSWI and the National Network. The aims and objectives of the NAPSWI are stated on its website (http://www.napswionline. org/). The NAPSWI aims to

"advance excellence in education, training and practice of professional social work through—Education, Research, Training, Networking, Advocacy, Resource Development" with the objective of "promoting the highest professional standards and ethics in the practice of professional social work; advancing the knowledge and practice base of social work interventions that enhance quality of life and standard of living of persons, their family and environment; fostering faster communication and support among professional social workers; promoting social change, empowerment and liberation of people to enhance their well-being adhering to the principles of human rights and social justice; and undertaking research, action and other forms of continuing education for knowledge up-gradation of members."

In its report (Nadkarni and Desai, 2012), the National Network states that it aims to

> rearticulate the vision of the profession of social work in the light of the changing socio-economic scenario; act as a quality enhancement and a standard setting body; provide space for continuing education, sharing of ideas and resources, and promote innovations in curriculum and pedagogy of social work education; advocate for the establishment of a national council on social work profession; provide visibility to the profession of social work in India both nationally and internationally; address the emerging grievances of institutions of social work which may come before the network once it is in place; strengthen the profession at four levels: (i) Teaching; (ii) Fieldwork; (iii) Field Action Projects; (iv) Research; help in the qualitative growth of new and emerging institutions of social work; define the professional content of the profession in terms of its role, functions and boundaries; establish the minimum standards of social work curriculum in the country with scope for innovation and flexibility keeping in mind the local context of each institution; and contribute to policy framing on social issues.

The comparative analysis of the aims of these two bodies suggests that some of their objectives are similar. Thus, there are some anxieties and questions about the existence of several bodies. Will they compete with each other? Will they cooperate with each other? Will they work hand in glove with each other? Will they fight with each other? Will they be subjected to dominance by vested interests? Will they constructively contribute to the development of the profession? Will they live in isolation? Learning from the past, it is better to be proactive. Anticipating the future, it is important to develop some operational guidelines and procedures based on democratic and cooperative federation principles, so that all the associations and their development will build a strong national professional body, which will contribute to the development of the profession and in turn possess the power to express articulated views on certain contemporary issues and debates and contribute to the national- and regional-level policy-making process and influence the policies that matter to their partners-the poor, disadvantaged and marginalized, and local-level communities. Leaders in professional social work and social workers generally have great potential to shape these professional bodies in such a way that they will focus on social and community development practice, drawing on indigenous knowledge and strengths, without mimicking the Western social work practice models.

Values, Virtues and Role Models

One of the important functions of professional organizations is to follow certain philosophical approaches in terms of values and virtues for the profession and social workers (see Chapter 9) and demonstrate such values and virtues through operating as role models. Some explicit ideologies, values and principles are indispensable in any professional training. It is not right to suggest what ideologies and values they should follow and practise, but they should have their own choice and demonstrate it whenever opportunities exist. The total commitment to the training is often built into and flows from such values, virtues and role models. Social work trainees need good role models around them, particularly when they are being trained. Essentially, the gap between what is preached and practised has to be minimized. Social work educators demonstrating what they preach will produce good models and great results. No one will deny the importance of such universal values and virtues as equality, social justice, service, human dignity and worth, honesty, commitment, courage, faith, various practices and procedures related to the operation of democracy, non-discrimination and non-judgemental attitudes and professional judgement when and where it is needed.

Implementation and Speed

Implementation and speed are two vital steps that can bring the profession back on track. For the most part, the suggested recommendations and remedies are not new. Therefore, the situation does not call for a new orientation but a reorientation. Since the first UGC report released in 1965, a number of good recommendations have been readily available in the above-referred committee reports and in social work educators' and practitioners' writings.

1. First, such useful information needs to be disseminated to all those who are concerned (there are issues of access to information).

2. Then the need is to discuss these ideas and suggestions wherever the opportunities exist.
3. We should also find out what are the difficulties, and their causes, in implementing the recommendations.
4. By working on those causes and difficulties, we should implement the relevant suggestions at the individual level, school level and overall at the professional level.

Another very important factor closely related to the implementation is speed and time, particularly for social work professionals. A long delay in the consideration and implementation of these recommendations will kill the ideas embedded in them and the enthusiasm of the people involved in implementing them. Therefore, speed of a careful implementation process needs to be enhanced. There is really no reason why we should not begin implementing these recommendations now.

New Social Work Schools

In view of the requirement of a large number of social work professionals to participate in social and community development and poverty alleviation programmes at various levels, there is a great need for the expansion of social work training. However, the trend of opening new social work schools without necessary infrastructure (Menachery and Mohite, 2001) and admitting students on the basis of donation (Nadkarni and Desai, 2012) must be stopped immediately. I am not sure which professional body will have the teeth to do so, and it is also not clear whether only the proposed council will be able to stop it. And till the council's formation (nobody knows for sure when this will be), this trend will cause a lot of damage to the profession. Supplementary mechanisms need to be developed immediately to cease this unwarranted activity.

Desai (1994) rightly suggests a feasibility study before establishing new social work schools. Undoubtedly, new schools are needed as the present uneven distribution of schools is heavily concentrated in urban centres with only a small number of schools located in rural areas. Whenever such rural-based schools are established, even though a few are located in remote areas, established schools should be approached for help and cooperation; instead, they are often kept at a distance or are completely hegemonized. They need to be constructively helped and supported by respecting their self-determination and reliance. The National Network has listed this task on its agenda (Nadkarni and Desai, 2012) and it is hoped that it will address it.

Multiply Opportunities

There are a number of sensitive issues in power, authority and hierarchy relationships, particularly among the professionals in schools and the concerned organizations. Often, growing young professionals experience stagnated careers and denial of opportunities. Mutually beneficial relationships and collegial attitudes need to be developed and nurtured.

Often, the sharing of opportunities will multiply opportunities, and the deliberate denial of opportunities will result in stagnation and wastage of opportunities, to the detriment of one and all. However, it may be noted that career paths and opportunities cannot be charted by others or the systems. Thus, individuals must be fully involved in developing their own career paths and in creating and sharing opportunities because often systems do not do this for individuals.

In relation to the professional bodies and associations, with due respect to the knowledge and wisdom of senior professionals, I am of the view that those who are nearing retirement and retired should renounce their craving for acquiring positions and holding chairs. They should respectfully take advisory roles and generally encourage young professionals to lead the profession.

Professional Approach to Heads and Students

The recruitment of non-social work professionals as heads of social work schools must be stopped, unless there are exceptional circumstances. I hope senior social work professionals' conscience will prevail on this. A number of alternatives are possible for filling these gaps, especially through the cooperative efforts of other schools. Senior staff from other schools may act as heads (on honorary basis or deputation) and demonstrate their professional leadership to build new schools.

Desai's (1994) findings and my own experience of recruiting students for social work training suggest that some reforms are needed in students' recruitment procedures and methods. Some recruitment criteria, such as participation in co-curricular activities and leadership roles, are not related to high motivation and are often biased against the disadvantaged students (see Desai, 1994). It is necessary to research reliable and valid criteria that will help identify highly motivated and committed students in the recruitment process and then prepare them for social and community development practice.

Formal or informal support services, through alumni associations or other bodies, need to be established to support the needy young graduates to venture into the field and thus reduce their career confusions.

Sever Labour Welfare and Personnel Management from Social Work

Separation of the labour welfare and personnel management specialization from social work programmes and removing them from social work departments need no further consideration and discussion. It has been well demonstrated that this unholy alliance has caused a lot of damage to the profession and drained the limited resources of the schools. Thus, Desai (1994) has persuasively argued that Labour Welfare and Personnel Management programmes have to be severed from social work education and training.

Conclusion

In conclusion, I should admit that this chapter is not comprehensive and not intended to provide all the answers to all the professional issues. It is limited to my experience, observations and what I have read. I am also aware that some readers may disagree with my views. However, I believe that solution to any issue begins with its acceptance. If the chapter has stimulated the thought process of readers on these issues, it has achieved its objective. American influence, remedial education model, dated curricula, certain professional issues related to a national professional association and social work training, and various other factors have hampered the development of the profession and thereby reduced the opportunities to reach out to the neediest in local-level communities. To overcome these factors, some reorientation and practical strategies have been suggested. These particularly include an emphasis on social and community development and poverty alleviation, the development of indigenous social work knowledge and, accordingly, revision of curricula, professional development and a professional approach to dealing with various issues.

About 80 years of social work, PEP in India has, undoubtedly, contributed to the well-being of some needy people. However, it has the potential to contribute to the well-being of the larger needy population and to society at large by focusing on social and community development practice. It is important to clarify the point of shifting the focus from the individual- or casework-oriented remedial model of social work to a developmental model of social work that emphasizes social and community development practice. I am not against clinical or casework practice, and I am aware that it represents an important body of knowledge that is essential to any social worker. However, most of the current social work courses are dominated by this remedial model, and I hope to see a reversal of this trend by the provision of a major focus on developmental social work in the course while at the same time keeping an appropriate place for casework practice. They are not antithetical to each other. The reality in India and in many developing countries cries for the indigenous developmental approach, and we need to shape our profession to respond to it. In her reconceptualization of community organization in India, in the conclusion, Andharia (2007, p. 115) raises important questions: "Can community organization be viewed as a separate discipline requiring sharper positioning and greater flexibility within the education process? Or is it best located within the discipline of social work in India?" I believe, if the social work profession and education adapts itself to the social and community development approach, as discussed in this book, such reconceptualized community organization fits quite well within social work. If social work will not rise to this opportunity, other disciplines will pounce on it, and this is already beginning to happen. So it is time to evolve the social work profession so as to embrace, to a much greater degree than at present, social and community development practice.

Notes

1. I would like to clarify that the meaning of 'social work profession, education and practice in India' differs from that of 'Indian social work profession, education and practice'. The former refers to alien and transplanted social work in India, and the latter refers to Indian and/or an indigenized form of social work PEP.

2. The first review committee was jointly appointed by the University Grants Commission (UGC) and Ministry of Education, Government of India, in March 1960 (UGC, 1965). The second review committee was appointed in April 1975 by the UGC (UGC, 1980). The third review committee has been established in 1997–1998, and the committee is planning to begin its exercise in the near future.

8

SCD Education through Distance Mode: An Unexplored Potential

Introduction

Social and community development education and training through distance mode, as a main stream developmental social work course and/or on its own standing where and if it exists, needs to be systematically and rationally explored and, if practical, used on its own merit without compromising quality. I have the experience of providing social work education and training through direct on-campus and distance modes. Having first taught students directly or face to face, the thought of social work education through distance mode never occurred to me. When I was recruited to teach social work through distance education at Charles Sturt University, the leading distance education provider in Australia and perhaps in the Pacific region, I did not know how it worked and how it differs from direct on-campus programmes. As a social work educator, I approached social work distance education with an open mind and a willingness to learn from such an open method of knowledge dissemination for the greater good of the society. I have been in the social work distance education programme now for nearly two decades. I have taught several social work subjects through distance education mode to both Bachelor of Social Work and Master of Social Work students. Two of the subjects I have taught are Social Work and Social Policy Practice and International Social Development. I have also undertaken field-work placement and liaison and lectures in residential schools for distant education students. The available and growing access to information technology is an important factor in distance education. The 21st-century distance education cannot be equated with the old correspondence courses in many universities. I teach students by using emails, telephones, internet forum, chat room, well-prepared learning materials and well-designed assessments. Students' questions are answered in a reasonably short time. Students' feedback below, as an example, testifies to the usefulness and effectiveness of the distance education subjects students undertake.

> "I thoroughly enjoyed the content, readings, and both assignment for this unit. It was a great learning experience for me, and it will no doubt prove invaluable to my future career as a social worker."

> "Your assistance as a teacher has been incredible. You really go above and beyond in your work role, and I appreciate that. So thank you once again."

> "Thank you for your prompt response to this and every question I have posted or emailed to you throughout this subject."

> "Would like to thank you for your assistance and for opening up the world of social policy to us. This was a subject which I initially thought would be dry; however, I was surprised by how much I have learnt. I now see the links between direct practice and the policies which direct practice, either by their presence or absence. This subject has increased my understanding of what sits behind policy development and structures to assist me in influencing current and future policies."

Reflecting on my nearly two decades of social work distance education experience, I am writing this chapter to convince social work educators and students and education-providing institutions to consider this option as another avenue for reaching out to those learners who otherwise would not be able to access social work and social and community development education and training. By looking at distance education in general, this chapter provides justifications for the introduction of social and community development distance education programme and examines its strengths and weaknesses and the opportunities for, and threats to, such an option. The analysis appears to indicate that there is a lot of potential for carefully operated social and community development distance education programme. Finally, it explores some modalities for initiating certain steps towards this goal so that social and community development education may be provided to many more people.

Distance Education

Kaye (1985) has identified two basic elements of distance education: first, the physical separation of teacher and learner; second, the changed role of teacher, who may meet students only for 'selected tasks' such as counselling, giving tutorials or seminars or solving study problems. In addition, Holmberg (1981, cited from Kaye, 1985) has identified six main categories of description for the term 'distance education'.

- Use of pre-produced courses as the main basis for study;
- Existence of organized two-way communication between the student and a supporting organization, that is, the university, college or school, with its tutors and counsellors;
- Planned and explicit catering for individual study;
- Cost-effectiveness of the educational use of mass communication methods when large numbers of students follow the same pre-produced courses;
- Application of industrial work methods to the production of learning materials and to the administration of a distance education scheme (Peters, 1973, cited from Kaye, 1985); and
- Notion of distance study as a mediated form of guided didactic conversation.

According to Kaye (1985), distance education can be equated with the combined, systematic and flexible use of at least three major elements: print-based communication, broadcasting and/or other technologies and face-to-face contact, in support of an independent learner. Although these concepts have the core elements of distance education, in the 21st century, 'distance' will be somewhat different as the physical distance and time are reduced through the use of information and communication technology and access to learning resources are enhanced. There are also accountability checks as emails and postings on forums have to be appropriately responded to in a reasonably specified time. In most of the social work distance education courses, there are the mandatory minimum face-to-face contact requirements as part of the course accreditation. In India, such guidelines need to be developed and implemented by social work distance education providers to maintain quality, as a professional accreditation body did not exist as of 2013.

The use of distance education method has expanded at unprecedented rates since the 1960s in both developed and developing countries (Asian Development Bank [ADB], 1990; Guy, 1991; Pardasani et al., 2012). Some estimates suggest that perhaps less than half of the courses offered by universities will be taught in a traditional classroom. The new distance technologies will greatly change the conception of what a university is; of how students, faculty and staff do their work; and of where they do their work (Hollister, 1996). The crux of the 21st-century distance education learning is blended and boundary-less learning; it is not the old correspondence learning. It is the mixture of well-developed educational resources, the use of network and multimedia technology and the understanding of dynamic social pedagogy (Iiyoshi and Vijay Kumar, 2008). All over the world enrolments in distance education are increasing. For example, Pardasani et al. (2012), drawing on previous studies conducted in the USA, indicated that, in 1994, 11 per cent of the social work programmes reported utilization of distance education technology (Jennings et al.,1994); in 1998, 16 per cent of the programmes included distance education (Siegel et al., 1998); and in 2009, 41 per cent of the BSW and 52 per cent of the MSW courses were delivering distance education courses and others planned to do so (Vernon et al., 2009). Trembaly's (2011, p. 30) review of distance education in the context of globalization suggests that "India is one of the countries in the world where distance education and research on it are the most advanced." The National Network consultation in its Western region report stated, "Distance education in social work is becoming popular in Maharashtra state, where currently 800 students were enrolled for social work education through this mode" (Nadkarni and Desai, 2012). The School of Social Work at IGNOU has enrolled 3,000 students in its BSW programme and another 3,000 students in its MSW programme. The total number of enrolled students in its social work and related programmes is about 25,000 (Thomas, 2013).[1] Of the 620 universities in India (UGC, 2013), about 174 are dual-mode universities and/or educational institutions, 14 are open universities (Distance Education Council, 2011) and about 21 universities/institutions offer social work distance education programmes.[2] These figures suggest that nearly one-third of Indian universities have a distance education provision, but of these only 11 per cent have social work distance education.

As there are nearly one-third of universities and 14 open universities that offer distance education programmes, there is every reason to assume that the number of distance education users has also increased. However, distance education in India has faced a number of problems relating to status of the institutes and teachers, training, study norms, duplication of courses, finance, accommodation, private appearance, media and student support services, approval by the university bodies, course material, evaluation of response sheets, personal contact programme and administration, although it has evolved its own remedies for dealing with these (see Mullick, 1987).

Despite such problems, the persistence of distance education has been attributed to economic factors and the goals of national development (see Guy, 1991). However, that persistence has not extended to social work education. Perhaps, social work educators and practitioners would be concerned about the credibility of such a programme. These concerns appear to emerge from many 'sacred cows' and many myths about distance education (see Bush and Williams, 1989). Bush and Williams (1989) have listed some of these myths. They are as follows: distance education is solely correspondence teaching, at best tentative and inadequate, cheap, second best, inherently unsatisfactory, expensive if trying to compare with on-campus standards, ineffective and inefficient in terms of expected student outcomes and may lack face-to-face teaching. They argue that

> a growing body of research suggests that not only are many of these assumptions quite wrong but that, in some instances, the very rigour of distance teaching and learning has reversed some of these traditional stereotypes. (p. 4)

Bush and Williams (1989) interestingly further argue that some elements of distance education already exist in social work education. To them social work fieldwork education is distance education. Lange (1986, pp. 61–62, cited from Bush and Williams, 1989) persuasively observes that

> despite years of research showing that technologically-delivered education can be as good or better in terms of results, many academics persist in viewing distance education as inferior to traditional methods. The basis of this view is ignorance and fear and unless academics and administrators

are themselves given education and training in the new education technologies, they will remain a source of opposition and sabotage.

Thus, open and informed discussion on social and community development distance education is needed by social work professionals.

Open-minded and Informed Discussion and Decision-making

Whether social work educators and practitioners and related educational institutions have an open mind and whether they make informed decisions about social work distance education programmes is not clear. Desai (1994) suggests a need to visualize distance education covering the length and breadth of this country for workers who have no certification in social work and are scattered among the numerous NGOs and GOs. Responding to such a visualization, as stated above, about 21 social work distance programmes[3] appear to be operating in India, as of 2013, though accurate figures are not available. The most noted one is the social work distance education programme offered by the Indira Gandhi National Open University (IGNOU). It would be relevant to explore how they operate these programmes and what can be learned from their experience.

However, many social work educators and educational institutions appear to have set their minds against social work distance education programmes. Some have rejected the idea altogether, some have postponed a decision with the view that 'we are not yet ready for it,' some might not have thought about it and some others may be simply questioning and doubting its validity and quality. At any reckoning, the thought of social work distance education in India appears to create many questions, fears, inhibitions, reservations, doubts and concerns in the minds of social work educators and practitioners and of educational institutions. Some of these may be real and some may not be well founded. Hearsay evidence suggests that such concerns, whether real or unreal, have resulted in halting attempts to begin social work distance education. For example, a Bangalore University's Board of Studies resolution stated, "It's practically not viable and professionally unethical to introduce social work through correspondence/distance education" and rejected the idea of having social work distance education (*The Times of India*, 2011). The National Network consultation, held in 2012, suggested that the profession take another look at distance education in social work. Although many members of the consultation were of the view that they "should do away with the system of distance education," others suggested that "instead of (distance education being) a post-graduate course, it should be converted to a certificate or diploma course" (Nadkarni and Desai, 2012). Given such extreme views on such a provision, it is important to dispassionately examine and discuss it rather than accept outright rejection. Based on my experience of social work education in India and social work distance education in Australia, I believe it has great potential and offers new opportunities and challenges through which social workers can prove their creativity and innovativeness. Therefore, it is important to look at the justifications for offering social and community development training through distance education.

Justifications for Social Work Education through Distance Mode in India

Need and Scope for Carefully Operated Social Work and Social and Community Development Distance Education Programmes

The general sense of need and scope emanates from the current developmental needs and social problems in the country. For example, the Twelfth Five Year Plan, 2012–2017, Volume 3, that looks at social sectors envisages several policies and programmes in the areas of health, education, employment and skills development, women and children, and social inclusion of excluded people and groups such as scheduled castes (SCs) and scheduled tribes (STs) and other backward classes (OBCs; Planning Commission, 2013). The plan has proposed significant outlays for each sector. In the social inclusion sector alone,

a tentative Gross Budgetary Support of ₹32,684 crore has been earmarked for the Ministry of Social Justice and Empowerment for the welfare and development of SCs, OBCs, DNTs (De-notified tribes), PWDs (persons with disabilities) and other vulnerable groups. Similarly, tentative allocations of ₹7,746 crore and ₹17,323 crore have been made for the Ministry of Tribal Affairs and Ministry of Minority Affairs, respectively for the welfare and development of STs and Minorities. (p. 274)

There are more than 21 poverty-targeted programmes with expenditures exceeding ₹1 billion (Srivastava, 2004). In each one of these social sectors, social and community development workers can have a meaningful role. Central and state governments and thousands of NGOs have launched many developmental programmes in which trained social workers can play an effective role in facilitating the overall social and community development process. The Planning Commission in its document, "Approach Paper to the Ninth Five Year Plan—1997–2002," states:

Awareness building among the people needs to be given top priority. The government machinery, voluntary organisations and self-help groups will be involved in the process of advocacy and organising the people, especially the poor (India, GOI, 1996, pp. 113–114).

Since the declaration of the "Year of the Gram Sabha" in 1999–2000 by the Government of India (Patil, 1999), in every village there is a need for trained social and community development workers to facilitate the participation of people in the 'Gram Sabha'. Mr R.M. Patil, President of the Federation of Voluntary Organization for Rural Development in Karnataka, when leading a movement of 'Gram Sabha', looked for trained social workers to join the movement. Then, given the perceived response, he vehemently questioned: Where are the social workers? In every village, trained social and community development workers can play crucial roles in social development.

In the 2001 census, 2.11 per cent of the population, as much as 20 million, were placed in the 'persons with disabilities' category (Planning Commission, 2013). The majority of them lived in rural areas possessing limited facilities for treatment and rehabilitation (Nanavatty, 1997b). An estimated 10 to 12 million people suffer from severe mental disorders and about 50 million people have common mental disorders (*The Hindu*, 2013), which suggests the need for community approaches. There are other growing social issues such as preventive and promotive health, drug abuse, AIDS, the elderly, illiteracy, child labour, women, juvenile justice and corrections, scheduled categories and environmental protection, all of which could benefit from the same approaches. As stated above, thousands of workers in GOs and NGOs are working on these issues without professional social work training. Thus, it is natural to assume that trained social workers are needed at various levels and that they can positively participate in addressing these issues. The massive developmental activities and social issues and the increasing emphasis on the social development perspective (Cox et al., 1997b; Gore, 1997; Mandal, 1989) make the need and scope for expanding social and community development training axiomatic.

Uneven Geographic Distribution and Concentration of Social Work Training in Urban Centres

The density of social work schools is relatively higher in South and Western India and lower in North and North-Eastern India (UGC, 1990), for example, Himachal Pradesh, Jammu and Kashmir, and many North-Eastern states, although recently a few new schools have been opened. The present social work training is not only unevenly spread across the length and breadth of the country but is also urban based. As stated earlier, the concentration of social work schools is highly skewed towards urban centres (Cox et al., 1997c; Pawar, 1999b), though some rural schools have recently emerged. Thus, the current social work training is mostly urban based, and its capacity to reach out to small towns and rural and remote areas is very limited. Social and community development distance education has the potential to bridge this gap by reaching out to areas that are not covered currently by social work schools and, thus, enhancing access to the training. For example, IGNOU's social work school has achieved this aim to some extent, though it is too early to draw a conclusion from one example.

Access and Affordability

Access and affordability to education is a critical issue in India as it has an ancient history and culture of denial of education to people on the basis of caste and birth. Education has been the prerogative of only some people. That situation has significantly changed, and now the constitution guarantees education as a matter of right to all citizens. However, the prerogative of caste-based education appeared to have changed to class-based education where relatively economically better-off people can better afford higher education, although theoretically everybody has access to it and several positive discrimination provisions (reservations) have been introduced. Those who are poor and disadvantaged due to their rural or remote location or for other social reasons are not able to have access to and afford higher education. Thus, all those who are interested in receiving professional social work training, to whatever degree, may not be in a position to access and afford the available training, largely because the available training schools are far away from potential students' places and, as stated above, are mostly urban based; moreover, many students may not be able to meet the cost of such training. In some ways, current social work training appears to be somewhat elitist, and that raises serious equity and access issues, particularly for those who are living in rural and remote areas or are numbered among the disadvantaged groups. Generally, social justice, equity and access issues are close to the heart of the social work profession. Social work distance education programme helps to address these issues within the profession, and it seems to be an ethically responsible approach if it is implemented properly. In the out-dated social work concept, clients came to the agency to seek or receive services, but today that concept has radically changed, and more commonly, social workers go to where clients and communities are to work with them. Similarly, distance education can be available wherever students are, so it should very much appeal to the social work profession.

Shortage of Trained Social Workers

Given the range of poverty alleviation programmes funded by both central and state governments (see Srivastava, 2004), the number of disabled people and people with mental health issues and the predicted size of the ageing population and other social problems, the number of available trained social workers is not adequate. The

National Network consultation report stated that there are more than 300 schools of social work. As stated earlier, if we restrict this number to 300 schools and conservatively estimate that 30 trained social workers will graduate per school per year, the available schools will graduate 9,000 trained social workers per year. Thus, on a per capita basis, every 1 million Indian population will have 9 trained social workers! Given this preposterous ratio, professional social workers are virtually non-existent. The current number of social and community development workers is also not adequate to effectively contribute to developmental programmes launched by both GOs and NGOs. Thus, it is hardly surprising that many GOs and NGOs have employees for social work-kind positions without social work training. Carefully operated social work distance education programme has the potential to reduce this shortage.

Need for Expanding Social Work Training at Certificate, Diploma and Degree Levels

Most of the available social work training is at postgraduate level. According to Desai (1994), the current expansion of social work training is occurring at the wrong level. Earlier studies have recommended that there is a need to expand social work training at certificate (paraprofessional), diploma and undergraduate levels (see Cox and Pawar, 2013; Cox et al., 1997c; Desai, 1994; UGC, 1980). Existing social work schools have not been able to attend to this need. Social work distance education programmes have the potential to impart training at these levels, and it is hoped that in the future there will be more distance education programmes to achieve this potential.

Students Can Work and Study at Their Own Pace

The availability of an articulated social work distance training at the above levels enhances the possibility for many employees in relevant GOs and NGOs to continue with their work, except during field work placements, and undertake study at their own pace. It also can operate as short-term in-service training for many employees as well as continuing professional education for social work professionals. The current social work training is full time and on campus and does not have flexibility. And it also does not have in-service and continuing professional education programmes.

Opens up Another Important Avenue to Study Social and Community Development Work

Only a small number of open universities in India are offering social work programmes, although the distance education method is gaining increasing recognition. Social work distance education programmes, prepared and offered by qualified social work educators and practitioners, perhaps in collaboration with Open Universities, will unfold another important avenue for the study of social and community development practice.

SWOT Analysis of Social and Community Development Practice Distance Education

To identify and examine key issues involved in social and community development distance education in India, a modified, rudimentary SWOT (strengths, weaknesses, opportunities and threats) analysis has been undertaken. The technique itself involves listing the opportunities, threats of the environment and the strengths and weaknesses of the profession as an organization (Joyce and Woods, 1997). Such an analysis will help the social work profession to objectively reflect on why should and should not the profession act on the distance education option. Furthermore, by making the profession aware of its SWOT, the analysis would lead the profession to adequately prepare itself to overcome weaknesses and face or avoid threats. The analysis may also help the profession develop itself. The following table (Table 8.1) shows lists of SWOT that are neither exhaustive nor inclusive but only indicative. Similar SWOT may be further identified to enrich the analysis.

Table 8.1:
Strengths and weaknesses of, opportunities for and threats to the profession

Strengths	Weaknesses
• Existence of the profession for nearly 80 years • Rapid growth in the number of schools of social work • Talented and innovative social work educators and practitioners • Somewhat active professional bodies • Ongoing contribution to social work and social sciences research and literature • Forthcoming social work education council • Declaration of ethics for professional social workers • Periodic review of social work education by the UGC • Desire to indigenise the curricula • Advancements in information and communication technology	• Quality concerns • Relatively lack of coordination and joint work • Dominance of remedial curricula and little emphasis on a developmental approach • Relatively little indigenous material and uneven access to textbooks • Urban centred and unevenly distributed education • The current training levels • The current rate of production of social work graduates does not match the demand • Lack of trained social and community development workers in rural and remote areas • Lack of the indigenisation of the curriculum • Lack of a strong professional body • The current growth of low quality schools • Relatively limited access to information and communication technology
Opportunities	*Threats*
• Demand • Rapid growth in NGOs • Massive developmental programmes and social development emphasis • Explicit interest in social work distance education programmes by open universities • Technical support and cooperation from International NGOs and Universities	• Introduction of the programme by other than social workers • Credibility: Image/recognition/integrity of the profession • Other professions/disciplines taking the opportunities • Intervention by Teachers' Unions as distance education affects staff recruitment

As many social work educators and practitioners may be aware of these SWOT, instead of a detailed discussion of them, these and similar SWOT may be cross-tabulated (see Smith, 1994, cited from Joyce and Woods, 1997) and four questions may be raised to further identify issues (see Table 8.2).

Table 8.2:
Cross-tabulating opportunities and threats by strengths and weaknesses

	Opportunities	*Threats*
Strengths	Can you use (exploit) the opportunities while using strengths?	Can strengths be used to face or avoid threats?
Weaknesses	Can opportunities be used to correct weaknesses?	Can threats that test weaknesses be handled?

Source: Based on Smith (1994), p. 41, cited from Joyce and Woods (1997).

Can You Use (Exploit) the Opportunities While Using Strengths?

By looking at the strengths of the profession in terms of long years of its existence and contribution to society, published or unpublished papers, articles, surveys and theoretical research (see Desai, 1997), talented and leading social work educators, growing professional bodies (see Chapter 7 and Pawar, 1999a), growth in the number of schools and some highly reputed schools, its own code of ethics (TISS Social Work Educators' Forum, 1997), periodic UGC review reports (Nadkarni and Desai, 2012; UGC, 1965, 1980, 1990) and the proposed social work education council, one could confidently say that there are opportunities that can be systematically used for the development of both society and the profession. Of course, we all need to put in concerted efforts to make use of the listed opportunities, as the challenge of doing so is indeed significant.

Can Strengths Be Used to Face or Avoid Threats?

I have listed four possible threats, although there could be many others. Available evidence suggests that the profession has already been able to use its strengths to face and or stop some outside threats. For example, it has strongly resisted the opening of new social work schools without necessary resources and has raised serious concerns about the current status of some social work schools and set out some strategies for the future (Nadkarni and Desai, 2012). The image, recognition and integrity of the profession as perceived by the public can be a threat or strength, depending on the type of perception held by the public. Inappropriate perceptions are a real threat to the profession. Even the basic acceptance of social work as a profession is problematic, within and outside the profession, particularly in the Indian context (see Gore, 1997). However, social workers' words and actions can greatly contribute to boost the image, recognition and integrity of the profession. I believe the profession's strengths can be used to deal with these threats.

Regarding the third threat, that the profession will be replaced by other professions, the profession can do very little except by ensuring that it uses its strengths to pursue the many opportunities that exist. Otherwise, some other profession will exploit them. The profession is capable of facing the fourth threat as that would be of a general nature.

Can Opportunities Be Used to Correct Weaknesses?

I am of the belief that the listed opportunities offer great avenues for correcting some of the profession's weaknesses. Many of the weaknesses or criticisms, such as the lack of developmental emphasis and indigenous material (Nagpaul, 1993) in the programme, dominance of remedial curricula, concentration of training at Bachelor's and Master's levels and in urban centres and the shortage of trained personnel can be appropriately and comparatively easily corrected by using the existing opportunities. The introduction of social work distance education calls for the preparation of study material on social work theory and practice subjects, social work practicum and electives. These materials may be prepared with a developmental focus and by using indigenous material. This will also somewhat help to overcome the problem of textbooks (see Nagpaul, 1993) as each distance education student will receive basic reading material in the form of a mail package on each subject of the programme. The training programme may be tried at certificate, diploma and bachelor levels. This enhances the possibility of providing training in rural and remote areas, thereby reducing the shortage of trained personnel in such areas. The availability of a better option might discourage students from going to poor-quality social work schools. In turn, this might result in either improving the quality of, or ensuring the closure of, such schools. This question also addresses some of the above-discussed justifications. It may be reiterated that, on the whole, the opportunities available can be used to correct at least some of the weaknesses.

Can Threats That Test Weaknesses Be Handled? (Is This Clear?)

This is a crucial question that raises some important issues. Many social work educators and practitioners would agree that this is a real challenge to the profession. Reservations regarding the expansion of social work education, whether it is on-campus or distance mode, stem from external threats and internal weaknesses. Social work professional bodies, educators and practitioners are concerned about the quality of social work training. Generally, inadequate resources and ineffective fieldwork education affect the quality. This has a direct bearing on the image, recognition and integrity of the profession—the external threat. In addition, a few programmes of one open university had experienced some problems that may lead some to view the social work distance education proposal with scepticism. How can we be sure that students will read study materials and prescribed textbooks and will write their assignments independently? How can we be sure that students will honestly and sincerely undertake the social work practicum? How can we overcome the initial problem of lack of trained social workers as fieldwork educators in rural and remote areas? How can we fill the gap created by the non-existence of a strong professional body? Will the proposed social work education council have adequate teeth?

I have observed and experienced frequent use of electronic communication systems such as telephone, fax, email and Internet by the students and staff of a social work distance education programme in Australia. I am aware that some students in India may not be able to have the same level of access to these communication systems as their cost will be prohibitive, though the availability of these systems is rapidly increasing. The social work distance education method may have to employ a combination of communication provisions in line with the existing open university systems.

On the basis of strengths and opportunities that can be used to correct weaknesses, one could optimistically think that some of the threats that test weaknesses can be handled. To see whether other threats that test weaknesses can be handled or not, we need to practically test social and community development education in the field as some open universities have been doing. The distance education option offers great opportunities for social work educators and practitioners to prove their creativity and innovativeness. By trialling and testing various approaches, locally effective training systems can certainly be eventually developed. If social workers do not undertake this, non-social work professionals will and that could cause more harm to the profession.

However, I would like to suggest that in the beginning a carefully planned social work distance education programme should operate only on a small scale. Moreover, before launching any programme, it is essential to have a good plan, trained social work staff and the preparation of necessary reading material. Initially, the carefully devised programme should begin on a pilot basis with a small number of students. On the basis of firsthand experience and feedback, the operation of any social work distance programme needs to be regularly refined. As already some universities have been offering social work distance education programmes, their operation and experience should also be evaluated by independent researchers, and this feedback may be used to improve and expand programmes.

Some Suggestions for Initiating Distance Education for Social and Community Development Practice

It is important to meet three core requirements when initiating distance education for social and community development practice. First, all those involved need to adhere to distance education ethics; second, they need to follow a consultative and collaborative process; and third, quality education must be ensured in terms of transfer of knowledge and development of competencies and practice skills. The meeting of the first two requirements should result in meeting the third requirement.

In addition to standard ethical guidelines, Farahani (2012) has referred to four ethical principles in distance education: (1) commitment to the student, (2) commitment to the distance education system, (3) commitment to the profession and commitment as a professional educator and (4) ethical commitment of instructional designers in distance education system. I would like to add a fifth one, that is, commitment of students to learning, as distance education is based on self-motivation to learn. If everyone does their job in the manner suggested, quality education and outcomes will emerge.

A consultative and collaborative process is essential in distance education, as a range of stakeholders is involved. Like-minded people need to come together and objectively discuss the demand for social and community development training through distance education mode and the profession's potential to realize this mission. It is also important to note that some reservations and scepticism have been common wherever distance education methods have been introduced. We need to heed those views and carefully address them in the consultative process. The consultative and collaborative process requires organizations/institutions and individuals to work together in a spirit of multilateral cooperation and understanding. At least four professional experts are involved in any distance education programme. These are subject experts and teachers who are responsible for producing high-quality learning materials, learning experts who are responsible for the learning process and for following the course requirements, technological experts who are responsible for introducing appropriate technology and its use and administrative experts who are responsible for operating the whole enterprise of distance education. Shortcomings in any of these quarters will be reflected in the quality of the distance education delivered to students.

As already some universities are providing social work education through the distance mode, it is important to explore their experience both from the provider and receiver point of view and identify strengths and weaknesses in the programmes. Building on that experience and by constituting subject development committees consisting of social work practitioners, educators, technology experts and educational designers, detailed subject curricula need to be developed in the social and community development practice area that are relevant in the local contexts. The core content may be common or some modules can be contextualized to make it region specific. Such open learning resources can be developed by and channelled through existing subject-based networks, such as the Network of Social Work Education led by the Tata Institute of Social Sciences. Social work educators and distance education providers can also take advantage of academic reforms proposed in the Twelfth Five Year Plan, which proposed the introduction of a choice-based credit system and the undertaking of the regular revision of curricula to incorporate contemporary and future needs (see Planning Commission, 2013). There is a great opportunity to develop social and community development model curricula, along with open learning resources in the form of lectures and textbooks in a reusable, digitized content form so that they can be regularly updated and disseminated through distance education providers. It also offers an important opportunity to indigenize the curriculum and that must be done as much as possible, in whatever language texts are written.

Field work placement is the core element of social work education. Social work education should not be provided without an adequate fieldwork placement component, whether it is direct or distance mode. Those who are new to social work may not understand this or are not able to appreciate this field placement requirement. In any social and community development distance education programme, necessary field placement arrangements in communities under the supervision of qualified professionals must be organized. Actual learning and skill development occur more in community field placements than in (digitized) textbooks or recorded lectures, though these are also most important. This presents a real challenge when thousands of students are enrolled, but innovative methods must be discovered.

Conclusion

Although some universities/institutions are already offering social work education through distance mode, it is still a contentious issue and will continue to be seriously debated, and opinions on it at best will probably remain divided. However, that contest, debate and discussion should occur on an informed basis and not steered by individual idiosyncrasies. As stated earlier, the aim of this chapter has been to present a case for social and community development practice education provided through distance education with the view of meeting the dire need in many local-level communities and the social work profession's obligations to reach out to these communities. Towards that end, the chapter has presented justifications for social and community development education through distance mode as an option, provided a framework for analysis and made a few suggestions for initiating the process. Iiyoshi and Vijay Kumar (2008) are anticipating three dramatic improvements in the future. These are increased quality of tools and resources, more effective use of these and greater individual and collective pedagogical knowledge. I hope this will also hold true for social and community development practice in India and beyond.

Notes

1. These figures were obtained by my telephonic discussions with Professor Gracious Thomas, Director of the School of Social Work, IGNOU, on 18 June 2013.
2. Ibid.
3. Ibid.

9

Social Work's Code of Ethics and Ethics-based SCD Practice

Introduction

Philosophical questions relating to human nature and human goodness inherently interest me, though I am not a professionally trained philosopher or ethicist. However, I have been engaged in social work ethics-related thinking and other relevant scholarly activities since the 1990s. When I was teaching at the Tata Institute of Social Sciences (TISS), Mumbai, India, I was a member of the TISS Social Work Educators' Forum that took an interest in a social work code of ethics for the Indian context. Some members of the forum assumed responsibility for drafting different sections of the code, and various drafts were discussed in a series of meetings. The outcome was the Declaration of Ethics for Professional Social Workers (TISS Social Work Educators' Forum, 1997). The details of the declaration will be discussed in the last section of this chapter. Having been involved in the draft preparation of the declaration and exposed to the Australian Association of Social Workers' (AASW) Code of Ethics, I was curious to consider the similarities and differences between the two. This comparative analysis of the two codes was published in the *Australian Journal of Professional and Applied Ethics* (Pawar, 2000a), and this chapter will, inter alia, draw on those ideas. I also had the interesting opportunity to supervise/guide a PhD thesis that to some extent focused on the relevance of virtues for social workers. All these experiences led to the preparation of a joint research proposal to further explore the place of virtues in the social work profession and practice. This chapter is based on my engagement with the question of ethics through these various opportunities.

Since many codes of ethics include values, principles, competencies and minimum standards, they should be a driving force for maintaining minimum standards and achieving excellence in any professional practice for at least some members of the profession. Is this happening in the social work profession and practice? Although a number of social workers are sincerely working with and trying to help individuals, families and communities, what keeps bothering me is whether we are doing our best in this area and thereby facilitating value-based change and social development in communities. When we generally compare the work of professionally trained social workers with that of non-professionally trained social workers, particularly in the area of community development practice, the visibility of the former is generally blurred. Trained social workers' contribution to community development is generally not as discernible as it should be, though there will clearly be exceptions. For example, look at the work of Anna Hazare, Baba Ampte, Kalyana Sundaram, Bunker Roy, Dr H. Sudarshan and so on. None of these people was a professionally trained social worker, yet their contribution to social and community development is so great. What is the difference between the way they work and social worker's work? What do social workers lack? Is it that our code of ethics, or lack of it, is failing us, or are we ourselves failing because we have failed to develop certain qualities that are needed for community development work? What can social workers learn from highly accomplished community development workers?

Bearing in mind these and similar critical questions, this chapter introduces the concept of ethics and briefly discusses the significance of ethics for social and community development practice. Furthermore, it shows how social work can draw from a range of theoretical formulations to develop its code of ethics and presents a comparative summary of current codes of ethics. In the final section, by discussing the main features of the Declaration of Ethics for Professional Social Workers it explores the potential for developing an indigenous code of ethics for social and community development work in India and similar countries. In the declaration, the meaning of non-English words are as follows: 'Bhakti' means devotion; 'Swarajya' means self-reliance, self-rule and self-governance; 'Lokniti' means equity and social justice for all; 'Sarvodaya' is an ideology that mainly emphasizes 'Swarajya' and 'lokniti' values; and 'Ahimsa' means non-violence.

The Concept of Ethics and Its Significance

It is difficult to clarify the meaning of ethics by presenting a definition of it, as any explanation of ethics includes contestable matter such as morality, values, virtues, rights and wrongs, judgements and standards for conduct. Interpretations of these may differ according to different disciplinary traditions. The understanding of it is further complicated when we look at the equivalence of ethics in the Indian literature. According to Crawford (2003, p. 11), "The Sanskrit word for ethics is 'dharma' [to hold], which upholds or embodies law (not static), custom and religion. Dharma is activity mobility and is possessed of catalytic qualities." Unlike Aristotelian or Thomistic models, the Hindu scriptures do not have systematic discussions of moral doctrines, but they are filled with certain theoretical statements that define the shape of reality and the nature of things, along with prescriptive and practical sayings, aimed at the cultivation of moral behaviour. By studying such sayings we should be able to construct models of systematic ethics (Crawford, 2003), but that is a mission to be completed by many social work educators and practitioners and is not for the present chapter.

Ethics is a branch of philosophy. It is derived from the Greek word 'ethos', which means custom, habit, character or disposition. The BBC (2013) website states that ethics is a system of moral principles that affect how people make decisions and lead their lives. Ethics covers issues such as how to lead a good life, what are one's rights and responsibilities, what is right and what is wrong, and moral decisions—what is good and what is bad? Velasquez et al. (2010) explain the meaning of ethics from two perspectives: First, "ethics refers to well-founded standards of right and wrong that prescribe what humans ought to do, usually in terms of rights, obligations, benefits to society, fairness, or specific virtues." Since feelings, behaviour, laws and social norms can deviate from what is ethical, it is important to examine such so as to make sure that ethical standards are adhered to. Thus, second, "ethics refers to the study and development of one's ethical standards that involves the continuous effort of looking at our own moral beliefs and our moral conduct, and striving to ensure that we, and the institutions we help to shape, live up to standards that are reasonable and solidly-based."

For social work and social and community development practice a code of ethics is crucial. As stated in an earlier chapter, Dean (2010) rightly says that social development is essentially an ethical project. The core agenda is to create good and happy communities in which people can realize their potential and lead a good quality of life. The means and processes of making progress towards achieving that end should follow right behaviour. That is why we have discussed in Chapter 3 four core values and principles for social and community development practice. Existing social arrangements and social structures appear to be often hurdles along the path. Ethics has the capacity to empower social workers to overcome such hurdles. Appropriate training and practice help to develop certain qualities in workers that enable them to take appropriate decisions and effectively implement them. They also ensure that no harm is caused in the process of working with individuals, families, groups, communities and their institutions. It is common to come across moral dilemmas in practise. For example, material well-being (consumerism) versus ecological well-being poses significant dilemmas in community development practice. Or there is the question of who should own community resources (land, water and forest). Ethics helps to effectively deal with such dilemmas by clarifying issues and offering choices. By strengthening the self, ethics helps individuals to focus on social/community issues and needs rather than remaining self-centred. In the case of conflicts and aberrations, ethics offers procedures to resolve them and makes people accountable for decisions and consequences. Overall, ethics help to maintain standards and achieve excellence in practice depending on the ethical framework followed. Ethics is all about creating good human beings and good communities.

Different Theoretical Formulations for the Development of Ethics in Social Work

India and many similar countries do not have a well-developed social work code of ethics due to the current status of professional social work and professional bodies (see Chapter 7). However, where professional social work is well established—for example, Australia, Canada and the USA—a social work code of ethics has been relatively well developed and members of the associations are expected to practise in the spirit of and according to that social work code of ethics. As stated earlier, codes of ethics generally include a preamble; a definition of social work, values, principles, standards and competencies; and guidelines/procedures for dealing with conflicts and complaints. What are the bases of such codes of ethics? Ethical codes can be developed on the basis of a range of theoretical formulations as presented in Figure 9.1. Although the range is wide, it is not necessary that all theories equally influence social work codes of ethics. Depending on the influence of these theories, the focus of various social work codes of ethics differs and, hence, the practice focus and outcomes. Thus, it is important to understand in brief these theoretical formulations and their strengths and weaknesses, as all of them to different degrees seem to influence the code of ethics.

Figure 9.1:
Theoretical bases of social work codes of ethics

Deontology (Kant, 1964) focuses on moral rules for action based on reason/rationality, objectivity, impartiality, unbiasedness, duty and respect for others. Kant's idea of 'categorical imperative' shows the importance of right motive and duty. Under Kant's categorical imperative principle, irrespective of specific situations, a set of injunctions are non- negotiable, unconditional and non-contingent and must be applied universally. For example, some of these imperatives are: 'do unto others as you would expect them to do to you'; 'treat people as ends in their own right' and 'never as a means to an end only'; and, as a way of respect, allow people to self-determine for themselves. Some of the major criticisms of Kant's deontological approach are that it does not help to resolve situations where moral rules are inconsistent or in conflict with each other, and social workers do face such conflicts in the field. Nor does it address cultural relativism issues (the same rules may not be applicable in all the different cultures), and it does not recognize the ambiguous, messy, indeterminate and uncertain nature of social life (Rossiter, 2006). In other words, it disconnects the decision-maker from the real world (Crigger and Godfrey, 2011)

The ethic of consequentialism is based on the tenets of hedonism—maximizing pleasure and minimizing pain—and utilitarianism—greatest happiness to the greatest number of people. Here the consequence or the outcome is more important than the process, though the action or the process of producing the outcome has to be morally right. Furrow (2005, p. 45) argues, "Simply by clarifying what counts as a best consequence and specifying the kind of reason that will produce the best consequence we can systematise all of our moral reasoning." Bowles et al. (2006, p. 61) argue that the influence of this approach is important in social work ethics as most of what is done is designed to or intended to have positive effects. Consequentialism/utilitarianism has, however, been subjected to significant criticism. Some of the main ones are as follows. It focuses on consequences of acts and undermines motives and the actor. It does not define the nature of what is good in social life. By following majority views, it can disregard well-respected virtues and ways of behaving (Harstell, 2006; Houston, 2012). For the sake of obtaining beneficial outcomes, any methods can be justified. If consequences are not known or uncertain, it is not fair to judge an action as right or wrong. The principle of utilitarianism is antithetical to the core social work value of human dignity and worth. How have these deontological and utilitarian influences shaped the being/self of a social worker?

Countering the influences of deontology and the consequentialism/utilitarianism approach and to overcome their weaknesses, McBeith and Webb (2002) contend that social work ethics needs to significantly draw on virtue ethics. Social workers on a daily basis deal with complex, unpredictable and uncertain situations, and ways of doing or intervening in such situations cannot be defined or prescribed in terms of strict rules, procedures or dutiful conduct. Rather than only focusing on the action and outcomes, it is useful to focus also on the actor. What social workers are is as important as what they do. Once the core virtues are developed in them, those virtues will help them to effectively deal with unpredictable and uncertain situations. McBeith and Webb (2002, p. 1020) state, "Virtue ethics can be used to offer an account of the modes of moral existence shaping *the being* of a good social worker." More simply then, the basic question is not what is good social work, but rather what is a good social worker? A small number of social work ethicists are also of the view that virtue ethics are relevant for social work (see Banks, 2006; Bowles et al., 2006; Hugman and Smith, 1995). The virtue theory is broadly influenced by the Platonic and Aristotelian notions of what is excellent (arête), what is practical and wise (phronesis) and what typifies human flourishing (eudaimonia), though Aristotle first emphasized the good of the larger community and then the good of the individual (Aristotle, 1976). Aristotle's doctrine of mean provides the basis for virtues. Prudence or temperance of a worker helps to choose between two extremes in a balanced way that suits the situation. Although the role of virtues in social work is gaining increasing recognition, Aristotelian virtue theory has also come in for some criticism. According to Harman (1999, p. 328), "Aristotelian style virtue ethics shares with folk psychology a commitment to broad-based character traits of a sort that people simply do not have" (2002, p. 93). Miller (2013) articulates Doris's argument that "there is not widespread possession of the traditional virtues and vices understood as global character traits" and builds on the rarity response along with other leading responses to defend the significance of virtues in society (see Miller, 2013).

Houston (2003) argues that the Aristotelian concept of virtues suffers from an ill-disguised tautology, falls prey to relativism, appears to draw on the utilitarian ground that it rejects, falls prey to inner biases and prejudices, fails to establish why virtues are paramount and suggests the need to draw on Habermas' ideas of critical hermeneutics and communication, which seem to strengthen the place of virtues in social work. Gray and Lovat (2007) persuasively make a case that Habermas's communicative action and discourse ethics theory makes a way for cultivating Aristotle's virtues concept. Habermas's ideas are around emancipatory knowing, a critical reflection on the self's beliefs and values and their consistency in action, egalitarian dialogue and social interaction to help character formation (Gray and Lovat, 2007; Swanton 2003). Drawing on Haberrmas's ideas, Swanton (2003) has categorized dialogical virtues into virtues of focus, imaginative and analytic virtues and facilitation.

Another strand of Aristotle's virtue ethics, though somewhat different from it, is ethics of care as an emerging theory. This theory emphasizes the significance of caring relationships and that caring as a virtue needs to be cultivated. Embedded in the virtue of care is the caring relationship and attentiveness, responsiveness and responsibility at both interpersonal and institutional policy levels (Gilligan, 1982; Gray, 2010; Houston, 2012; Hugman, 2005; Sevenhuijsen, 1998, 2000, 2003; Tronto, 1993).

By linking Aristotelian virtues ethics to the principles embedded in Buddhism (see Keown, 2001; Withehill, 1994), Ovrelid (2008) makes a persuasive case for the cultivation of the moral character of a social worker (see also Clark, 2006). Many theologians refer to the use of cardinal and theological virtues in practice (Geach, 1977; Lewis, 2001). Wisner (2011, p. 386) states,

> Personal self-awareness on the part of the practitioner, consideration of the multiple contexts of religious belief systems through understanding their theoretical underpinnings, and understanding a particular religion's broad structure may facilitate effective social work practice with such client populations.

It has the potential to lead to personal spiritual awakening, resulting in social, political and economic change at different levels (Bond, 2004; Macy, 1983). Challenging the influences and practices of deontology and consequentialism/utilitarianism in social work, some social workers have proposed that social work education and practice need to include a faith and spiritual dimension (Canda, 2001; Canda and Furman, 2010; Knitter, 2010; Ortiz et al., 2000; Sheridan, 2009).

Despite such a plea, it is not clear whether and how social workers use faith and spirituality as part of their being/self as a virtue in practice. In the social work literature, generally, social workers' being/self is devoid of faith and spirituality, despite the fact that many people and communities are influenced by, and have a faith derived from, Buddhism, Judeo-Christianity, Confucianism, Hinduism, Islam and similar religions or faith systems of the world. What place faith and spirituality have in virtues and whether these are/should be used to influence social workers' being/self in practice are not clear.

Finally, a pluralistic approach suggests that social workers need to use all of these social work ethics theories within their practice, depending always on the field context, as each theoretical perspective has its own strengths and weaknesses (Berlin, 2003; Bowles et al., 2006, p. 56; Houston, 2012; Hugman, 2005, p. 166;). Houston (2012, p. 661) suggests,

> Practitioners need to be open to the pluralistic ethics of both the 'head' (deontology/utilitarianism) and the 'heart' (virtue ethics and ethics of care), even though they may present countervailing arguments and colliding sentiments. Adherence to ethical monism will just not do. Justice, duty and reason need to be held in a creative equilibrium, where possible, with emotion, caring, intuition and aspirations towards virtue. The apparent collision of these divergent ethical positions needs to be softened and embraced in a creative tension, as both Berlin and Sevenhuijsen have argued.

So has Hugman (2005, p. 166) whose view is that this tension "augments and enriches the ethical vocabulary of the caring professions without any one approach being seen as an absolute position." Does this mean that social workers' being/self should consist of all these virtues, holding them in tension? If so, it is useful to explore how they can hold them in tension and use them in practice and how and when they mask some characters/qualities and unmask others. When social workers' 'being/self' is viewed in terms of virtues or characters, several theories or philosophical positions—deontology, consequentialism/utilitarianism, Aristotelian virtues, Habermas's communicative action and discourse ethics, faith and spirituality and pluralistic ethics—appear to theoretically contribute to the formation of social workers' being/self/virtues. It would be interesting and useful to examine the influence of these ethical theories on social work codes of ethics.

232 Social and Community Development Practice

Social Work Codes of Ethics

As discussed earlier, social work codes of ethics are important from several perspectives. According to Banks (1998), codes of ethics have four general functions. First, they are a guide to conduct and ethical decision-making; second, they protect users from malpractices or abuse; third, they contribute to the 'professional status' of social work; and fourth, they establish and maintain professional identity. In my view, they also should function to create good communities. Despite such intended good functions, codes of ethics are never final. They continually evolve to make them more relevant to a changing society. Codes of ethics developed by professional bodies have often been subject to favourable and unfavourable critiques (see Bowles et al., 2006; Hugman, 1998). The issue of what is an appropriate code of ethics remains unresolved and is always a matter of debate. Questions include: Do codes of ethics guide actions of helping professionals for the larger benefit of society or serve only professionals' interests? Do they represent ideal or attainable aspirations? Do social workers really use them? These are important concerns for both professionals and the general public. Despite such critical concerns and the often unfavourable criticism, codes of ethics are established by professional associations and are applied to their members. The subject of ethical practice based on a code of ethics has become an important part of professional training and is commonly found in social work textbooks (see Baird, 1999; Bowles et al., 2006; Compton and Galaway, 1999; Gambrill and Pruger, 1992; Hugman, 2013; Linzer, 1999; O'Connor et al., 1998; Preston, 1994; Sampford and Preston, 1998; Shardlow, 1998). A well-developed code of ethics and its inculcation in social workers is frequently seen as empowering both social workers and their practice and people and communities.

Not all countries where professional social work exists have their own professional code of ethics, but most do. However, those countries that do not have their own codes of ethics may adopt or adapt 'the Statement of Ethical Principles' developed by the International Federation of Social Workers (IFSW) and International Association of Schools of Social Work (IASSW) (IFSW, 2013; for details visit: http://ifsw.org/policies/statement-of-ethical-principles/). Although each country's code of ethics may be different in some respects and should be so to make it relevant to the local contexts, all of them do have some core common elements. To explore such common elements, Bowles et al. (2006, pp. 91–94) have compared the social work codes of ethics of the IFSW/IASSW with six countries, as presented in Table 9.1. Their analysis identified the following three common themes:

1. Respect for the inherent dignity and worth of all people and the human rights that follow from this, including respecting self-determination, promoting participation, treating people as a whole and identifying and developing strengths;
2. Responsibility to promote social justice, both in relation to society in general and the people with whom we work, including challenging negative discrimination, acknowledging diversity, distributing resources equitably, challenging unjust policies and practices and working in solidarity with those who are subjugated, excluded or stigmatized; and
3. Professional behaviour that is ethically sound or 'virtuous', including being competent, acting with integrity, being compassionate and empathic, not putting their own needs above the needs of the people who use their services, being accountable, engaging in ethical debate, caring for themselves professionally and so on.

This analysis by Bowles et al. (2006) further suggests that the first theme closely relates to the deontological ethical framework, the second to consequentialist and the third to virtues. In our view it is difficult to relate the three themes to the three ethical frameworks in such a compartmentalized manner. Equally important are the other emerging themes—care, ecology, faith/spirituality—which need to be incorporated. By comparing the IFSW/IASSW statement of principles with code of ethics for British social workers, Gilbert (2009) argues that both codes face "challenges from alternative traditions and emerging ethical frameworks that reject liberal orthodoxy and the hegemony of Western forms of thought and both the documents are contradictory to their aims." Despite its emphatic commitment to social justice, the Australian code is tilted more towards individualized practice with clients (Pawar, 2000a). Our analysis suggests

Table 9.1:
Comparison of values and principles in some countries' codes of ethics

IFSW Ethics in Social Work Statement of Principles	Australian Code of Ethics (2010)	National Association of Social Workers (USA) Code 1999	British Association Code of Ethics (2002)	Canadian Association Code of Ethics (1996)	Association of Social Workers in Turkey (undated)	Declaration of Ethics for Professional Social Workers (India 1996)
Human rights and human dignity	Human dignity and worth	Service	Human dignity and worth	Maintain best interest of client	Unique value of every human	Inherent worth and dignity of people, needing to live in harmony with other non-human existence
Social justice	Social justice	Social Justice	Social justice	Integrity and objectivity	Self-fulfilment	Working towards the overall well-being of people in the spirit of 'Sarvodaya'*
	Service to humanity	Dignity and worth of the person	Service to humanity	Competence	Society should function for maximum benefit of members	Solidarity and partnership with the marginalised people
	Integrity	Importance of human relationships	Integrity	Non-exploitation (limit on professional relationship)	Human rights – UN Declaration	Peaceful and non-violent approaches in the spirit of 'Ahimsa'**
	Competence	Integrity	Competence	Confidentiality		
		Competence		Outside interest	Service	
				Limit on private practice	Struggle against social inequality	
					Social change and justice goals	

Ethical responsibilities to workplace	Competence
	Confidentiality and privacy
	Informed consent and participation of clients
	Self-determination, minimum compulsion
	Anti terrorism, torture or brutal means
	Accept the association's principles and responsibilities

Source: Bowles (2006, pp. 92–93).

* 'Sarvodaya' is an ideology that mainly emphasizes 'swarajya' (self-reliance, self-rule and self-governance) and 'lokniti' (equity and social justice for all; Pawar, 2000a). As part of the description of this value in the declaration, three goals are identified: (a) Equity, non-hierarchy and non-discrimination of human groups; (b) Social, economic, political and legal justice; ensuring satisfaction of basic needs and integrity and security; universal access to essential resources and protective safeguards for the marginalised people; and (c) People-centred development from micro to macro levels where people participate in determining their lifestyles and goals for development.

** 'Ahimsa' means non-violence (Pawar, 2000a).

that social work codes of ethics could do well to make virtue ethics more explicit within them. Several social work educators and ethicists have asserted that moral philosophy related to virtues has not received much consideration in social work (Gray, 2010; Houston, 2003; Pullen-Sansfacon, 2010). Gadamer (1981) states that a moral agent with virtues of judgement, experience, understanding, reflection and disposition is best fitted to social work under the fluid conditions of a complex social system. Clark (2006, p. 86) argues,

> In the first place, it is a delusion to suppose that the professional's moral character is irrelevant to the specific qualities they will bring to their professional role. On the contrary, their character and values will certainly be transmitted in the services and relationships they offer to clients.

Furthermore, Clark (2006, pp. 85–86) points out

> There is a perpetual tension between the abstract requirements of universal liberal rights and the specific readings of them to be discovered and created in particular contexts. This tension cannot be resolved by reading off from the texts of professional ethics; it must be squarely faced in the everyday judgements made by practising professionals.

McBeath and Webb (2002, p. 1033) suggest,

> The virtuous worker must learn to bring together strength of mind, judgement, perception of situation, and action in a highly analytical way, sorting through alternative courses of action as competing expressions of the good life—of eudaimonia; and these are capacities which have been much discounted by the dilution of the demands of social work training.

Thus, they recommend that we "develop means by which professionals nurture virtues" (p. 1016). It is also important to note that, in the literature, social workers' 'being/self' is often discussed in the therapeutic context (Coady and Wolgien, 1996; Edwards and Bess, 1998; Elliott, 2000; Goldstein, 1994; Reupert, 2006) while community development contexts have been largely ignored. Therefore, it is important to think about what kind of virtues or being or self is needed for social and community development workers. While discussing virtues or codes of ethics generally, Hugman (2005, p. 448) advises that we regard ethical statements as living traditions in the manner of an ongoing conversation. As codes of ethics are open to continual debate and reconsideration, the task for each social worker is to be prepared to take part in the conversation and to ensure that the ethical tradition of social work remains alive and continues to grow.

An Indigenous Code of Ethics for Social Work and Social and Community Development Practice

Social work educators and practitioners in India and similar countries perhaps need to heed the advice of Hugman and take part in the conversation of code of ethics that is relevant to their context, not the one adopted from overseas (Goswami, 2012). A few social workers have already initiated this process, and their efforts have resulted in the Declaration of Ethics for Professional Social Workers (TISS Social Work Educators' Forum, 1997). To facilitate further conversation of this work, the main features of the declaration are reviewed here.

The declaration consists of three parts: preamble, a value framework and ethical practice responsibilities. The preamble of the declaration consists of four elements. First, it makes clear who it applies to and the basis of the declaration. Second, it refers to the philosophical/ideological basis of 'Bhakti movement', Socialism and 'Sarvodaya'. Third, it expresses the profession's commitment to solidarity with marginalized people. Fourth, it recognizes that marginalized people need to be empowered. It aims to bring about social change/systemic change.

The value framework includes the inherent worth and dignity of people, working towards the overall well-being of people in the spirit of 'Sarvodaya', solidarity and partnership with marginalized people and peaceful and nonviolent approaches in the spirit of 'Ahimsa'.

The value framework has not explicitly included any principles. It is written in the first person, and social workers are expected to take a pledge as each statement begins with the phrase 'I pledge to'. Social workers are expected to promote the value framework within themselves and their work as well as in the profession and in society. Several areas of responsibilities are set out as follows.

Responsibilities to the Profession

The declaration expects social workers to uphold the dignity and integrity of the profession, review and criticize the profession and work towards its development and excellence. The declaration states that social workers have the responsibility to promote networking among social work professionals and other like-minded individuals and organizations and work towards the developing and strengthening of professional associations. They also have the responsibility to facilitate the development of new entrants to the profession and work towards people-centred development.

Responsibilities to Self

The declaration expects social workers to constantly seek an understanding of themselves and to change those attitudes and prejudices that may adversely affect their work. Social workers should respect the feelings and thinking of others, understand behaviours, avoid stereotypes and recognize individuality in every person.

Responsibilities to Clients/the Marginalized and Other People in Need

The declaration expects social workers to give priority to the interests of clients/marginalized people, promote self-determination, ensure informed consent, maintain confidentiality and records, and appropriately terminate or interrupt the service. The declaration states, "Social workers' primary professional response and accountability should be to the marginalized and other people in need and their commitment and professional stand should be with them." Furthermore, it is social workers' responsibility to

> empathise with people's marginalisation and thereby respect and give credence/value to their life experiences; to work towards changing the systemic and contextual forces which marginalise people, on behalf of and in partnership with them; and to nurture a relationship of partnership with people that promotes mutual reflection on their life situation and their development. (TISS Social Work Educators' Forum, 1997)

Responsibility to Co-workers/Colleagues

Social workers' responsibilities include relating to, and cooperating and working with, colleagues with respect, integrity and courtesy while seeking to understand differences in viewpoints and practice. Social workers should also learn from other disciplines to promote and expand ideas, knowledge and skills. According to the declaration, social workers shall respect the inherent worth and dignity of co-workers, contribute to the process of collective reflection and democratic decision-making when working as a team, respect confidences shared by co-workers in the course of their professional relationships and transactions and promote a practice of mutual evaluation with co-workers for their professional development.

Responsibility to Employing Organizations

It is a responsibility of social workers to use the resources of employing organizations honestly/judiciously and only for their intended purpose. The declaration states that social workers should promote humanistic values and ethical practices in implementing the organization's policies and practices. Social workers should periodically monitor and evaluate the organization's policies and programmes by maintaining records and by self-reflection on people's and co-workers' feedback. When the social worker becomes an employer/contractor, she or he should ensure clarity of goals in delegation of roles and responsibilities and give opportunities for co-workers' growth.

Responsibility to Social Work Education

Social workers are responsible for possessing and maintaining necessary knowledge, skills and methods and for teaching within the value framework of the profession. The declaration states that it is the responsibility of social workers to be conversant with the learners' needs, readiness and goals; to recognize the importance of partnership between practitioners and educators; to develop nurturing relationships with students, encouraging openness and self-study;

to undertake demonstration of people-centred field action projects for the purpose of research and documentation, training and replication; and to share their knowledge with other social educators and practitioners.

Responsibility to Social Work Research

These include careful selection of the research topic and considerations of its consequences, protection of the privacy and dignity of research participants, informed voluntary consent, protection from unwarranted physical and mental harm, confidentiality, accurate and objective report preparation with due acknowledgements and the sharing of results with participants. According to the declaration, social workers should consider the informants as co-partners in understanding the phenomenon, provide information services to participants as and when necessary and use the findings for the benefit of participants, by seeking to revise policies and programmes.

Responsibility to Society and the State

Social workers have responsibilities to promote the implementation of the Fundamental Rights and Directive Principles enshrined in the Indian Constitution; to work towards a society and a state that promotes equity, justice, 'Ahimsa' 'Swarajya' and 'lokniti'; to advocate changes in social systems and state policies and legislation to promote the above values; to encourage informed participation by the people in shaping state policies, legislation and programmes; and to respond and offer professional services in emergencies at all levels.

The declaration of ethics for professional social workers in India has some indigenous substance. It is unique in many ways. Its preamble and value framework have indigenous elements, and the declaration has, overall, an ideological and philosophical base. The application of relevant tenets from the 'Bhakti' movement, 'Sarvodaya', 'Swarajya', 'Lokniti' and 'Ahimsa' are highly commendable. The declaration recognizes the intrinsic worth of not only all human life but also non-human life. This is indeed a unique feature. Other striking features include living in harmony with other non-human existence, solidarity with marginalized peoples, empowerment and people-centred development.

Notwithstanding the idealism and the spirit and uniqueness of the declaration, I think it is still a document in the making. It has a sense of incompleteness. Looking at the Australian Code of ethics, Ife (1997a) aptly argued,

> The community-development aspect of social work, at present of relatively minor status within the profession (and so in the code), could become the most significant role for the future and could, if social workers have the vision and the courage to accept the new challenges, lead social work to becoming perhaps the most important of all professions for the future sustainable society. (p. 404; parenthesis added for emphasis)

I wonder whether such a comment applies to the Indian declaration and context. The declaration could do more in developing, organizing and presenting its contents. More important, the declaration should be able to communicate effectively with social workers and other interest groups. If social workers have the responsibility to be active social and community development workers and to engage with the thousands of local-level communities in need of such, they would do well to consciously develop the virtues of commitment, love, compassion, care, consistency, courage, conviction, honesty and so on. This they could do in part by following the example of the exemplary community organizers that India has produced. To achieve this goal, the Indian social work code of ethics needs to go beyond deontology and consequentialism and embrace the emerging ethical frameworks. Indian social cultural contexts (e.g. Dharma), social work educators and practitioners have a lot more to offer to their code of ethics, as well as to their communities and themselves, if they pursue the aforesaid lines of development.

Conclusion

Professional codes of ethics are expected to play crucial roles in building professional identity, preparing committed and integrated professionals, enhancing standards and improving practice for the benefit of the larger society. Towards that end, this chapter has

242 Social and Community Development Practice

discussed the meaning of ethics and its significance for professional social work and social and community development practice. It has shown how a social work code of ethics can draw from a range of ethical frameworks and how the current codes of ethics seem to be mostly preoccupied with deontology and consequences or seem to be not explicit about the implication of other ethical frameworks for practice. There appears to be a consensus on certain human values that should guide practice. Hence, various social work educators and practitioners have called upon the profession to look at virtue-led practice. The declaration of ethics for professional social workers in India has several indigenous and unique elements, and it represents an important initial step. However, through the broad engagement of the profession and individual social workers in its further development, a better declaration could be achieved. Moral rules and social and community development practice have to be ethics based, irrespective of the source of such ethics. Under the influence of liberal ideology and managerialism, current social work codes of ethics appear to be more rule bound and outcome focused. Deontology and consequentialism have to have their place in social work codes of ethics, but the profession and practice also have to progress beyond the rule and consequences orientation. As social workers on a day-to-day basis face unexpected, challenging and unpredictable situations, they need to make appropriate judgements and act accordingly. They need to enable and empower marginalized and disadvantaged groups, and their practice needs to be emancipatory. To achieve all this, for social workers 'what they are' is as important as 'what they do'. Thus, professional social work and its code of ethics need to focus more explicitly on developing virtues in social workers. Common sense and community development examples suggest that virtuous social workers and virtue-led practise can facilitate better social and community development practice.

Section IV

The Future of SCD

Gaining insights from the analysis of the first three sections, the last section reflects on the future of social work profession and its practice and the place of much-needed social and community development practice within it. In the course of that reflection, it is useful to raise this question: Where is the social work profession (education and practice) heading and where should it be heading? Unlike the previous sections, the last section includes only one, concluding, chapter. To visualize the future of social work, it briefly looks into the Indian and Western historical context in which social work began and how the Western social work model was replicated in many countries. One raises the question of whether such a reactive and remedial social work model is relevant for social and community development practice at local levels, as its purpose and context were quite different in the UK and USA settings than they need to be in India. The historical development of social work has been presented in terms of early beginnings and the consolidation of social work knowledge and skills, the spread of that social work knowledge and skills to developing countries and colonies, the questioning of the dominance of the casework model and making a case for developmental social work. It also appreciates the importance of contributions coming from empowerment and strengths-based, human rights and social justice-based, anti-oppressive and anti-discriminatory-based approaches; radical, critical and feminist social work; and from reflective practice. Despite such developments within the profession, the social work profession has been facing several challenges within and from outside. The concept of social work and its identity has been revisited several times, and a new definition of social work is being deliberated internationally. However, there appears to be consensus about what should be the agenda for social work profession, and that agenda is social work and social development.

The social work and social development agenda is befitting the contemporary and emerging Indian social, cultural, political and economic context where reducing poverty and creating a less unequal society along with economic prosperity are major challenges now and into the future. Such a context offers many opportunities as well. To effectively use those opportunities, people's and communities' capacities need to be developed by employing a social and community development approach at the local level. This is the major theme of the book, and the concluding chapter shows how relevant and necessary it is for social work in India and South Asian region generally to adopt and adapt the developmental perspective and practise social and community development at local levels.

10

Social Work and SCD Practice: Reflections and Foreflections

Introduction

I coin the words 'foreflect and foreflections' to refer to reflections about the future. This book is about my reflections on social and community development practice and how social work profession needs to facilitate such a practice. While engaged in these reflections, I keep visiting the same ideas again and again and raising critical questions. This book has helped me to share my reflections with others. Although three decades of learning, teaching, researching and writing is a long time, when it comes to learning, creative thoughts and contributing to society generally, I have a need to accomplish a lot more in all three areas than I feel I have done. Repeating the same ideas does not contribute to furthering this goal, though there is nothing wrong in repeating good ideas till they are picked up and implemented. This is what the book does; it sets out these ideas. It is like chanting 'slokas' in Sanskrit or devotional songs that some chant without understanding them. However, the way I understand social development and the social development approach has been presented in Chapter 1. Why and how such an approach needs to be applied within local communities is discussed in Chapter 2. While pursuing social development, what values and principles need to be followed and the dynamics of community practice likely to be faced are discussed in Chapters 3 and 4. To realize social development in local-level communities, it is inevitable and logical to focus on and draw from social policy practice and international social work, and these issues are covered in Chapters 5 and 6, respectively. However, to contribute to the social development of communities, the social work profession needs to resolve some issues of its own and reorient some of its strategies (Chapter 7), including arranging training of personnel by using a range of further options and, more particularly, distance education (Chapter 8), and to revisit, update and complete its ethics declaration with some new perspectives (Chapter 9). Facilitating the comprehensive social development of communities, according to the appropriate values and principles, is a challenging and skilful activity. The previous chapters help us to reflect on and act in regard to face those challenges and confidently develop the skills required to initiate the social development of communities, particularly at the local level. I believe that the themes and issues discussed in these chapters are relevant and, equally, of interest to social work students, educators and practitioners and to the profession as a whole.

Drawing on the analysis presented in the previous nine chapters, in this final chapter I foreflect on the future of social work in India/ South Asia. In thinking about that future, we need to look at where we are now and the path we have followed. That is what this chapter does by briefly exploring the evolution of professional social work over a period of more than one century. Then it presents the contemporary and future Indian context very broadly in terms of major problems and opportunities. To respond effectively to these problems and opportunities, it is suggested that social and community development practice must be a substantial aspect of the future of social work.

Social Work: Past, Present and the Future

Although it is important to look at the past in order to think about the future, where exactly to look in the past history of social work is complicated. The history of social work and its interpretation will be articulated differently, depending on the way social work is understood and the parameters that are set around such an understanding. It is reasonable to assume that, during different periods (ancient/Vedic, medieval and modern) and in different societies and communities, people and groups (e.g. religious) in formal and informal ways have been kind and helpful to each other, particularly under crisis conditions. Human history goes back thousands of years. Unearthing that kind of broadly understood mutual aid or social work history is an important research task that needs to be undertaken. However, the history of social work discussed here does not include that long past, though it is important and should be acknowledged.

A rich (non-professional) social work tradition was there much before professional social work was introduced to India, and likewise, in many other countries. Mostly rooted in religion, the social reform activities undertaken by Buddha, Mahavir, Basava, Kabir, Dnyaneshwar and Tukaram have been noted (Tope, 1987). There has also been a rich tradition of voluntary, individual and collective service. In the 7th century, a Chinese traveller, Hsuan-tsang, observed that "the Indian people were always in the habit of planting trees on the wayside to provide shade for travellers. They came together voluntarily to dig tanks and wells for drinking water for the community" (Gangrade, 1987, p. 221). Such observations suggest some ways of providing services to the community. In the 12th century, Basava, known as the Universal Guru, led in some social, economic and political radical reforms. During the medieval period, "through the 'adheenamas' system, the community had organised centres of learning and research where free boarding and lodging were provided to students" (p. 221). 'Dharmsalas' (rest houses) were built for travellers. During crisis situations, kings responded with royal charity doles. During the period of colonization from the 16th to the 19th century, both local reform movements and reforms and services introduced by Christian missionaries have been noted (Ratnam, 1987). Particularly during the 19th century, important religious reforms were introduced by establishing Raja Ram Mohan Roy's Atmiya Society in 1815, Unitarian Committee in 1822 and Brahmo Samaj in 1828 to fight against 'sati' system, to improve conditions of widows, to provide education for women and to remove caste restrictions. To fight these and similar causes, later on many organizations, such as the Prarthna Samaj in 1864 and the Arya Samaj in 1877, were established. Several institutions for the orphans, disabled and the destitute were established by Christian missionaries (Ratnam, 1987). Such indigenous reforms under the influence of Western thought, enlightenment ideals and rationalism continued through-out the 19th and early 20th century. Bose (1987, p. 197) observes,

> Before the independence, the role of the state in the execution of welfare programs was negligible, services established through voluntary effort were unevenly spread, depending upon the existence of responsive work-ers and appropriate leadership. The institutions were generally personality oriented and their functioning was not institutionalized. (Gangrade, 1987)

Tope (1987, p. 44) categorized social reforms into two areas. One focused on 'Dharmashastras' and its reinterpretation, and the second focused on social reforms based on reason. Tope argues that the first one soon faded from the horizon of social reform. It appears that the systematic colonization strategy did play a role in weakening indig-enous practices, both good and bad.

In the West, following the enlightenment, rationalism, indus-trial revolution, technological innovation and industrialization, life changed significantly during the 16th to 18th centuries. Rural to urban migration, poverty, destitution, sickness and the situation of children and elderly in urban centres in the midst of wealth creation were all disturbing phenomena that attracted the voluntary efforts of both individuals and organizations, such as charity societies and settlement houses in the UK and the USA. Both religion and ration-ality influenced this work, as churches were significantly engaged in addressing social issues by developing children's aid societies and similar efforts to help the needy much before formal social work training began. Payne notes that case work originated in the attempts of the London Charity Organization Society (COS) formed in 1870, and the first almoner (medical social worker) was appointed in 1895. According to Rowlings (1997, p. 113), the first knowledge-, skills-and value-based schools of social work were established in the UK and Netherlands in 1896, in Germany in 1899 and in France in 1907. Based on the UK COS model, the first COS was founded in New York in 1877, and the idea spread quickly to other cities. COSs tried to systematically organize voluntary charity efforts through 'friendly visitors' who looked in on poor families and corrected individual behaviour (Leighninger and Midgley, 1997, p. 10). The COS in New York offered the first formalized training programme for workers as a summer school in 1898. Later it became the School of Philan-thropy in 1904 and then the School of Social Work within Columbia

University. Later several social work schools were established in the USA. In the first decade of the 20th century, social work emerged as an occupation. Mary Richmond's role in the COS movement and her conceptualization of social work and publication of the book on social diagnosis in 1917 have significantly influenced the nature and development of social work profession (Stuart, 2013).

Another origin of social work may be traced to evangelical Christian and Victorian 'good works' ideas, which had an approach of 'We care for everyone who comes.' Through this approach, shelters for orphans and oppressed women were provided and university settlements were established (Payne, 1997). Following London's first settlement house, Toynbee Hall, Jane Addams and Ellen Gates Starr founded Chicago's Hull House, the most famous settlement house in the USA, in 1889. Settlement workers tried to organize and mobilize poor people around improving social and economic conditions by bringing change to welfare policies and provisions. These origins of social work are linked to community organization and development (Leighninger and Midgley, 1997, p. 10; Payne, 1997; Stuart, 2013), but they have mostly retained a backseat in social work education, practice and the profession.

These developments in the UK and the USA had significant influence in India, as we can see from the establishment of similar children's aid societies and settlement houses in Bombay. For example, Dr Clifford Manshardt, an American Protestant Missionary, established Nagpada Neighbourhood House in 1926 to address social problems such as poverty, gambling and prostitution in the growing city of Bombay, and he later established the first school of social work in India in 1936 (Desai, 1987).

During the first 20 to 30 years, between 1890 and 1920, social work was gradually established as an occupation and then a profession in the West, and Mary Richmond's casework approach became the torch light for social work education and practice. It was a kind of consolidation period for the development of social work knowledge and skills, and the consequences of World War I, among other things, lent themselves to such a practice. This form of organized, systematic and paid helping force, as if it were a new invention, was imposed on India, particularly in its growing cities, in order to address similar problems that had been encountered in the UK and the USA. During the next 20 to 30 years, between 1920 and 1950 or even 1960, Western social work education spread to many developing countries and colonies. Many educators in practice were trained in the USA to teach social work in India. It was truly the domination of Western social work education, which itself was dominated by Mary Richmond's case work model.

In the subsequent 20 to 30 years, between 1960 and 1990, many social work educators, practitioners and students kept wondering about this dominance of the case work, remedial/medical-oriented model and its relevance for the growing developmental problems of the country, including within such as local-level development, and many kept arguing that social work profession needed to have a developmental focus (Cox, 1995; Cox and Pawar, 2013; Midgley, 1995, 2014; Midgley and Conley, 2010; Pawar, 2000b). Although group work, community organization and development, welfare administration/social policy and a research methods subject were all taught as part of social work courses, somehow they remained at the periphery of the curriculum with the continuing dominance of the case work model. Even today, this is the situation in most schools.

However, in the past two and half decades, between 1990 and 2014, several new strands have, at the theoretical level, emerged within social work knowledge, which are significant developments. These are radical social work (Ferguson and Woodward, 2009; Fook, 1993; Mullaly, 2006), critical social work (Allan et al., 2009; Fook, 2012), feminist social work (Dominelli, 2002; White, 2006), empowerment and strengths-based practice (Lee, 2001), reflective practice (Knott and Scragg, 2013; Martyn, 2000; Webber and Nathan, 2010), human rights and social justice (Ife, 2012; Mapp, 2008; Reichert, 2011; Wronka, 2007), anti-oppressive and anti-discriminatory practice (Baines and Benjamin, 2007; Dalrymple and Burke, 2006; Dominelli, 2003), social development (Midgley, 1995, 2014; Midgley and Conley, 2010; Pawar and Cox, 2010c) and international social work (Cox and Pawar, 2013; Healy, 2008; Healy and Link, 2012; Lyons et al., 2012). As these new strands can in practice be applied both within the casework-dominated practice and beyond it, by and large social work education and practice seem to be clinging to the case work/remedial practice model, wherein working with individuals is the primary focus. What does it take to change this situation?

Contemporary social work and the social work profession seem to be having an identity crisis due to several complex and competing forces such as the role of other professions, market and privatization, the reduction of the welfare state, fragmentation and the nature and scope of its own activities and historical legacies. There is really no consensus on the concept of social work. The meaning keeps changing and evolving (see Gibelman, 1999). For example, the current international definition of social work has been regularly deliberated on, and now a new definition has been proposed for consideration.

Current definition

The social work profession promotes social change, problem solving in human relationships and the empowerment and liberation of people to enhance well-being. Utilising theories of human behaviour and social systems, social work intervenes at the points where people interact with their environments. Principles of human rights and social justice are fundamental to social work

New and revised proposed definition

The social work profession facilitates social change and development, social cohesion and the empowerment and liberation of people. Principles of social justice, human rights, collective responsibility and respect for diversities are central to social work. Underpinned by theories of social work, social sciences, humanities and indigenous knowledge, social work engages people and structures to address life challenges and enhance well-being.

The inclusion of many new elements in the definition, such as social development, indigenous knowledge and collective responsibility, seems to be in response to the critique of the earlier definition that it appeared to be individualistic and Eurocentric. Since 2010, leading professional social work organizations such as IFSW, IASSW and ICSW have come together and set a global agenda for social work for the future. Social development has now come into their vocabulary and it is part of the future agenda of these organizations and of the social work profession. Though these organizations do not clarify the concept of social development, the one proposed in the first and second chapter of this book may be readily employed. These organizations' global agenda for social work and social development includes addressing:

- social and economic inequalities within countries and between regions,
- dignity and worth of the person,

- environmental sustainability and
- importance of human relationships.

In the later discussion they have identified shared commitments and a renewed determination to promote social work and social justice. The representatives agreed that

- the full range of human rights are available to only a minority of the world's population;
- unjust and poorly regulated economic systems, driven by unaccountable market forces, together with non-compliance with international standards for labour conditions and a lack of corporate social responsibility, have damaged the health and well-being of peoples and communities, causing poverty and growing inequality;
- cultural diversity and the right to self-expression facilitate a more satisfactory intellectual, emotional, moral and spiritual existence, but these rights are in danger owing to aspects of globalization which standardize and marginalize peoples, with especially damaging consequences for indigenous and first nation peoples;
- people live in communities and thrive in the context of supportive relationships, which are being eroded by dominant economic, political and social forces;
- people's health and well-being suffer as a result of inequalities and unsustainable environments related to climate change, pollutants, war, natural disasters and violence to which there are inadequate international responses (Jones and Truell, 2012).

Their conference in 2012 focused on the action around, and the impact of, social work and social development agenda, and the conference in 2014 focused on social work, education and social development. These developments initiated by professional bodies seem to suggest that the future of social work lies in social development. Now, it is important to see how such a global social work and social development agenda are appropriate to contemporary Indian realities.

The General Indian Context

The aforementioned four global agenda items and the five shared commitments are relevant to the social, cultural, economic and political contexts in India. Politically, India is the largest democracy in the world and has stable and robust democratic structures. Its legislature, executive and judiciary are well established and have been working well for nearly three quarters of a century and have contributed to many specific reforms and overall development of the country, though they may need to improve their functioning to address some existing and emerging challenges. India has a well-developed constitution that includes directive principles of state policy, which guarantees fundamental rights to the people (see Chapter 5) and provides legitimate avenues for people's participation through 'gram panchayat' and 'gram shabha' in local-level communities. In the world of shrinking welfare, it has followed rights-based approaches to employment, health and education (Pawar, 2012; for example, the National Rural Employment Guarantee Act 2005 [NREGA] and the Unorganised Sector Workers' Social Security Act, 2008 [USWSSA]).

As stated earlier, the Indian economy is growing fast, and it is expected to remain doing so in the foreseeable future, despite temporary fluctuations in its growth rates. It has opened its market and is following economic liberalization policies. It has attained the growth rate of 9 per cent, and it has been estimated that the growth rate will hold at around that mark (7–9 per cent, World Bank, 2013). Its economy is the 9th largest in the world, and it is the 19th largest exporter and the 10th largest importer. Of the total nearly 500 million labour force, 53 per cent are engaged in agriculture, 28 per cent in services and 18 per cent in industry. However, only 17 per cent of GDP comes from agriculture, 18 per cent from industry and 65 per cent from services. Its unemployment rate is about 10 per cent (Index Mundi, 2013). Overall, India is an emerging power in the world (Cohen, 2001). Despite such economic achievements and its emerging power status, India faces several challenges from the social development perspective. Some of the important challenges that prevail in the current Indian context are summarized hereunder.

Undoubtedly, India is creating more wealth and income, and certainly its economic power is growing. Its greatest challenge is how it is going to distribute this wealth and income in such a way that it will create a less unequal society. Growing social and economic inequality is a fact in the Indian economy and society. Contributing to addressing inequality is one aspect of the global agenda of social work. About 30 per cent of the Indian population or 400 million people are below the poverty line, which is one of the biggest concentrations of poor people in the world. How the new economic riches can be used to lift these people out of poverty in a relatively short time is a difficult but extremely urgent challenge. Allowing poverty to continue to exist is causing other forms of violence and abuse and the violation of human rights.

Closely connected to poverty is the unemployment issue. Due to various social, economic and technological factors, the Indian occupational structure is changing. People are often pushed to move out from the agriculture sector with no recourse to any other employment opportunities. As generations of family members come and go, land holdings decrease to the extent that even the subsistence economy is no longer possible. By developing appropriate knowledge and skills the surplus labour available needs to be employed in the industry, service or knowledge sectors, which in turn need to be open to them. The unemployment issue is complicated by India having the highest number of youth population in the world, which is generally referred as Indian demographic divided or youngest India. It is estimated that a fifth of the world's working-age population will be in India. As a workforce it is a great asset and presents enormous economic opportunities; however, it is also a challenge to channel this workforce appropriately into further development of communities, the country and individuals. An article published by *India Knowledge* (2013) stated the following:

India will be one of the few countries in the world with a working age population that exceeds its number of retirees. 'By 2020, the average Indian will be only 29 years of age, compared with 37 in China and the U.S., 45 in Western Europe, and 48 in Japan,' Ramadorai pointed out. That means India will experience an age advantage for at least three decades, through 2040. 'So this is where I see an unprecedented opportunity,' he added. The future is bright 'if Indians skill themselves to suit the future demand for jobs both domestic and abroad'.

The Indian Twelfth Five Year Plan is aware of this demographic dividend and aims to create 100 million work opportunities by 2022— many in labour-intensive manufacturing sectors such as textiles, gems and footwear.

These economic and employment-related factors are predicted to result in massive rural to urban migration and increasing urbanization. As per the 2011 census, about 31 per cent of the population lived in urban areas, and by 2021 this is expected to increase to about 40 per cent (Ministry of Urban Unemployment and Poverty Alleviation and Ministry of Urban Development, Government of India, 2005). This means that about three-fifths of the Indian population will be based in rural areas, and those who migrate to cities will give rise to a different set of problems relating to the inadequacy of the urban infrastructure and individual and family settlement in substandard conditions (slum areas) and with limited support systems.

Associated with economic growth, industrialization and development and urbanization is the issue of global warming and climate change. With a growing middle class, India's material consumption has changed and increased, and this trend will create increasing pressure on production systems that require energy and water and that cause depletion and pollution of natural resources, resulting in damages such as deforestation and pollution of water and air. Such activities may also lead to natural disasters, displacement of people and changes in food production patterns. Climate change mitigation and adaptation and focus on green economy are important challenges and opportunities in the coming years.

The revolution in information and communication technology, its adaptation in both urban and rural areas and its influences on, and consequences for, social and cultural aspects of life could pose important behavioural problems that have implications for coping with intergenerational gaps and human relationship issues. Making these technologies affordable and accessible and bearing the consequences of the use of them will pose both material and human issues within families. For example, the de-traditionalization of roles, emerging gender issues, child-raising practices, increasing expectations of material fulfilment and handling the stresses of modern life all call for a focus on human behaviour and relationships and on culture and spirituality generally.

As pointed out earlier, recent reports have indicated that about 1 to 2 per cent of the population have severe mental health issues and about 5 per cent of the population have general mental health issues. This constitutes millions of people needing appropriate medical, social and emotional support. Similarly, there are millions of disabled people in India. Planning appropriate and adequate services and delivering the same for such groups of people, and, from the prevention point of view, building supportive communities are going to be among India's major challenges.

Coping with such socio-economic changes and their consequences calls for important measures. A public distribution system appears to be one such measure. The distribution of low-priced wheat or rice to people who need it is perceived in some quarters somewhat negatively, stating that it will lead to dependency, laziness and some people's unwillingness to work. Real or unreal, such perceptions need to be corrected by demonstrating that such programmes will not necessarily lead to dependency but could, instead, result in a better work culture. India has a rich culture of volunteerism. Within this cultural orientation, there is a value of working without expecting rewards/fruits—work is worship and work is divine. This cultural attitude or wisdom has to be used in cultivating a work culture.

Despite positive affirmation, reservations and other policies, there are significant structural barriers to opportunity distribution in India. Although opportunities are theoretically available to everyone, in practice not everyone is able to access them. An article published in the *Economist* (Banyan, 2013) magazine argued,

> that social mobility of all sorts has been slow in India, mostly because it has remained poor and predominantly rural for so long due to decades of wrongheaded economic policies. For a Dalits peasant or labourer the reservation policy is unlikely to make much difference; getting a job in a factory or a call centre would transform her/his life.

By looking at the reservations arrangements in the political system, Chin and Prakash (2011) have concluded that, for 'scheduled tribes' who are conveniently crowded near one another on electoral maps, greater political clout has indeed led to a small drop in poverty. However, for the 'scheduled castes', by contrast, it has made absolutely no difference at all. Thus, structural barriers to opportunity distribution and opportunity utilization must be addressed. The third volume of the Twelfth Five Year Plan (2012–2017) is especially devoted to the social sectors, which include health, education, employment and skill development, women's agency, child rights and social inclusion. The social inclusion sector covers scheduled castes, scheduled tribes, other backward classes, minorities and other marginalized and vulnerable groups such as persons with disabilities, senior citizens, street children, beggars and victims of substance abuse. The capacities of these groups in terms of Sen's (2001) freedoms need to be developed so that they can make use of the opportunities created by the overall development process.

As many as 11 Five Year Plans, that is, 55 years of planning and development flowing from top to the bottom or central to the local level, have not developed local-level communities or villages to the extent they should have. What is needed is social and community development at the local level so that these people can share in the benefits of central-level plans and programmes.

Social and Community Development—The Future of Social Work

The aforementioned and summarized Indian development context in general, both in terms of opportunities and challenges, shows how important it is to focus on social and community development at the local level from the perspectives presented in Chapters 1 and 2. Particularly in Chapter 2, I have presented the rationale and justification for focusing on social and community development at the local level. Fifty-five years of Indian development plans and history, though well intended, have shown that its percolation down to the local level is meagre. The majority of villages have been neglected, poverty and deprivation levels are high and unless we prepare the people in these villages by developing their capacities or freedoms (Sen, 2001), they will not be able to benefit from the above-presented developmental context and this will contribute to further inequality. Thus, it is crucial to focus on comprehensive development within local-level communities and not just on economic or political development.

It is also important to reflect on the Indian historical context, its rich cultural and spiritual traditions including volunteerism, working without expecting rewards, selfless sacrifice, significant social reforms against the caste system and certain other social evils, and to liberate men and women through education and other means, and also on the haunting colonization and decolonization experience. Similarly, it is important to reflect on developments in the West and in what context professional social work emerged in and was introduced throughout the West, and in what context, and how it was introduced to India. After doing so, it is hardly surprising to find that social work has not addressed the local-level community issues in India, or for that matter, the aboriginal context in Australia and similar situations in many other countries. Nobody, neither professional bodies nor individuals, can be blamed or held responsible for such a situation. The historical evolution of social work shows that social work was born to respond mainly to the ills of industrialization in urban centres resulting from peoples' migration from rural to urban areas, the breakdown of family ties, alienation, homelessness, settlements without services and, added to these, the mass consequences of the two World Wars. It was largely to help such groups in urban areas that, over the years, social work knowledge and skills have been developed. It is then important to critically examine to what extent this knowledge and skill is useful in the social development of local rural communities and what new knowledge is required for this task.

To realize the agenda of social work and social development within local-level communities, new and innovative approaches are needed, not only in practice but also in recruiting students, in training and preparing them for practice, in developing a value and virtue orientation, and in curriculum development and training levels (certificate, diploma and degree levels). For example, the way we initially orient and introduce new social work students to the social work field is very important. How do we socialize students in social work? Is it with class rooms, smart boards and other such technologies? Initially, if you take new students to orphanages, children's institutions, institutions for the disabled children or to slum areas, their understanding of social work and what needs to be done is perhaps entirely different from what it is if they are introduced to villages, 'gram panchayats', 'gram sabhas' and a range of developmental issues in villages. Taking students to communities and letting them experience them and exposing them to good community workers and their work might help develop better virtues in the next generation of social workers. The expansion of social work education and knowledge to villages in rural areas and a beginning orientation of those areas should be a major focus of social work now and into the future.

The social development approach presented in Chapter 1 and expanded in Chapter 2 provides a practical framework for social work in this area, with suggested goals, values, processes and strategies to focus on cultural, political, economic, ecological, education, health, housing, equity groups' and citizens' and their institutions' development in local-level communities or villages. As alluded to earlier, to what extent existing social work knowledge can be used, to what extent it can be revised and adapted and to what extent new knowledge can be drawn from people and communities and other relevant disciplines need to be examined.

Creative and new thinking, new learning and new approaches are certainly needed. Future communities will be very dynamic and I think different as information and communication technology and relative easy access to transport will play an important role in that dynamism. Even if nearly half the population migrate to urban areas they are likely to keep close links with rural areas or their communities. Urban–rural cultural influences and Western cultural influences through information and communication technology on rural areas cannot be denied. Many modern and technological developments need to be used to enhance the quality of life in local-level communities. It is practical to imagine the future where every home will generate its own solar electricity wherever this is possible. The ecological values practised by farmers need to be learned. How everything is recycled and reused in farming families would be an eye opener for many. Moreover, one has to be careful in introducing ecologically unfriendly ideas, or materials such as plastic products, in villages.

The importance of human relationship should not only include relationship with self and others but also the relationship with nature and ecology. How do we relate to nature and the geography surrounding us? Throwing rubbish and spitting on roads, puffing tobacco smoke into the atmosphere, defecating in public open places and polluting land and water and blocking rivers by building big dams all show how people are relating to nature, and it is necessary to raise awareness about how they could or should relate to nature in sustainable ways. Creating cooperative, conserving, tolerant and sharing communities is important as many resources available are limited or are at least portrayed as limited. In the longer run, such communities are likely to be a good weapon against the negative forces of the market, liberalization and globalization.

A clear shift from remedial to developmental social work is needed. Once India was a leader in community development, and its idea of community development spread from here to many countries. In the 21st Asian century, it has another opportunity to lead the world by showing how social and community development can be reactivated and how other communities and countries may adopt these ideas, with local contextualization of course, if they are found relevant and useful. Social workers are not alone in such an endeavour, and they need to bring in many other professionals and work with them to build communities. Attracting talented people and preparing them to be committed professionals with the virtues that will facilitate social and community development at local levels is an important challenge.

Conclusion

This book is about thinking, reflection and action around social and community development practice. It argues that social work needs to expand its nature and scope to refocus from remedial case work practice to social and community development practice if it is to address major issues such as the poverty and growing inequality that are confronting India and the South Asian region, particularly at local levels. In some respects, medical- or remedial-oriented work with individuals or case work practice does not include the local community level, but community practice does include work with individuals from a developmental perspective. The social and community development approach discussed in this book is not a romanticized concept; it is a real and practical approach in theory, and we need to make it so in practice within the Indian and South Asian context, and beyond.

The brief history of professional social work began through voluntary efforts, charity and religious institutions. For heuristic purposes, the 125 years of professional social work history (if we include the pre-professional training period) has been discussed in terms of the following: origin of professional social work and pre-origin activities and influences; the beginning of social work training in voluntary agencies, hospitals and universities; the development of a knowledge base around case work; the medical model or remedial social work; the spread of professional social work to developing countries and colonies; the questioning of the dominance of the medical or remedial model; and seeing the relevance of social and community development that is developmental social work, within which several other approaches such as critical/radical, reflective, empowerment/ strengths based and ecological may be considered. Further discussion shows how the global social work and social development agenda is relevant to the Indian social, economic and political context. It is an agenda that presents many challenges and opportunities, and the social work profession and social work educators need to reorganize themselves to focus on social and community development practice at local levels or villages and to further social development in all its dimensions.

Such a focus is needed because the legacy of colonization and the neo-colonization that is occurring through economic and political factors, information and communication technology revolution and globalization will impact life in local communities, particularly social, cultural and spiritual aspects. On reflection, these factors have certainly impacted me, and I am perhaps slowly losing my native culture. This reminds me of a Kannada popular film song that I used to sing as a young boy, the first line of which runs like this: 'Huttida ooranu bittu hodare kattuvarari nammura?' Its nearly equivalent English translation is, 'If birth village is left and disserted, who will build our village?' In today's rapidly globalizing world, many people are migrating internally and internationally to such an extent that some places are now called ghost villages/towns. I hope such a thing will not occur in Indian villages. While some people are leaving their villages for whatever reason, technological innovation and growing access to transport and communication are at the same time helping people to come closer together. Such a trend can be advantageously used to mobilize the resources needed to build local-level communities, irrespective of their location. On the other hand, the same technology and communication changes play an instrumental role in introducing the forces of market, liberalization and globalization, and I hope these forces do not crack the cultural and spiritual foundation of local-level communities. The suggested social and community development approach is expected to help strengthen the cultural and spiritual dimension of communities while achieving all the other dimensions of community development.

In concluding this book, I recall the late Professor M.S. Gore's words in his history and philosophy of social work class in which I was a first-year student: "Social work makes you a better human being" and "social work is not a readymade meal; you need to make it what you want." More than three decades have passed since I heard those words, and I find myself pondering: Have I become a better human being? Have I made what I want from social work? These questions may be reversed from a self-focus to an 'other' focus as: Does social work, meaning social workers, contribute to making better communities and better human beings? Do social work and social workers enable and empower communities to realize what they want? These are apt questions for present and future social work.

Acknowledgements

I thank the publishers of the following copyright material, written by me, for granting the permission to adopt and adapt them in this book:

1. Pawar, M. and Cox, D. (2010). Social Development. In M. Pawar and D. Cox (eds), *Social Development: Critical Themes and Perspectives*. New York: Routledge.
2. Pawar, M. and Cox, D. (2010). Local Level Social Development. In M. Pawar and D. Cox (eds), *Social Development: Critical Themes and Perspectives*. New York: Routledge.
3. Chapter 4, 'Values and Principles for Community Development', and Chapter 5, 'Practice Dimensions and Dynamics of Community Development', from Pawar, M. (2010). *Community Development in Asia and the Pacific*. New York: Routledge.
4. Pawar, M. (2004). Social Policy Curricula for Training Social Workers: Towards a Model. *Australian Social Work*, 57(1), 3–18 (journal website: www.tandfonline.com).
5. Pawar, M. (2010). Looking Outwards: Challenges for Teaching International Social Work in Asia. *International Journal of Social Work Education*, 29(8), 896–909 (journal website: www.tandfonline.com).
6. Pawar, M. (1999). Professional Social Work in India: Some Issues and Strategies. *Indian Journal of Social Work*, 60(4), 566–586.
7. Pawar, M. (2000). Social Work Education through Distance Mode in India: A Proposal. *The Indian Journal of Social Work*, 61(2), 196–211.
8. Pawar, M. (2000). Australian and Indian Social Work Codes of Ethics. *Australian Journal of Professional and Applied Ethics*, 2(2), 72–85.

Bibliography

AASW (Australian Association of Social Workers). (2000). *Policy and Procedures for Establishing Eligibility for Membership of AASW*. Canberra, Australia: AASW.

———. (2010). *Code of Ethics*. Canberra, Australia: AASW.

ADB (Asian Development Bank). (1990). *Distance Education*. Manila, Philippines: ADB.

———. (2008). *Food Prices and Inflation: Is Poverty Reduction Coming to an End?* Manila, Philippines: ADB.

Ahmadi, N. (2003). Globalisation of Consciousness and New Challenges for International Social Work. *International Journal of Social Welfare*, 12(1), 14–23.

Allan, J., Briskman, L. and Pease, B. (2009). *Critical Social Work: Theories and Practices for a Socially Just World*. Sydney, Australia: Allen & Unwin.

Alphonse, M. and Adsule, J. (2007). Book Review—International Social Work: Issues Strategies and Programs. *Perspective in Social Work*, 22(2), 36–38.

Alphonse, M., Purnima, G. and Moffatt, K. (2008). Redefining Social Work Standards in the Context of Globalisation: Lessons from India. *International Social Work*, 51(2), 145–158.

Andharia, J. (2007). Reconceptualizing Community Organization in India: A Transdisciplinary Perspective. *Journal of Community Practice*, 15(1/2), 91–119.

Andreas, F.A. and Vadlamannati, K.C. (2012). *The Needy Donor: An Empirical Analysis of India's Aid Motives*. Retrieved 5 June 2013 from http://www.uni-heidelberg.de/md/awi/professuren/intwipol/needy2.pdf

Argyrous, G. and Stilwell, F. (eds). (1996). *Economics as Social Science*. Sydney, Australia: Pluto Press.

Aristotle. (1976). *Nicomachean Ethics*. Harmondsworth, UK: Penguin.

Artner, A. (2004). Anti-globalization Movements: The Developments in Asia. *Contemporary Politics*, 10(3–4), 243–255.

Australian Institute of Health and Welfare. (1997). *Australian Welfare Services*. Canberra, Australia: Australian Institute of Health and Welfare.

Ayyar, R.V.V. (2010). *India: An Emerging Donor?* Retrieved 5 June 2013 from http://www.norrag.org/fr/publications/norrag-news/online-version/a-brave-new-world-of-emerging-non-dac-donors-and-their-differences-from-traditional-donors/detail/india-an-emerging-donor.html

Baines, D. and Benjamin, A. (2007). *Doing Anti-Oppressive Practice: Building Transformative, Politicized Social Work.* Winnipeg, Manitoba, Canada: Fernwood Publishing.

Baird, B.N. (1999). *The Internship, Practicum, and Field Placement Handbook: A Guide for the Helping Professionals* (2nd ed.). Upper Saddle River, NJ: Prentice-Hall.

Banks, S. (1998). Professional Ethics in Social Work—What Future? *British Journal of Social Work*, 28, 213–231.

Banks, S. (2006). *Ethics and Values in Social Work* (3rd ed.). Basingstoke, UK: Palgrave Macmillan.

BBC. (2013). *Ethics Guide: Ethics: A General Introduction.* Retrieved 20 June 2013 from http://www.bbc.co.uk/ethics/introduction/intro_1.shtml

Beecher, B., Reeves, J., Eggertsen, L. and Furuto, S. (2010). International Students' Views about Transferability in Social Work Education and Practice. *International Social Work*, 53(2), 203–216.

Banerjiv, O. (2012). *India's Trajectory from Aid Recipient to Donor Nation.* Retrieved 5 June 2013 from http://blogs.lse.ac.uk/indiaatlse/2012/12/07/indias-trajectory-from-aid-recipient-to-donor-nation/

Banyan. (2013). *Affirmative Action: Indian Reservations.* Retrieved 3 July 2013 from http://www.economist.com/blogs/banyan/2013/06/affirmative-action?zid=306&ah=1b164dbd43b0cb27ba0d4c3b12a5e227

Barefoot College. (2009). *Barefoot College.* Retrieved 9 March 2009 from http://www.barefootcollege.org/

Barker, R.L. (1999). *The Social Work Dictionary.* Washington, DC: National Association of Social Workers.

———. (2003). *The Social Work Dictionary* (4th ed.). Washington, DC: National Association of Social Workers.

Beilharz, P., Considine, M. and Watta, R. (1992). *Arguing about the Welfare State: The Australian Experience.* Sydney, Australia: Allen & Unwin.

Beresford, P. and Croft, S. (2000). User Participation. In M. Davies and R. Barton (eds), *The Blackwell Encyclopaedia of Social Work.* Oxford, UK: Blackwell.

Berlin, I. (2003). *The Crooked Timber of Humanity: Chapters in the History of Ideas.* London: Pimlico.

Berner, E. and Phillips, B. (2005). Left to Their Own Device? Community Self-Help between Alternative Development and Neo-Liberalism. *Community Development Journal*, 40(1), 17–29.

Billups, J. (1994). The Social Development Model as an Organising Framework for Social Work Practice. In R.G. Meinert, T. Pardeck and P. Sullivan (eds),

Issues in Social Work: A Critical Analysis (pp. 21–37). Westport, CT: Auburn House.

Bodhi, S.R. (2011). Professional Social Work Education in India. *Indian Journal of Social Work*, 72(2), 289–300.

Bond, G.D. (2004). *Buddhism at Work: Community Development, Social Environment and the Sarvodaya Movement*. West Hartford, CT: Kumarian Press.

Bose, A.B. (1987). Development of Social Welfare Services. In *Encyclopedia of Social Work*. New Delhi, India: Ministry of Social Welfare, Government of India.

Bowles, W., Collingridge, M., Curry, S. and Valentine, B. (2006). *Ethical Practice in Social Work: An Applied Approach*. Crows Nest, Sydney: Allen and Unwin.

Brigham, T.M. (1982). Social Work Education Patterns in Five Developing Countries: Relevance of US Microsystems Model. *Journal of Education for Social Work*, 18(2), 68–75.

Brokensha, D. and Hodge, P. (1969). *Community Development: An Interpretation*. Los Angeles, CA: Chandler Publishing.

Bryson, L. (1992). *Welfare and the State: Who Benefits?* Basingstoke, UK: Macmillan.

Burns, R. (2002). *The Adult Learner at Work*. Sydney, Australia: Business and Professional Publishing.

Bush, R.A. and Williams, C.J. (1989). *Distance Education: An Option for Social Welfare and Social Work Education in the 1990s* (Occasional Papers, No. 8). Wagga Wagga, Australia: Charles Sturt University.

Canda, E.R. (2001). Buddhism. In M. Van Hook, B. Hugen and M. Aguilar (eds), *Spirituality within Religious Traditions in Social Work Practice*. Pacific Grove, CA: Brooks/Cole.

Canda, E.R. and Furman, L.D. (2010). *Spiritual Diversity in Social Work Practice: The Heart of Helping*. New York: Free Press.

CESCR (Committee of Economic, Social and Cultural Rights). (1998). *The Domestic Application of the Covenant: CESR General Comment No. 9*. Geneva, Switzerland: CESR.

Clements, E. (2004). The Limits of Self-Determination. *Convergence*, 37(2), 65–77.

Chanana, D. (2010). *India's Transition to Global Donor: Limitations and Prospects*. Retrieved 5 June 2013 from http://www.realinstitutoelcano.org/wps/portal/rielcano_eng/Content?WCM_GLOBAL_CONTEXT=/elcano/elcano_in/zonas_in/ari123-2010

Chin, A. and Prakash, N. (2011). The Redistributive Effects of Political Reservation for Minorities: Evidence from India. *Journal of Development Economics*, 96(2), 265–277.

Chui, E., Tsang, S. and Mok, J. (2010). After the Handover in 1997: Development and Challenges for Social Welfare and Social Work in Hong Kong. *Asia Pacific Journal of Social Work and Development*, 20(1), 52–64.

Clark, C. (2006). Moral Character in Social Work. *British Journal of Social Work*, 36, 75–89.

Clarke, M. and Stewart, J. (1998). *Community Governance. Community Leadership and the New Local Government*. York, UK: Joseph Rowntree Foundation.

Coady, N.F. and Wolgien, C.S. (1996). Good Therapists' Views of How They Are Helpful. *Clinical Social Work Journal*, 24(3), 311–322.

Cohen, S.P. (2001). *India: Emerging Power*. Washington, DC: The Brooking Institution.

Compton, B.R. and Galaway, B. (1999). *Social Work Processes*. Pacific Grove, CA: Brooks/Cole.

Cornwall, A. (2008). Unpacking 'Participation': Models, Meanings and Practices. *Community Development Journal*, 43(3), 269–283.

Cox, D. (1994). The Role of Social Work in Bettering the Human Condition. *The Indian Journal of Social Work*, 55(3), 311–325.

———. (1995). Future Directions for Social Work and Social Work Education. In *Social Work Profession: Reflection and Future Directions, Twenty Years Celebration Conference* (17–20 November 1993). Asian and Pacific Association of Social Work Education and Tata Institute of Social Sciences, Mumbai, India.

Cox, D.R. (2006). Building Resilient Families and Caring Communities in a Troubled World: The Importance of Strengthening Social Capital. In J. Ariffin (ed.), *Facing up to Global Challenges, Proceedings of APFAM International Conference* (pp. 9–23). Kuala Lumpur, Malaysia.

Cox, D.A. and Britto, G.A. (1986). *Social Work Curriculum Development in Asia and the Pacific: A Research Report*. Melbourne, Australia: Department of Social Work, University of Melbourne.

Cox, D. and Pawar, M. (2006). *International Social Work: Issues, Strategies and Programs*. Thousand Oaks, CA: SAGE Publications.

———. (2013). *International Social Work: Issues, Strategies and Programs* (2nd ed.). Thousand Oaks, CA: SAGE Publications.

Cox, D., Gamlath, S. and Pawar, M. (1997a). Social Work and Poverty Alleviation in South Asia. *Asia Pacific Journal of Social Work*, 7(2), 15–31.

Cox, D., Pawar, M. and Picton, C. (1997b). *Introducing a Social Development Perspective into Social Work Curricula at All Levels*. Melbourne, Australia: RSDC, La Trobe University.

———. (1997c). *Social Development Content in Social Work Education*. Melbourne, Australia: RSDC, La Trobe University.

Crawford, C.S. (2003). *Hindu Bioethics for the Twenty-First Century*. New York: SUNY Press.

Crigger, N. and Godfrey, N. (2011). *The Making of Nurse Professionals: A Transformational Ethical Approach*. Sudbury, MA: Jones and Bartlett Learning.

Cuyvers, L. (2001). *Globalisation and Social Development: European and Southeast Asian Evidence*. Cheltenham, UK: Edward Elgar.

Dalrymple, J. and Burke, B. (2006). *Anti-oppressive Practice: Social Care and the Law*. Berkshire, UK: Open University Press.

Dalton, T., Draper, M., Weeks, W. and Wiseman, J. (1996). *Making Social Policy in Australia: An Introduction*. Sydney, Australia: Allen & Unwin.

Davis, G. (2004). *A History of the Social Development Network in the World Bank, 1973–2002*. Retrieved 6 June 2008 from http://siteresources. worldbank.org/EXTSOCIALDEVELOPMENT/Resources/244362-1164107274725/3182370-1164201144397/SocialDevelopment-History. pdf?resourceurlname=SocialDevelopment-History.pdf

De Kadt, E. (1982). Community Participation for Health: The Case of Latin America. *World Development*, 10, 573–584.

Deacon, B. (1997). *Global Social Policy: International Organizations and the Future of Welfare*. London: SAGE Publications.

Deacon, B. (2007). *Global Social Policy and Governance*. London: SAGE Publications.

Dean, H. (2010). The Ethics of Social Development. In M. Pawar and D. Cox (eds), *Social Development: Critical Themes and Perspectives*. New York: Routledge.

———. (2012). *Social Policy: Short Introductions*. Cambridge, UK: Polity Press.

Deci, E. and Ryan, R. (eds). (2002). *Handbook of Self-Determination Research*. Rochester, NY: University of Rochester Press.

Deci, E. and Ryan, R. (2008). Facilitating Optimal Motivation and Psychological Well-Being across Life's Domains. *Canadian Psychology*, 49, 14–23.

Department of Social Policy, London School of Economics. (2012). *What Is Social Policy?* Retrieved 1 June 2012 from http://www2.lse.ac.uk/ socialPolicy/aboutUs/introduction.aspx

Desai, A.S. (1987). Development of Social Work Education. In *Encyclopedia of Social Work*. New Delhi, India: Ministry of Social Welfare, Government of India.

———. (1994). *A Study of Social Work Education in India: Student, Educator and the Educational Process*. Mumbai, India: Tata Institute of Social Sciences.

Desai, M. (1991). Issues Concerning the Setting Up of Social Work Specialisations in India. *International Social Work*, 34, 83–95.

———. (1997). Literature on Social Work Profession in India, 1936–1996: An Overview. *The Indian Journal of Social Work*, 58(2), 149–160.

Desai, M., Monteiro, A. and Narayan, L. (1998). *Towards People-Centred Development* (Parts 1 and 2). Mumbai, India: Tata Institute of Social Sciences.

Dictionary.com (2007). *Development*. Retrieved 5 May 2008 from http://dictionary.reference.com/browse/development

Distance Education Council. (2011). *List of Universities/Institutions Approved by Distance Education Council (as on 16 August 2011)*. Retrieved 18 June 2013 from http://www.dec.ac.in/

Dominelli, L. (2002). *Feminist Social Work Theory and Practice*. Basingstoke, UK: Palgrave Macmillan.

———. (2003). *Anti-oppressive Social Work Theory and Practice*. Basingstoke, UK: Palgrave Macmillan.

Drucker, D. (1993). The Social Work Profession in Asia: Look Homeward 1968–1993. *Indian Journal of Social Work*, 54(4), 513–536.

Eade, D. (2007). Capacity Building: Who Builds Whose Capacity? *Development in Practice*, 17(4), 630–639.

Edwards, J.A. and Bess, J.M. (1998). Developing Effectiveness in the Therapeutic Use of Self. *Clinical Social Work Journal*, 26(1), 89–105.

Effrat, M.P. (1974). Approaches to Community: Conflicts and Complementarities. In M.P. Effrat (ed.), *The Community: Approaches and Applications* (pp. 1–32). New York: The Free Press.

Ejaz, F.K. (1991). Social Work Education in India: Perceptions of Social Workers in Bombay. *International Social Work*, 34, 299–311.

Elliott, C. (2000). Tuning and Practicing the Therapeutic Instrument: The Therapist's Life Experience. *Clinical Social Work Journal*, 28(3), 321–330.

ESCAP. (1996a). *Showing the Way: Methodologies for Successful Rural Poverty Alleviation Projects*. Bangkok, Thailand: ESCAP.

———. (1996b). *Making an Impact: Innovative HRD Approaches to Poverty Alleviation*. Bangkok, Thailand: ESCAP.

———. (2007). *Economic and Social Commission for Asia and the Pacific Map*. Retrieved 6 April 2009 from http://www.un.org/Depts/Cartographic/map/profile/escap.pdf

Eyben, R. (2003). Mainstreaming the Social Dimension into the Overseas Development Administration: A Partial History. *Journal of International Development*, 15, 879–892.

Farahani, M. F. (2012). Ethics Principles in Distance Education. *Procedia—Social and Behavioral Sciences*, 46, 890–894.

Farrar, A. and Inglis, J. (1996). *Keeping It Together: State and Civil Society in Australia*. Sydney, Australia: Pluto Press.

Fawcett, B., Goodwin, S., Meagher, G. and Phillips, R. (2010). *Social Policy for Social Change*. Melbourne, Australia: Macmillan.

Ferguson, I. (2008). *Reclaiming Social Work: Challenging Neoliberalism and Promoting Social Justice*. Thousand Oaks, CA: Sage.

Ferguson, I. and Woodward, R. (2009). *Radical Social Work in Practice: Making a Difference*. Bristol, UK: Policy Press.

Figueira-McDonough, J. (1993). Policy: The Neglected Side of Social Work Intervention. *Social Work*, 38(2), 179–188.

Fook, J. (1993). *Radical Casework: A Theory of Practice*. Sydney, Australia: Allen & Unwin.

———. (2012). *Social Work: A Critical Approach to Practice*. London: SAGE Publications.

Frankovits, A. and Patrick, E. (2000). *Working Together: The Human Rights Approach to Development Cooperation*. The Human Rights Council of Australia. Presented at the Stockholm Workshop, 16–19 October, in Stockholm, Sweden.

Freire, P. (1972). *Pedagogy of the Oppressed*. London: Sheed and Ward.

Furrow, D. (2005). *Ethics: Key Concepts in Philosophy*. New York: Continuum.

Gadamer, H.-G. (1981). *Reason in the Age of Science*. Boston, MA: MIT Press.

Gal, J. and Weiss-Gal, I. (2013). *Social Workers Affecting Social Policy: An International Perspective on Policy Practice*. Bristol: Policy Press.

Gambrill, E. and Pruger, R. (1992). *Controversial Issues in Social Work*. Boston, MA: Allyn & Bacon.

Gangrade, K.D. (1987). Development of Voluntary Action. In *Encyclopedia of Social Work*. New Delhi, India: Ministry of Social Welfare, Government of India.

Geach, P. (1977). *The Virtues*. Cambridge, UK: Cambridge University Press.

Ghai, Y. (2001). *Human Rights and Social Development: Toward Democratization and Social Justice*. Retrieved 18 February 2009 from http://www.unrisd.org/unrisd/website/document.nsf/(httpPublications)/ECD0417EB-1177C5280256B5E004BCAFA?

Gibelman, M. (1999). The Search for Identity: Defining Social Work—Past, Present, Future. *Social Work*, 44(4), 298–309.

Gilbert, T. (2009). Ethics in Social Work: A Comparison of the International Statement of Principles in Social Work with the Code of Ethics for British Social Workers. *The Journal of Social Work Values and Ethics*, 6(2).

Gilbert, N. and Terrell, P. (2012). *Dimensions of Social Welfare Policy*. Boston, MA: Allyn & Bacon.

Gilligan, C. (1982). *In a Different Voice: Psychological Theory and Women's Development*. Harvard, MA: Harvard University Press.

Girgis, M. (2007). The Capacity Building Paradox: Using Friendship to Build Capacity in South. *Development in Practice*, 13(3), 353–363.

Goldstein, E.G. (1994). Self-Disclosure in Treatment: What Therapists Do and Don't Talk About. *Clinical Social Work Journal*, 22(4), 417–433.

Gore, M. (1973). *Some Aspects of Social Development*. Hong Kong: Department of Social Work, University of Hong Kong.

———. (2003). *Social Development: Challenges Faced in an Unequal and Plural Society*. Jaipur, India: Rawat Publications.

Gore, M.S. (1988). Levels of Social Work Provisions in Relation to Needs in a Developing Society. *The Indian Journal of Social Work,* 49(1), 1–9.

———. (1997). A Historical Perspective of the Social Work Profession. *The Indian Journal of Social Work*, 58(3), 442–455.

Goswami, I. (2012). Adherence to Ethical Guidelines in Practice by Social Workers: An Empirical Study in India. *Practice: Social Work in Action*, 24(2), 105–121.

Government of India (GOI). (2013). *Economy Survey, Human Development, Chapter 13*. Retrieved 1 June 2013 from http://indiabudget.nic.in/es2012-13/echap-13.pdf

Gray, M. (2010). Moral Sources and Emergent Ethical Theories in Social Work. *British Journal of Social Work*, 40, 1794–1811.

Gray, M. and Lovat, T. (2007). Horse and Carriage: Why Habermas's Discourse Ethics Gives Virtue a Praxis in Social Work. *Ethics and Social Welfare*, 1(3), 310–328.

Graycar, A. and Jamrozic, A. (1993). *How Australian Live: Social Policy in Theory and Practice* (2nd ed.). Melbourne, Australia: Macmillan.

Guy, R. (1991). Distance Education and the Developing World: Colonisation, Collaboration and Control. In T. Evans and B. King (eds), *Beyond the Text: Contemporary Writing on Distance Education* (pp. 152–175). Geelong, Victoria, Australia: Deakin University Press.

Hammoud, H.R. (1988). Social Work Education in Developing Countries: Issues and Problems in Undergraduate Curricula. *International Social Work*, 31, 195–210.

Harman, G. (1999). Moral Philosophy Meets Social Psychology: Virtue Ethics and the Fundamental Attribution Error. *Proceedings of the Aristotelian Society*, 99(3), 315–331.

———. (2002). *No Character or Personality*. Retrieved 30 September 2012 from http://www.princeton.edu/~harman/Papers/Character.pdf

Harstell, B. (2006). A Model for Ethical Decision-Making: The Context for Ethics. *Journal of Social Work Values and Ethics*, 3(1). Accessed online at http://www.socialworker.com/jswe

Hazare, A. (2003). *My Village—My Sacred Land*. Ralegan Siddhi, Maharashtra, India: Ralegan Siddhi Pariwar.

Healy, L. (2001). *International Social Work: Professional Action in an Interdependent World*. New York: Oxford University Press.

———. (2008). *International Social Work: Professional Action in an Interdependent World* (2nd ed.). New York: Oxford University Press.

Healy, L.M. and Link, R.J. (eds). (2012). *Handbook of International Social Work: Human Rights, Development, and the Global Profession*. New York: Oxford University Press.

Hicks, J., Basu, P.K. and Sappy, D. (2010, May). Education and Potential for Growth in China and India. *Connections*, 21, 2.

Hillery, G.A. (1955, 20 June). Definitions of Community: Areas of Agreement. *Rural Sociology*, 20, 111–123.

Hoff, M.D. (ed.). (1998). *Sustainable Community Development: Studies in Economic, Environmental and Cultural Revitalization*. Boca Baton, FL: Lewis.

Hokenstad, M.C., Khinduka, S.K. and Midgley, J. (1992). The World of International Social Work. In M.C. Hokenstad, S.K. Khinduka and J. Midgley (eds), *Profiles in International Social Work* (pp. 1–11). Washington, DC: NASW Press.

Hokenstad, M.C. and Midgley, J. (2004). *Lessons from Abroad: Adapting International Social Welfare Innovations*. Washington, DC: NASW Press.

Hollister, D. (1982). The Knowledge and Skills Bases of Social Development. In D.S. Saunders (ed.), *The Developmental Perspective in Social Work* (pp. 31–42). Manoa, Hawaii: University of Hawaii Press.

Hollister, C.D. (1996). *Distance Education Technologies and Social Development*. A Paper Presented at the Ninth International Symposium on Social Development on 15–19 July 1996, Organised by the Inter-University Consortium for International Social Development, Oporto, Portugal.

Hollnsteiner, M.R. (1977). Community Participation in the Planning of Human Settlements. *Assignment Children*, 43, 11–47.

———. (1982). The Participatory Imperative in Primary Health Care. *Assignment Children*, 59/60, 35–56.

Hornby, A.S. (1993). *Oxford Advanced Learner's Dictionary*. Oxford, UK: Oxford University Press.

Houston, S. (2003). Establishing Virtue in Social Work: A Response to McBeath and Webb. *British Journal of Social Work*, 33, 819–824.

———. (2012). Engaging with the Crooked Timber of Humanity: Value Pluralism and Social Work. *British Journal of Social Work*, 42, 652–668.

HRCA (Human Rights Council of Australia). (2001). *Submission to the Joint Standing Committee of Foreign Affairs, Defence, and Trade Inquiry into the Link between Aid and Human Rights*. Retrieved 20 January 2009 from http://www.hrca.org.au/wp-content/uploads/2008/05/link-between-human-rights-and-aid-submission-to-parliament-2001.pdf

Hugman, R. (1998). *Social Welfare and Social Value: The Role of Changing Professions*. London: Macmillan.

———. (2005). *New Approaches in Ethics for Caring Professions*. Basingstoke, UK: Palgrave Macmillan.

———. (2010). *Understanding International Social Work: A Critical Analysis*. Basingstoke, UK: Palgrave Macmillan.

———. (2013). *Culture, Values and Ethics in Social Work: Embracing Diversity*. Oxon, UK: Routledge.

Hugman, R. and Smith, D. (1995). Ethical Issues in Social Work: An Overview. In R. Hugman and D. Smith (eds), *Ethical Issues in Social Work* (pp. 1–15). London: Routledge.

Hugo, G. (2005). The New International Migration in Asia: Challenges for Population Research. *Asian Population Studies*, 1(1), 93–120.

Hussein, M.K. (2006). Capacity Building Challenges in Malawi's Local Government Reform Program. *Development Southern Africa*, 23(3), 371–383.

Ife, J. (1997a). Australia. In N.S. Mayadas and T.D. Watts (eds), *International Handbook on Social Work Theory and Practice*. Westport, CT: Greenwood Press.

———. (1997b). *Rethinking Social Work: Towards Critical Practice*. Melbourne, Australia: Longman.

Ife, J. (2001). *Human Rights and Social Work: Towards Rights-Based Practice.* Melbourne, Australia: Cambridge University Press.

———. (2012). *Human Rights and Social Work: Towards Rights-Based Practice* (3rd ed.). Melbourne, Australia: Cambridge University Press.

———. (2013). *Community Development in an Uncertain World: Vision, Analysis and Practice.* Melbourne: Cambridge University Press.

Ife, J. and Fiske, L. (2006). Human Rights and Community Work. *International Social Work*, 49(3), 297–308.

IFSW (International Federation of Social Workers). (2013). *The Statement of Ethical Principles.* Retrieved 15 June 2013 from http://ifsw.org/policies/statement-of-ethical-principles/

Iiyoshi, T. and Vijay Kumar, M.S. (2008). Conclusion: New Pathways for Shaping the Collective Agenda to Open Up Education. In T. Iiyoshi and M.S. Vijay Kumar (eds), *Opening Up Education: The Collective Advancement of Education through Open Technology, Open Content, and Open Knowledge* (pp. 429–440). Cambridge, MA: MIT Press.

ILO (International Labour Organization). (2013). *Social Protection Floor.* Retrieved 16 May 2013 from http://www.ilo.org/secsoc/areas-of-work/policy-development-and-applied-research/social-protection-floor/lang-en/index.htm

Index Mundi. (2013). *Indian Economy Profile 2013.* Retrieved 3 July 2013 from http://www.indexmundi.com/india/economy_profile.html

India Knowledge. (2013). *India Demographic Dividend: Asset or Liability?* Retrieved 3 July 2013 from http://knowledge.wharton.upenn.edu/india/article.cfm?articleid=4717

Inglis, J. and Rogan, L. (1993). *Beyond Swings and Roundabouts—Shaping the Future of Community Services in Australia.* Sydney, Australia: Pluto Press.

IWGIA (International Working Group on Indigenous Affairs). (2009). *What Is Self-Determination?* Retrieved 23 February 2009 from http://www.iwgia.org/sw228.asp

Jacobsen, D.A., Eggen, P. and Kauchak, D. (1999). *Methods for Teaching: Promoting Student Learning.* Upper Saddle River, NJ: Merrill/Prentice-Hall.

Jaensch, D. (1992). *The Politics of Australia.* Melbourne, Australia: Macmillan.

Jennings, J., Siegel, E. and Conklin, J.J. (1994). Social Work Education and Distance Learning: Applications for Continuing Education. *Journal of Continuing Social Work Education*, 6(2), 3–7.

Johnson, H.W. (1996). International Activity in Undergraduate Social Work Education in the United States. *International Social Work,* 39(2), 189–199.

Jones, M. (1996). *The Australian Welfare State: Evaluating Social Policy* (4th ed.). Sydney, Australia: Allen & Unwin.

Jones, J.F. and Pandey, R.S. (eds). (1981). *Social Development: Conceptual, Methodological and Policy Issues.* Delhi, India: Macmillan.

Jones, D.N. and Truell, R. (2012). The Global Agenda for Social Work and Social Development: A Place to Link Together and Be Effective in a Globalized World. *International Social Work*, 55(4), 454–472.

Joyce, P. and Woods, A. (1997). *Essential Strategic Management: From Modernism to Pragmatism*. Oxford, UK: Butterworth Heinemann.

Kailash, K.K. (2013). Sub-national Comparative Social Policy: A Review of the Literature on India. *Comparative State Politics and Public Policy (CSPPP) Working Paper 2, February 2013*. Retrieved 31 May 2013 from http://www.cspppindia.org/docs/9005comparative-subnational-social-policy-india-review.pdf

Kannan, K.P. and Breman, J. (eds). (2013). *The Long Road to Social Security: Assessing the Implementation of National Social Security Initiatives for the Working Poor in India*. New Delhi, India: Oxford University Press.

Kant, I. (1964). *The Groundwork of the Metaphysics of Morals*. New York: Harper and Row.

Kar, K. (2005). *Practical Guide to Triggering Community-Led Total Sanitation*. Retrieved 28 June 2007 from http://www.ids.ac.uk/ids/bookshop/wp/Wp257%20pg.pdf

Karger, H.J. (1994). Toward Redefining Social Development in the Global Economy: Free Markets, Privatization, and the Development. *Social Development Issues*, 16(3), 32–44.

Kauchak, D. and Eggen, P. (1998). *Learning and Teaching: Research-Based Methods*. Boston, MA: Allyn & Bacon.

Kaye, A.R. (1985). Distance Education. In T. Husen and T. Neville Postlethwaite (eds), *The International Encyclopedia of Education: Research and Studies* (Vol. 3, pp. 1432–1438). Oxford, UK: Pergamon Press.

Kenny, S. (2007). *Developing Communities for the Future* (3rd ed.). Melbourne, Australia: Thomson.

Keown, D. (2001). *The Nature of Buddhist Ethics*. New York: Palgrave Macmillan.

Knitter, P.F. (2010). Social Work and Religious Diversity: Problems and Possibilities. *Journal of Religion and Spirituality in Social Work: Social Thought*, 29(3), 256–270.

Knott, C. and Scragg, T. (2013). *Reflective Practice in Social Work* (3rd ed.). London: SAGE Publications.

Korten, D.C. (1980, September–October). Community Organisation and Rural Development: A Learning Process Approach. *Public Administration Review*, pp. 480–511.

———. (1995). *When Corporations Rule the World*. London: Earthscan.

Kwok, J. (2008). Regional Perspectives from Asia: Social Work and Social Development in Asia. *International Social Work*, 51(5), 699–704.

Laksmono, B.S., Pattiasina, C., Sirojudin, A. and Osburn, L. (2008). Policy and Historical Context of Disaster Relief in Aceh: Relevant Factors in Social Work Assessment. *Asia Pacific Journal of Social Work and Development*, 18(2), 6–18.

Lavalette, M. and Pratt, A. (eds). (1997). *Social Policy: A Conceptual and Theoretical Introduction*. London: SAGE Publications.

Ledwith, M. (2005). *Community Development: A Critical Approach*. Bristol, UK: The Policy Press.

Lee, J.A.B. (2001). *The Empowerment Approach to Social Work Practice*. New York: Columbia University Press.

Leighninger, L. and Midgley, J. (1997). United States of America. In N.S. Mayadas, T.D. Watts and D. Elliot (eds), *International Handbook on Social Work Theory and Practice*. Westport, CT: Greenwood Press.

Lepper, M.K., Greene, D. and Nisbett, R. (1973). Undermining Children's Intrinsic Interest with Extrinsic Reward: A Test of the 'Overjustification' Hypothesis. *Journal of Personality and Social Psychology*, 28, 129–137.

Lewis, C.S. (2001). *Mere Christianity*. London: Harper One.

Linzer, N. (1999). *Resolving Ethical Dilemmas in Social Work Practice*. Boston, MA: Allyn & Bacon.

Lokur, V. (undated). *Ralagen Siddhi: Rural Transformation through People's Participation*. Ralagen Siddhi, Maharashtra, India: Sant Yadav Baba Shikshan Prasarak Mandal and Notre Specialised Publishing Division.

Lowe, G.R. (1995). Social Development. In *Encyclopaedia of Social Work* (19th ed.). Washington, DC: NASW Press.

Lyons, K. (1999). *International Social Work: Themes and Perspectives*. Burlington, VT: Ashgate Publishing.

Lyons, K., Hokenstadt, T., Pawar, M., Huegler, N. and Hall, N. (eds). (2012). *The SAGE Handbook of International Social Work*. London: SAGE Publications.

Lyons, K., Manion, K. and Carlsen, M.S. (2006). *International Perspectives on Social Work: Global Conditions and Local Practice*. Basingstoke, UK: Palgrave Macmillan.

Macy, J. (1983). *Dharma and Development: Religion as Resource in the Sarvodaya Self-Help Movement*. West Hartford, CT: Kumarian Press.

Majeres, J. (1977). *Popular Participation in Planning and Decision Making for Basic Needs Fulfilment*. Geneva, Switzerland: ILO.

Maltby, T. (2002). Participation. In P. Alcock, A. Erskine and M. May (eds), *The Blackwell Dictionary of Social Policy*. Oxford, UK: Blackwell.

Mandal, K.S. (1989). American Influence on Social Work Education in India and Its Impact. *International Social Work*, 32, 303–309.

Mapp, S.C. (2008). *Human Rights and Social Justice in a Global Perspective: An Introduction to International Social Work*. New York: Oxford University Press.

Martinez-Brawley, E.E. (1980). Historical Perspectives in on Rural Social Work: Implications for Curriculum Development. *Journal of Education for Social Work*, 16(3), 43–50.

Martyn, H. (2000). *Developing Reflective Practice: Making Sense of Social Work in a World of Change*. Bristol, UK: Policy Press.

McBeath, G. and Webb, S.A. (2002). Virtue Ethics and Social Work: Being Lucky, Realistic, and Not Doing Ones Duty. *British Journal of Social Work*, 32, 1015–1036.

Meinert, R.G. and Kohn, E. (1987). Towards Operationalization of Social Development Concepts. *Social Development Issues*, 10(3), 4–18.

Menachery, J. and Mohite, A. (2001). Whither Social Work Education in Maharashtra. *Indian Journal of Social Work*, 62(1), 106–122.

Midgley, J. (1981). *Professional Imperialism: Social Work in the Third World*. London: Heinemann.

———. (1984). Poor Law Principles and Social Assistance in the Third World: A Study of the Perpetuation of Colonial Welfare. *International Social Work*, 27, 19–29.

Midgley, J. (1986). *Community Participation, Social Development and the State*. London: Methuen.

———. (1992a). Introduction: Perspectives on Social Development and the State. *Social Development Issues* 14(1), 1–9.

———. (1992b). The Challenge of International Social Work. In M.C. Hokenstad, S.K. Khinduka and J. Midgley (eds), *Profiles in International Social Work* (pp. 13–27). Washington, DC: NASW Press.

———. (1994). Defining Social Development: Historical Trends and Conceptual Formulations. *Social Development Issues*, 16(3), 3–19.

———. (1995). *Social Development: The Developmental Perspective in Social Welfare*. London: SAGE Publications.

———. (2003). Social Development: The Intellectual Heritage. *Journal of International Development*, 15, 831–844.

———. (2014). *Social Development: Theory and Practice*. London: SAGE Publications.

Midgley, J. and Conley, A. (2010). *Social Work and Social Development: Theories and Skills for Developmental Social Work*. New York: Oxford University Press.

Miller, C. (2013). The Problem of Character. In S. van Hooft and N. Saunders (eds), *The Handbook of Virtue Ethics*. Durham, NC: Acumen Press.

Milnes, A. (2007). *Community Hero: Bunker Roy*. Retrieved 4 March 2009 from http://www.myhero.com/myhero/hero.asp?hero=Bunker_Roy_06

Ministry of Urban Employment and Poverty Alleviation and Ministry of Urban Development, Government of India. (2005). *Jawaharlal Nehru National Urban Renewal Mission (JNNURM) Toolkits*. New Delhi, India: GOI.

Mishra, B. (1996). *A Successful Case of Participatory Watershed Management at Ralegan Siddhi Village in District Ahmadnagar, Maharashtra, India*. Retrieved 6 March 2009 from http://www.fao.org/docrep/x5669e/x5669e06.htm

Mohan, B. (2010). Toward a New Social Development. In M. Pawar and D. Cox (eds), *Social Development: Critical Themes and Perspectives* (pp. 205–223). New York: Routledge.

Mohan, B. and Sharma, P. (1985). On Human Oppression and Social Development. *Social Development Issues*, 9(1), 12–23.

Moni, M.H. (2008). Japan and South Asia: Toward a Strengthened Economic Cooperation. *Asia-Pacific Social Science Review*, 7(1), 1–26.

Moore, E. and Pawar, M. (2007). Promoting International Social Work Discourse through Conference Participation: Praxis and the Solidarity Fund of Global Social Work 2004. *Advances in Social Work and Welfare Education*, 9(1), 27–44.

Mullaly, B. (2006). *The New Structural Social Work: Ideology, Theory, Practice*. New York: Oxford University Press.

Mullick, S.P. (1987). Distance Education in India. In *Distance Education in Asia and the Pacific* (Vol. 2, pp. 15–93), Manila, Philippines: Asian Development Bank.

Muzumdar, K. (1997). Teaching Material for Social Work Education. *Indian Journal of Social Work*, 58(2), 233–243.

Nadkarni, V.V. and Desai, K.T. (2012). *National Consultation on National Network of Schools of Social Work for Quality Enhancement of Social Work Education in India*. Mumbai, India: School of Social Work, Tata Institute of Social Sciences.

Nagpaul, H. (1988). The Profession of Social Work in Contemporary India. *The Indian Journal of Social Work*, 29(4), 339–354.

———. (1993). Analysis of Social Work Teaching Material in India: The Need for Indigenous Foundations. *International Social Work*, 36, 207–220.

Nanavatty, M.C. (1997a). Professional Associations of Social Work: An Analysis of Literature. *The Indian Journal of Social Work*, 58(2), 287–300.

———. (1997b). India. In N.S. Mayadas and T.D. Watta (eds), *International Handbook on Social Work Theory and Practice*. Westport, CT: Greenwood Press.

Noble, C. (2004). Social Work Education, Training and Standards in the Asia-Pacific Region. *Social Work Education*, 23(5), 527–536.

Nyoni, S. (1987). Indigenous NGOs: Liberation, Self-Reliance and Development. World Development, 15(1 Suppl.), 51–56.

Oakley, P. (1995). *People's Participation in Development Projects* (INTRAC Occasional Papers Series 7). Oxford, UK: INTRAC.

O'Connor, I., Wilson, J. and Setterland, D. (1998). *Social Work and Welfare Practice*. Melbourne, Australia: Longman.

OPHI (Oxford Poverty and Human Development Initiative). (2010). *OPHI and the UNDP Human Development Report Launch the Multidimensional Poverty Index*. Retrieved 16 July 2010 from http://www.ophi.org.uk/

Ortiz, L., Villereal, S. and Engel, M. (2000). Culture and Spirituality: A Review of the Literature. *Social Thought*, 19(4), 21–36.

Overlid, B. (2008). The Cultivation of Moral Character: A Buddhist Challenge to Social Workers. *Ethics and Social Welfare*, 2(3), 243–261.

Paiva, J.F.X. (1982). The Dynamics of Social Development and Social Work. In D.S. Saundes (ed.), *The Developmental Perspective in Social Work* (pp. 1–11). Manoa, Hawaii: University of Hawaii Press.

Palmer, G. and Short, S. (1989). *Health Care and Public Policy.* Melbourne, Australia: Macmillan.

Pandey, R. (1981). Strategies for Social Development: An International Approach. In J. Jones and R. Pandey (eds), *Social Development: Conceptual, Methodological and Policy Issues* (pp. 33–49). New York: St. Martin's Press.

Pardasani, M., Goldkind, L., Heyman, J.C. and Cross-Denny, B. (2012). How Much Does the Distance in Distance Education Matter? Our Students Speak. *Social Work Education*, 31(4), 406–421.

Parker, K. (2000). *Understanding Self-Determination: Basics.* Retrieved 23 February 2009 from http://130.94.183.89/parker/selfdet.html

Patel, L. (2005). *Social Welfare and Social Development in South Africa.* New York: Oxford University Press.

Pateman, C. (1970). *Participation and Democratic Theory.* Cambridge, UK: Cambridge University Press.

Pathak, S. (1987). Social Development. In *Encyclopaedia of Social Work in India* (Vol. 3, pp. 53–63). New Delhi, India: Ministry of Social Welfare, Government of India.

———. (1997). Social Welfare, Social Work and Development: Review of Literature. *The Indian Journal of Social Work*, 58(2), 161–184.

———. (2012). *Social Work and Social Welfare.* Bangalore, India: Nirutha Publications.

Patil, B. (1999). *A Letter Formally Conveying the Declaration of 1999–2000 as the 'Year of the Gram Sabha'.* New Delhi, India: Minister for State (Independent Charge) for Rural Areas and Employment, Government of India.

Pawar, M. (1997). Special Review Essay: Social Development: The Developmental Perspective in Social Welfare by James Midgley. *Indian Journal of Social Work*, 58(2), 342–349.

———. (1999a). Professional Social Work in India: Some Issues and Strategies. *Indian Journal of Social Work*, 60(4), 566–586.

———. (1999b). Social Work Schools and Social Development Prospects in the Asia-Pacific Region. *Social Development Issues*, 21(1), 62–69.

———. (2000a). Australian and Indian Social Work Codes of Ethics. *Australian Journal of Professional and Applied Ethics*, 2(2), 72–85.

———. (2000b). Social Development Content in the Courses of Australian Social Work Schools. *International Social Work*, 43(3), 277–288.

———. (2005). Participatory Welfare: Conceptual and Practice Issues. In M. Pawar (ed.), *Capacity Building for Participation: Social Workers' Thoughts and Reflections*. Wagga Wagga, New South Wales, Australia: CRSR/ILWS.

———. (2008). The Flood of Krishna River and the Flood of Politics: Dynamics of Rescue and Relief Operations in a Village in India. *Asia-Pacific Journal of Social Work and Development*, 18(2), 19–35.

Pawar, M. (2010). *Community Development in Asia and the Pacific*. New York: Routledge.

———. (2012). The Adoption of a Rights-Based Approach to Welfare in India. *Journal of Comparative Social Welfare*, 28(1), 27–39.

———. (2013). Water Insecurity: A Case for Social Policy Action by Social Workers. *Australian Social Work*, 66(2), 248–260.

———. (2014). *Water and Social Policy*. Basingstoke: Palgrave Macmillan.

Pawar, M. and Cox, D. (2004*). Communities' Informal Care and Welfare Systems: A Training Manual* (2nd ed.). Wagga Wagga, New South Wales, Australia: CRSR.

———. (2010a). Social Development. In M. Pawar and D. Cox (eds), *Social Development: Critical Themes and Perspectives* (pp. 13–36). New York: Routledge.

———. (2010b). Local Level Social Development. In M. Pawar and D. Cox (eds), *Social Development: Critical Themes and Perspectives* (pp. 37–53). New York: Routledge.

———. (2010c). *Social Development: Critical Themes and Perspectives.* New York: Routledge.

Pawar, M., Sheridan, R. and Georgina, H. (2004). International Social Work Practicum in India. *Australian Social Work*, 57(3), 223–236.

Pawar, M. and Tsui, M. (2012). Social Work in Southern and Eastern Asia. In K. Lyons, T. Hokenstadt, M. Pawar, N. Huegler and N. Hall (eds), *The SAGE Handbook of International Social Work*. London: SAGE Publications.

Payne, M. (1997). United Kingdom. In N.S. Mayadas, T.D. Watts and D. Elliot (eds), *International Handbook on Social Work Theory and Practice*. Westport, CT: Greenwood Press.

Payne, M. and Askeland, G.A. (2008). *Globalization and International Social Work: Postmodern Change and Challenge*. Burlington, VT: Ashgate Publishing.

Planning Commission. (1996). *Approach Paper to the Ninth Five Year Plan (1997–2002)*. Faridabad, UP, India: GOI Press.

———. (2013). *Twelfth Five Year Plan (2012–2017), Social Sectors* (Vol. 3). New Delhi: SAGE Publications.

Popple, P.R. and Leighninger, L. (2001). *The Policy-Based Profession: An Introduction to Social Welfare Policy Analysis for Social Workers*. Boston, MA: Allyn & Bacon.

Pearse, A. and Stiefel, M. (1979). *Inquiry into Participation: A Research Approach*. Geneva, Switzerland: UNRISD.

———. (1981). *Debater Comments on Inquiry into Participation: A Research Approach*. Geneva, Switzerland: UNRISD.

Pedersen, M.B. (2008). *Promoting Human Rights in Burma: A Critique of Western Sanctions Policy.* Lanham, MD: Rowman & Littlefield.

Pierson, J. and Thomas, M. (2010). *Dictionary of Social Work*. Berkshire, UK: Open University Press.

Preston, N. (1994). *Ethics for the Public Sector: Education and Training*. Sydney, Australia: The Federation Press.

Pullen-Sansfacon, A. (2010). Virtue Ethics for Social Work: A New Pedagogy for Practical Reasoning. *Social Work Education*, 29(4), 402–415.

Putnam, R.D. (1993). The Prosperous Community: Social Capital and Public Life. *The American Prospect*, 4(13), 36–42.

Ramachandran, V. (2010). *India Emerges as an Aid Donor*. Retrieved 5 June 2013 from http://www.huffingtonpost.com/vijaya-ramachandran/india-emerges-as-an-aid-d_b_751008.html

Ratnam, D.L.G. (1987). History Social Reform among Christians. In *Encyclopedia of Social Work*. New Delhi, India: Ministry of Social Welfare, Government of India.

Rees, S. (1991). *Achieving Power*. Sydney, Australia: Allen & Unwin.

Rees, W.E. (2006). Globalization, Trade and Migration: Undermining Sustainability. *Ecological Economics*, 59(2), 220–225.

Reichert, E. (2011). *Social Work and Human Rights: A Foundation for Policy and Practice* (2nd ed.). New York: Columbia University Press.

Reupert, A. (2006). The Counsellor's Self in Therapy: An Inevitable Presence. *The International Journal for the Advancement of Counselling*, 28(1), 95–105.

Richardson, A. (1983). *Participation*. London: Routledge and Kegan Paul.

Rossiter, A. (2006). The 'Beyond' of Ethics in Social Work. *Canadian Social Work Review*, 23, 139–44.

Rowlands, A. and Tan, N.T. (2008). Social Development following the Indian Ocean Tsunami: An International Social Work Response through the Fast Project. *Social Development Issues*, 30(1), 47–58.

Rowlings, C. (1997). Europe. In N.S. Mayadas, T.D. Watts and D. Elliot (eds), *International Handbook on Social Work Theory and Practice*. Westport, CT: Greenwood Press.

Roy, B. (1997). The Barefoot College Project, Tilonia. In B. Saraswsati (ed.), *Integration of Endogenous Cultural Dimension into Development*. New Delhi, India: IGNCA and D.K. Printworld. Retrieved 30 May 2007 from http://www.ignca.nic.in/cd_05021.htm

Sampford, C. and Preston, N. (1998). *Public Sector Ethics: Finding and Implementing Values*. Sydney, Australia: The Federation Press.

Saunders, P. (1994). *Welfare and Inequality: National and International Perspectives on the Australian Welfare State*. Melbourne, Australia: Cambridge University Press.

Schimmelfennig, F. (2007). Europeanization beyond Europe. *Living Reviews in European Governance*, 2(1). Retrieved 3 March 2009 from http://europeangovernance.livingreviews.org/open?pubNo=lreg-2007-1&page=articlesu2.html

Schuler, D. (1996). *New Community Networks: Wired for Change*. New York: CAN Press.

Scott, D. (2011). *Reflections on Social Work: Past, Present and Future*. Retrieved 15 June 2013 from http://socialwork.unimelb.edu.au/alumni

Sen, A. (2001). *Development as Freedom*. Oxford, UK: Oxford University Press.

Sevenhuijsen, S. (1998). *Citizenship and the Ethics of Care*. London, Routledge.

————. (2000). Caring in the Third Way: The Relation between Obligation, Responsibility and Care in Third Way Discourse. *Critical Social Policy*, 20(1), 5–37.

————. (2003). Principle Ethics and the Ethic of Care: Can They Go Together? *Social Work/Maatskaplike Werk*, 39(4), 393–399.

Shardlow, S. (1998). Values, Ethics and Social Work. In R. Adams, L. Dominelli and M. Payne (eds), *Social Work Themes, Issues and Critical Debates*. London: Macmillan.

Shari, I. (2000). Globalization and Economic Disparities in East and South East Asia: New Dilemmas. *Third World Quarterly*, 21(6), 963–975.

Sheridan, M.J. (2009). Ethical Issues in the Use of Spiritually Based Interventions in Social Work Practice: What Are We Doing and Why? *Journal of Religion & Spirituality in Social Work: Social Thought*, 28, 99–126.

Siegel, E., Jennings, J., Conklin, J. and Napoletano Flynn, S.A. (1998). Distance Learning in Social Work: Results and Implications of a National Survey. *Journal of Social Work Education*, 34(1), 71–80.

Singh, S., Gumz, E.J. and Crawley, B.C. (2011). Predicting India's Future: Does It Justify the Exportation of US Social Work Education? *Social Work Education*, 30(7), 861–873.

Smillie, I. (2001). Capacity Building and the Human Humanitarian Enterprise. In I. Smillie (ed.), *Patronage or Partnership: Local Capacity Building in Humanitarian Crisis* (pp. 7–23). Bloomfield, CT: Kumarian Press.

So, A.Y. (1990). *Social Change and Development*. Thousand Oaks, CA: SAGE Publications.

Specht, H. and Courtney, M.E. (1994). *Unfaithful Angels: How Social Work Has Abandoned Its Mission*. New York: The Free Press.

SPF (Social Protection Floor). (2013). *Social Protection Floor*. Retrieved 16 May 2013 from http://www.socialprotectionfloor-gateway.org/index.html

Spicker, P. (1995). *Social Policy: Themes and Approaches*. London: Prentice Hall.

————. (1990). Social Work and Self-Determination. *British Journal of Social Work*, 20(3), 221–236.

Srivastava, P. (2004). *Poverty Targeting in Asia: Country Experience of India* (Asian Development Bank Institute Discussion Paper No. 5). Retrieved 2 June 2013 from http://www.adbi.org/files/2004.02.05.dp005.poverty.india.pdf

Stepney, P. and Popple, K. (2008). *Social Work and the Community: A Critical Context for Practice*. Basingstoke, UK: Palgrave Macmillan.

Stuart, P.H. (2013). Social Work Profession: History. In C. Franklin (ed.), *Encyclopedia of Social Work*. New York: National Association of Social Workers/Oxford University Press.

Swanton, C. (2003). *Virtue Ethics: A Pluralistic View*. Oxford, UK: Oxford University Press.

Tan, N.T., Rowlands, A. and Yuen, F.K.O. (2006). *Asian Tsunami and Social Work Practice: Recovery and Rebuilding*. New York: Haworth.

Thachil, G. and Kumar, A. (1997). Social Work Employment and Human Power: Review of Studies. *The Indian Journal of Social Work*, 58(2), 265–286.

The Ashden Awards for Sustainable Energy. (2003). *Barefoot College, India 2003*. Retrieved 9 March 2009 from http://www.ashdenawards.org/files/reports/Barefoot%20college2003%20Technical%20report.pdf

The Hindu. (2013). *New Mental Health Bill Bans Electric Shocks without Anaesthesia, Gives Right to Treatment*. Retrieved 18 June 2013 from http://www.thehindu.com/sci-tech/health/policy-and-issues/new-mental-health-bill-bans-electric-shocks-without-anaesthesia-gives-right-to-treatment/article4820430.ece

The National Centre for Education Statistics, US Department of Education. (1998). *Distance Education in Higher Education Institutions: Highlights*. Available online at http://www.wested.org/hyper-discussions/deos-fwl/9422.html

The University of Queensland. (2009). *What Is a Sub-prime Mortgage?* Retrieved 21 February 2009 from http://www.studyatuq.net/what-sub-prime-mortgage

Thirlwall, A.P. (1989). *Growth and Development: With Special Reference to Developing Economies* (4th ed.). Basingstoke, UK: Macmillan.

Thomas, G. (2013). Supportive Role of the 'CBCI Chair' at IGNOU in ODL Programme Development. *Asian Association of Open Universities Journal*, 8(1), 83–89.

The Times of India. (2011). *BU Rejects Correspondence Course in Social Work*. Retrieved 17 June 2013 from http://articles.timesofindia.indiatimes.com/2011-04-07/bangalore/29392347_1_social-work-distance-education-correspondence

TISS Social Work Educators' Forum. (1997). Declaration of Ethics for Professional Social Workers. *The Indian Journal of Social Work*, 58(2), 335–341.

Titmuss, R.M. (1974). *Social Policy*. London: Allen & Unwin.

Todaro, M.P. (1997). *Economic Development* (6th ed.). London: Longman.

Tope, T.K. (1987). History of Social Reform amongst Hindus. In *Encyclopedia of Social Work*. New Delhi, India: Ministry of Social Welfare, Government of India.

Trembaly, G. (2011). Distance Education in the Context of Globalization: A Francophone Perspective. *The American Journal of Distance Education*, 25(1), 21–32.

Tronto, J.C. (1993). *Moral Boundaries: A Political Argument for an Ethic of Care*. New York: Routledge.

UGC (University Grants Commission). (1965). *Social Work Education in Indian Universities*. New Delhi, India: UGC.

———. (1980). *Review of Social Work Education in India*. New Delhi, India: UGC.

UGC (University Grants Commission). (1990). *Report of the Curriculum Development Centre in Social Work Education.* New Delhi, India: UGC.
————. (2013). *Total No. of Universities in the Country as on 11.02.2013.* Retrieved 18 June 2013 from http://www.ugc.ac.in/oldpdf/alluniversity.pdf
UN Centre for Regional Development. (1988). *Explorations in Local Social Development Planning: 1988 Synthesis Report.* Nagoya, Japan: UN Centre for Regional Development.
UNDP. (1992). *Human Development Report.* New York: Oxford University Press.
————. (1997). *Capacity Development.* New York: Management and Development and Governance Division, UNDP.
————. (2003). *Human Development Report 2003, Millennium Development Goals: A Compact among Nations to End Human Poverty.* New York: Oxford University Press.
UNDSPD (United Nations Division of Social Policy and Development). (2013). *United Nations Social Development Network.* Retrieved 1 May 2013 from http://unsdn.org/
UNESCAP (United Nations Economic and Social Commission for Asia and the Pacific). (1992). *Social Development Strategy for the ESCAP Region towards the Year 2000 and Beyond.* Bangkok, Thailand: UNESCAP.
————. (1996a). *Making an Impact: Innovative HRD Approaches to Poverty Alleviation.* Bangkok, Thailand: UNESCAP.
————. (1996b). *Showing the Way: Methodologies for Successful Rural Poverty Alleviation Projects.* Bangkok, Thailand: UNESCAP.
UNGA (United Nations General Assembly). (2010). *Keeping the Promise: A Forward-Looking Review to Promote an Agreed Action Agenda to Achieve the Millennium Development Goals by 2015* (Report of the Secretary-General) Retrieved 9 May 2010 from http://www.un.org/ga/search/view_doc.asp?symbol=A/64/665
UNHCR. (2005). *Handbook for Self-Reliance.* Retrieved 20 February 2009 from http://www.unhcr.org/pubs/self_reliance/handbook_for_self_reliance.pdf
United Nations. (1975). *Popular Participation in Decision Making for Development.* New York: United Nations.
————. (1981). *Popular Participation as a Strategy for Promoting Community Level Action and National Development.* New York: United Nations.
————. (1992). *Teaching and Learning about Human Rights: A Manual for Schools of Social Work and the Social Work Profession.* Geneva, Switzerland: The UN Centre for Human Rights.
————. (1995). *World Summit for Social Development Report.* New York: United Nations.
United Nations Centre for Regional Development. (1988). *Explorations in Local Social Development Planning: 1988 Synthesis Report.* Nagoya, Japan: United Nations.
UNRISD (United Nations Research Institute for Social Development). (1980). *The Quest for a Unified Approach to Development.* Geneva, Switzerland: UNRISD.

UNSDN (United Nations Social Development Network). (2013). *United Nations Social Development Network*. Retrieved 16 May 2013 from http://unsdn.org/

Uphoff, N. (1986). *Local Institutional Development: An Analytical Sourcebook with Cases*. West Hartford, CT: Kumarian.

Uvin, P. (2004). *Human Rights and Development*. Bloomfield, CT: Kumarian Press.

Velasquez, M., Andre, C., Shanks, S.J.T. and Meyer, M.J. (2010). *What Is Ethics?* Retrieved 20 June 2013 from http://www.scu.edu/ethics/practicing/decision/whatisethics.html

Verba, S., Nie, N.H. and Kim, J. (1978). *Participation and Political Equality*. Cambridge, UK: Cambridge University Press.

Vernon, R., Vakalahi, H., Pierce, D., Pittman-Munke, P. and Adkins, L.F. (2009). Distance Education Programs in Social Work: Current and Emerging Trends. *Journal of Social Work Education*, 45(2), 263–275.

Wearing, M. and Berreen, R. (eds). (1994). *Welfare and Social Policy in Australia: The Distribution of Disadvantage*. Sydney, Australia: Harcourt-Brace.

Webber, J. and Nathan, M. (2010). *Reflective Practice in Mental Health: Advancing Psychosocial Practice with Children, Adolescents and Adults*. London: Jessica Kingsley Pub.

Webley-Smith, T. (2007). The Limits of Self-Determination in Oceania. *Social and Economic Studies*, 56(1&2), 182–208.

Weeks, W. (1994). *Women Working Together—Lessons from Feminist Women's Service*, Melbourne, Australia: Longman Cheshire.

Weeks, W. and Wilson, J. (1995). *Issues Facing Australian Families: Human Services Respond*. Melbourne, Australia: Addison-Wesley Longman.

Weiss, I., Gal, J., Cnaan, R. and Majlaglic, R. (2002). What Kind of Social Policy Do Social Work Students Prefer? *International Social Work*, 45(1), 59–81.

White, A.T. (1982). Why Community Participation? *Assignment Children*, 59/60, 17–34.

White, V. (2006). *The State of Feminist Social Work*. New York: Routledge.

Whitehill, J. (1994). Buddhist Ethics in Western Context. *Journal of Buddhist Ethics*, Vol. 1. Available online at http://www.buddhistethics.org

Wilson, J., Thomson, J. and Mcmahon, A. (1996). *The Australian Welfare State: Key Documents and Themes*. Melbourne, Australia: Macmillan.

Wisner, B.L. (2011). Exploring the Lived Religion of Buddhists: Integrating Concepts from Social Work and Religious Studies. *Journal of Religion & Spirituality in Social Work: Social Thought*, 30(4), 385–404.

World Bank. (2005). *The Effectiveness of Word Bank Support for Community-Based and -Driven Development*. Retrieved 12 March 2012 from http://books.google.com.au/books?id=QmCGZHmrHkkC&pg=PA1&lpg=PA1&dq=Evaluation+of+CDD+projects&source=bl&ots=G-JkEfL-WS&sig=GseQCpoNoR8v6kagSPoWX2qOFNc&hl=en&ei=3eu4SZmHD

tLEkAW5w_meCA&sa=X&oi=book_result&resnum=5&ct=result#PP
P1,M1

World Bank. (1997). *World Development Reports: The State in a Changing World.* New York: Oxford University Press.

———. (1999/2000). *World Development Reports: Entering the 21st Century.* New York: Oxford University Press.

———. (2000/2001). *World Development Reports: Attacking Poverty.* New York: Oxford University Press.

———. (2001). *Understanding and Measuring Social Capital.* Washington, DC: World Bank.

———. (2013). *India Development Update. Economic Policy and Poverty Team, South Asian Region.* Retrieved 3 July 2013 from http://www-wds. worldbank.org/external/default/WDSContentServer/WDSP/IB/2013/04/ 30/000356161_20130430105728/Rendered/PDF/770810WP0P13240nt0 Update0April02013.pdf

Wronka, J. (2007). *Human Rights and Social Justice: Social Action and Service for the Helping and Health Professions.* Thousand Oaks, CA: SAGE Publications.

Xiong, Y. and Wang, S. (2007). Development of Social Work Education in China in the Context of New Policy Initiatives: Issues and Challenges. *Social Work Education,* 26(6), 560–572.

Yuen, A.W.K. and Ho, D.K.L. (2007). Social Work Education in Hong Kong at Crossroads: Challenges and Opportunities amidst Marketization and Managerialism. *Social Work Education,* 26(6), 546–559.

Yuen-Tsang, A.W.K. and Wang, S. (2002). Tensions Confronting the Development of Social Work Education in China: Challenges and Opportunities. *International Social Work,* 45(3), 375–388.

Index

general Indian context, 253–257
GO. *See* Government organization
(GO)
GOI. *See* Government of India (GOI)
Government of India (GOI), 132, 152,
194, 210
Government organization (GO), 95
grassroots-level communities, 97
Gray, M., 230
Greek civilizations, 11
gross domestic product (GDP), 253

Handbook for Self-reliance
(UNHCR), 74
Hazare, Anna, 104*b*–105*b*
Hillery, G.A., 39
*A History of the Social Development
Network in the World Bank,
1973–2002* (Davis), 17
Hobhouse, Leonard, 13, 14
Hodge, P., 75
Houston, S., 230
HRCA. *See* Human Rights Council of
Australia (HRCA)
Hsuan-tsang, 247
Hugman, R., 230
Human Development Index, 26
human rights
community development practice,
71–72
critiques and obstacles, 69–71
meaning of, 66–69
in Ralegan Siddhi, 100*b*–101*b*
values and principles, 72
Human Rights Council of Australia
(HRCA), 72
Hussein, M.K., 114

IASSW. *See* International Association
of Schools of Social Work
(IASSW)
ICSD. *See* International Consortium
for Social Development (ICSD)

ICSW. *See* International Council on
Social Welfare (ICSW)
Ife, J., 65, 70
IFSW. *See* International Federation of
Social Workers (IFSW)
IGNOU. *See* Indira Gandhi National
Open University (IGNOU)
ILO. *See* International Labour
Organization (ILO)
IMF. *See* International Monetary
Fund (IMF)
India Knowledge, 254
Indian civilizations, 11
Indian Journal of Social Work
(Pawar), 3–4, 176
The Indian Society of Professional
Social Work (ISPSW), 182
Indian Society of Professional Social
Work (ISPSW), 182, 195
Indian Technical and Economic
Cooperation (ITEC), 156
Indira Gandhi National Open
University (IGNOU), 206, 208,
211
INGO. *See* international
non-government organization
(INGO)
Integrated Chid Development
Services, 186
Integrated Rural Development
Programme, 186
Integrated Tribal Development
Projects, 186
International Association of Schools
of Social Work (IASSW), 18, 163,
166, 251
International Consortium for Social
Development (ICSD), 163
International Council on Social
Welfare (ICSW), 18, 163
The International Court of Justice, 78
International Covenant on Economic,
Social and Cultural Rights, 67

About the Author

Manohar Pawar, PhD, is professor of social work at the School of Humanities and Social Sciences, Charles Sturt University (NSW, Australia) and is also the President of the Asia-Pacific branch of the International Consortium for Social Development. Earlier, he has taught at the Tata Institute of Social Sciences, Mumbai, and La Trobe University, Melbourne. He has more than 30 years of experience in social work education, research and practice in Australia and India.

Professor Pawar has received a number of awards, including the *ICSSR Doctoral Fellowship* located at the Centre for the Study of Developing Societies, New Delhi (1986–1988); the *Citation Award for Outstanding Contributions to Student Learning* (2008, from the Australian Learning and Teaching Council); and *Quality of Life Award* (2001, from the Association of Commonwealth Universities).

His current areas of interest include international social work, development and social policy practice, social consequences of climate change and water, social work education, virtues and social work practice, informal care and ageing, NGOs and community development. He is the lead chief investigator of research funded by the Australian Research Council's Discovery Project that focuses on virtues and social work practice.

His publications include *Social Work Practice Methods: Reflections on Thinking, Doing and Being* (2015); *Water and Social Policy* (2014); *International Social Work: Issues, Strategies and Programs* (2013); *The SAGE Handbook of International Social Work* (2012); *Social Development: Critical Themes and Perspectives* (2010); and *Community Development in Asia and the Pacific* (2010).